D1036150

Developing Leaders
for the Small Church

Also by Glenn C. Daman

Shepherding the Small Church
Leading the Small Church

Developing Leaders for the Small Church

A GUIDE TO SPIRITUAL TRANSFORMATION
FOR THE CHURCH BOARD

Glenn C. Daman

Kregel
Academic & Professional

Developing Leaders for the Small Church: A Guide to Spiritual Transformation for the Church Board

© 2009 by Glenn C. Daman

Published by Kregel Publications, a division of Kregel, Inc., P.O. Box 2607, Grand Rapids, MI 49501.

Library of Congress Cataloging-in-Publication Data
Daman, Glenn.
    Developing leaders for the small church : a guide for spiritual transformation for the church board / Glenn C. Daman.
    p. cm.
Includes bibliographical references
1. Church trustees. 2. Small churches. I. Title.
BV705.D36   2009   254—dc22   2008050615

ISBN 978-0-8254-2455-7

Printed in the United States of America

09 10 11 12 13 / 5 4 3 2 1

To my brothers, Paul Daman and Keith Daman,
who have modeled spiritual leadership while serving on
the board at Tensed Community Church.

To my sister, Lynette Daman, who led me to Christ
when I was young.

To the family of my wife, Becky: Terry and Phyllis Landsem and
Mark and Kimberly Landsem, who have been faithful servants
of Christ and an encouragement to our ministry.

Contents

Introduction

Understanding what it means to be a church board member begins with our perspective of the roles, responsibilities, and requirements of being a leader of the church. When we enter into our role as leaders, we do not do so with a clean slate. We have previously formulated views of what it means to serve in leadership. Sometimes these are derived from our understanding of Scripture. More often they are determined by our cultural background, our past history within the church, and what we have personally observed in the church. This perspective influences our conception of the role that the pastor has within the church. It governs our understanding of the board and their responsibilities. Some of these preconceived ideas are biblically sound, some are unrealistic expectations we have of the pastor and/or the board, and some are a mistaken understanding of what we can contribute to the leadership team within the church. These misunderstandings can hinder our ministry by undermining our confidence (I have nothing to give) or by resulting in self-elevated pride (Everyone should listen to me).

✳ ✳ ✳

For years, the board at First Community Church had functioned as the caretakers of the building. While the board had a desire to be biblically governed, they left the spiritual work to Pastor Dave. In their minds, their role was to take care of the facilities and oversee the budget. However, Ken, who served as the chairman of the board, recently raised the question concerning the role of the board. As he had been reading Scripture, he was challenged by the amount of responsibility God assigned the elders of the church.

So at the next board meeting, he asked the question, "Who are the elders we read about in the New Testament, and what is our biblical role as board members?"

During the discussion that followed, Pastor Dave smiled. For years he had been praying that the board would start thinking about their biblical responsibility. Maybe this was the catalyst that would start that discussion.

❋ ❋ ❋

Dispelling the Myths of Leadership

We begin our journey of discovery concerning the role and responsibility of the board by first dispelling some of the more prevalent misconceptions we have regarding ourselves, the pastor, and what it means to be on the board. These misconceptions, if allowed to remain and influence our thinking, will cloud our perspective, ultimately undermining our effectiveness as leaders within the church.

Myth #1: "I'm Just a _____"

Often we allow our society and culture to determine our opinion of ourselves and others. Because of this, we approach leadership with a negative view. At times in rural areas, we easily fall prey to the thinking that "I'm just a farmer, and I don't have the abilities to do anything significant within the church." In more suburban areas, when we are in occupations that society determines to be a non-leading role, we assume that we have nothing to contribute and we cannot be effective as a leader within the church. For example, we might assume that because we are blue-collar workers we do not possess leadership qualities.

This is further compounded because we often lack training in both general leadership and church leadership, which results in apprehension about serving as a board member. The problem, however, is not a lack of training, nor is it in our perception of ourselves; rather it is in our perception of God. What we fail to realize is that spiritual leadership is not based upon abilities, talents, or training; rather it is based upon character and empowerment by the Holy Spirit (1 Cor. 2:1–5; 2 Cor. 1:12). We can serve effectively, not because of who we are, but because of what God can do through us (Jer. 9:23–24). When we are faced with difficult decisions in the church, we can have confidence in knowing that God has equipped and empowered us to be fully prepared to meet any challenge we face (Matt. 10:19–20; Phil. 4:13). Often the most effective board members are not the ones who are leaders in the secular world but the ranch hands, the blue-collar workers, the carpenters—the average individuals who manifest a deep love for Christ, a commitment to and knowledge of God's Word, and a reliance upon the Holy Spirit for guidance and direction.

※   ※   ※

John began to feel uncomfortable as they discussed the biblical roles of the elders and deacons. It was not that he did not want to do what God desired; it was just that he felt so inadequate. All his life he had been a laborer for a construction company. He never saw himself as a leader, especially one who was to be a spiritual leader of others. He did not mind overseeing the care of the building; after all, he understood construction. As the conversation carried over to the next several board meetings, he realized he needed to rethink his role.

※   ※   ※

Myth #2: "We're Just a Small Church"

It was a long day. The people were tired and hungry. For hours they had sat upon the hillside listening to the itinerate preacher proclaim the word of God with authority. However, as the sun began to set in the western sky, many were faced with a long walk home. There were no fast-food restaurants. There were no supermarkets to stop at along the way. The only food available was a small lunch prepared by a loving mother for her young son. To the disciples such a small lunch seemed ridiculously insignificant in the face of a crowd that perhaps numbered as high as fifteen to twenty thousand. However, in the hands of the living God, the lunch was more than sufficient to accomplish his purpose (see Matt. 14:13–21).

Like the disciples, we often look at the size of our church and wonder how we can do anything significant with the limited number of people, the inadequate facilities, and the insufficient resources. Because the church has only a handful of people, we assume that we cannot accomplish much. When confronted with the opportunities and challenges of ministry, we fall back on the response that "We are just a small church; what can we do?" We look at what we lack rather than at the strengths we possess.

The problem is not the smallness of our congregation but the smallness of our vision of what God can accomplish. What we see as limitations to effectiveness God sees as opportunities for his glory to be revealed. When we look within the pages of Scripture, we discover a number of times when God takes the insignificant and inconsequential and accomplishes the eternal and supernatural. Moses reminds Israel that "the LORD did not set his affection on you and choose you because you were more numerous than other peoples, for you were the fewest of all peoples" (Deut. 7:7). God used twelve average, untrained men to turn the Roman world upside down (Acts 4:13). He used a church of 120 to radically transform Jerusalem (Acts 1:15). It is never a question of size, but of availability and empowerment by the Holy Spirit.

Myth #3: "We Must Fill All the Board Positions"

In many small churches there are a minimal number of people who can serve on the board. This problem is further compounded by the fact that many constitutions have a specified number of positions that are to be filled on the board. The result is that people who are not spiritually qualified are placed on the board. Because the church is under pressure to fill each position, the requirement of spiritual maturity is abandoned in the quest to find people willing to serve. When positions are empty, a church may even use the position as a way to attempt to get a person more involved in the church. In this case a person is placed on the board in the hope that the person will start coming more regularly as a result.

However, Scripture makes it clear that the focus of leadership is not upon organizational needs, but upon character. As we will see in chapter 2, selection to serve on the board is not to be based upon organizational requirements or even family connections but upon the level of spiritual maturity the person manifests. It would be better to leave a position open than to place someone in it who is not spiritually qualified for the position. Rather than fill the position, the church should develop a strategy to train and disciple individuals to become qualified.

Myth #4: "We Don't Have Enough Board Members to Be Effective"

When a small church does place only spiritually qualified leaders on the board, the result can be a minimal number of individuals on the board. It is not uncommon for small churches to have only one or two people on the board besides the pastor. In these situations, we can easily conclude that the board cannot be effective with such a limited number. If we are on a small board, we can feel overwhelmed by the biblical responsibilities that are given us.

We must keep in mind, however, that the number of

Being Effective with Few

- Recognize that it is not the number of individuals that is crucial but the quality of individuals. One person who is serving as a biblical leader is far more valuable than five who are only running an organization.
- The most important contribution a leader gives is his personal holiness. It is not the number of individuals that influence people, but the spiritual quality of the individuals.
- For many small congregations, the pastor and one or two individuals can provide spiritual care.
- The priority of the leadership should be to develop more leaders.

board members needed to be effective is never stipulated in Scripture. While Scripture does imply that there is to be a plurality of leaders, it does not mandate any specific number. It is not the size of the board that determines effectiveness but the holiness that governs their actions and the empowerment of the Holy Spirit. Certainly our desire should be to have a larger number on the board. But we should not think that the ministry of the church is hindered if we do not have enough individuals available. God can use any number of people to accomplish his purpose.

Myth #5: "All Leaders Are Visionaries"

Perhaps the most prevalent myth today, even in writings on church leadership, is that a true leader is a visionary. That is, the leader is someone who has the ability to see into the future and project what the church organizationally is to be and become and then move the church in that direction.

It is important to realize that this "vision" is not one derived from Scripture but from the ability to assess the present and future setting of the church. Certainly it is true that the church needs a sense of vision and direction. It is important for the church to have an awareness of what God desires it to accomplish in the present and future. Often God equips individuals within the church with the ability to keenly discern what he desires it to accomplish. However, more often than not, the vision for the church grows out of the whole congregation rather than one individual. Our concept of vision is derived from a secular model, where the focus is upon organizational growth and leadership.

A biblical leader is one who has an understanding of God's Word and insight into how it should be applied within the present context. Nehemiah was a great leader, not because he had a grand vision to rebuild Jerusalem, but because he understood the Scriptures that promised that God would rebuild Jerusalem if the people turned back to him (Neh. 1:8–9). The greatest need within the church today is for leaders who understand Scripture and can apply it to the issues confronting people within the congregation, the community, and the world in which we live.

Myth #6: "Leaders Possess a Certain Temperament and Certain Gifts"

When we consider the job description of leaders, we often focus on certain temperaments and gifts. We expect the person to be forceful and driven, a hard worker who will see a project through to completion. He is someone who is charismatic and appealing. We assume the person will be an excellent communicator who is comfortable being in front of people, teaching others the truths of Scripture. However, as we examine Scripture, we discover that there is a difference between spiritual gifts and their function within the church on the one hand, and the position of leadership on the other. The "pastor" is to be one who is gifted as a pastor-teacher (Eph. 4:11). This position within the church is related to the spiritual gift. However, nowhere in Scripture do we find the position of an elder (i.e., board member) restricted to a specific spiritual gift. Rather the qualifications relate to character rather than giftedness. While the person should be able to teach (that is, communicate the truth of God's Word to others), that does not mean that the person must demonstrate the gift of teaching. Just because a person is not able to get in front of people and teach a Sunday school class does not mean that the person is unable to teach.

Myth #7: "That Is What We Hired the Pastor to Do"

Often in the small church when we are confronted with the responsibility of overseeing the spiritual health of the congregation and ministering to the needs of people, our response is, "That is what we hired the pastor to do!" When someone is in the hospital and in need of spiritual comfort, we call the pastor, expecting him to do the visitation. When someone is going through a time of testing and difficulty, needing the encouragement and support of prayer, we rely upon the pastor to fulfill the role. If someone comes to church with questions about his or her relationship with God, we refer that person to the pastor.

Nevertheless, when we examine the pages of Scripture, we find that there is no such distinction in the New Testament. The pastor is not the only one who is responsible for the spiritual well-being of the congregation; rather, it is the responsibility of all those in leadership. The board is accountable to ensure the doctrinal integrity of the congregation. The board is to provide prayer, encouragement, and counsel for those going through times of testing and difficulty (James 5:14). The board, not just the pastor, oversees the spiritual health and well-being of the people within the church (Heb. 13:17). All those in leadership are responsible to live in such a way that their lives become a testimony to others (1 Peter 5:3). The pastor is one who is given the task of teaching and preaching, but it is the board that is responsible for the spiritual vitality of the congregation.

Myth #8: "The Board's Primary Role Is to Maintain the Peace"

Because the small church is relationally driven, the board often develops the perspective that its primary role is to maintain unity and peace within the church. As Aubrey Malphurs points out, "Though most aren't aware of it, many boards believe that their purpose is to keep everybody happy for the sake of peace and church unity. While this is true in both small and large churches, it's characteristic of many small churches that pride themselves in being one happy family. The board's goal is to keep it that way."[1] Consequently, decisions are based not upon Scripture or upon the goal of transformation but upon the goal of maintaining relationships.

When "keeping the peace" becomes the driving force, we become reluctant to make hard decisions, decisions that are necessary and mandated by Scripture but unpopular with people in the pew. For example, we become reluctant to exercise church discipline because it might damage the relationships that exist within the church. It is important that we always remember that the board ultimately is not accountable to the congregation but to God (Heb. 13:17). Like the people in Jesus' day, we can become pressured to gain the approval of men but in the process violate our responsibility before God. In John 12:42–43 we find this sad indictment of the religious leaders: "Yet at the same time many even among the leaders believed in him. But because of the Pharisees they would not confess their faith for fear they would be put out of the synagogue; for they loved praise from men more than praise from God." Unity is a critical indicator of the health of the church, but it should never come at the cost of biblical truth.

Myth #9: "I Don't Have Enough Time"

We live in an increasingly fast-paced society. The nostalgia of the small town has painted a picture of a slow-paced society, where people have time to sit at the local diner visiting with friends and neighbors. Our view of rural America often corresponds to Mayberry RFD, where the men spend the day at the local barbershop playing checkers, talking about sports, and arguing about politics. The women gather together to tie quilts for the next local church bazaar and discuss the latest scandalous town gossip.

However, reality is often far different from the myths that color our perspective. Farms have increased in size while the amount of manpower available (and needed) has decreased. As a result the farmer must do more work with fewer helpers. More and more people are still living in the small town but driving an hour to the next town to work. The old adage that one works from sunup to sundown is not only true for the local farmer; it is true for the businessman as well. The women likewise spend their day at work, as more and more families need two wage earners to keep up with the rising cost of living. The result is a significant decrease in the amount of time people have to give to the ministry of the church. When the pastor brings up the topic of the board becoming more involved in ministry, there is a collective and audible groan as exhausted board members baulk at one more thing on their plate. Many of us object to doing more than just meeting once a month because "we don't have the time."

In utilizing our time, we must recognize again that perception is often different from reality. While the perception may be that we do not have the time, the reality is that we do. The issue is not about time but priorities. We find the time to do what is important to us. This is true from the busiest farmer to the overworked businessman. We always find time to attend local sporting events or a local farm auction. We find time to go golfing with a business associate. We find time to pursue a hobby. We do so because these things are important to us.

It is also critical that we realize that God never calls us to a task without first giving us everything we need to accomplish the task. The very nature of God demands that he supply all our needs to accomplish all his demands. This includes not only the resources needed for the task but adequate time as well. The issue is not an issue of time but an issue of God's calling and our priorities. If God has called us to be spiritual leaders within the church, then we must make it a high priority.

Finally, we need to recognize that the amount of time required is not nearly as extensive as we may think. Calling someone on the phone to see how they are doing takes little time but is critical to providing spiritual and emotional support to someone who is facing struggles. Stopping by at the hospital when we are in town will cost only twenty to thirty minutes of our time, but it brings great spiritual encouragement to people. In most cases we do not need to spend more time visiting with people; we just need to be more focused in the time we spend with them. Instead of talking about the weather, sports, and local politics, we need to talk about how things are going with them spiritually and how we can be praying for them.

* * *

During the third board meeting, Steve raised an issue that was troubling him. As a farmer, he worked twelve to fourteen hours a day, six days a week. It became apparent that what they were talking about would require far more time then he had. In the meeting he voiced his frustrations, asking how they could minister to people when they had so little time in their schedules. As he did so, he saw nods of agreement from Ken and John as well.

Pastor Dave agreed. "This is a significant issue and one that we all wrestle with." So he wrote the question on the whiteboard, "How can we minister to the needs of people when we are all so busy?"

As they talked about this question, the pastor asked each board member to come up with one way they could minister to people that would not require a great deal of time. He wrote their suggestions on the whiteboard:

- Plan a visit with someone in the hospital when you are already in town.
- When you are waiting for the fertilizer truck to come, take time to call someone in the church and pray with that person.
- When attending a local sporting event, look for someone who may be facing difficulties in life and take a few moments to visit with him or her.
- Take ten minutes after the service on Sunday to talk with someone about how things are going in his or her life and/or ministry. Then pray with the person.

As Dave wrote these ideas down, each board member soon realized that there was much that a person could do that was significant but did not take a great deal of time. It just took creativity and effective use of the time each person had.

✻   ✻   ✻

Developing a Right Perspective

In response to the misconceptions we have about leadership, it is important that we develop a biblical perspective. Instead of viewing our responsibility as leaders through the eyes of our society and the business model it follows, we must develop a biblical model, one that is derived from and governed by the biblical teaching regarding the role and responsibilities we have as board members within the church. We need to examine the pages of Scripture to understand what our role is and then how we can apply these responsibilities within the small church context. The call to be a leader within the church is one of the greatest privileges and yet one of the most challenging responsibilities we find in the pages of the Bible. While we should not shrink from the task in fear, we should be driven to the Bible for clarification and to the Holy Spirit in humility and prayer to seek supernatural empowerment to fulfill the task. As we shall see, we are not in the position of leadership because we are chosen by a congregational vote; we are in this position because of God's sovereign appointment as he guided the church in our selection to serve as leaders. As long as we are in this position, we must seek to fulfill these responsibilities with faithfulness and integrity so that God can and will accomplish his purpose in the church through his guidance in and through us.

Leadership Is Spiritual Rather Than Organizational

Often when we gather for the monthly board meeting, the focus is on the physical and organizational administration of the church. We spend time discussing the problems faced with an old building. Discussion focuses on who will repair the leaky roof, when it should be repaired, how much it will cost, and how the church will raise the necessary funds. Time is then spent talking about any problems in the church, which are usually related to organizational issues. We examine how programs are running, who is in charge of what, and when things will happen within the church calendar. As long as everything is running with few problems and there are no pressing facility needs, the meetings are short and the conversation moves to the latest market trends.

However, when we examine Scripture we find a different emphasis. The priority of leadership established in the book of Acts makes it clear that our priority is spiritual rather than organizational. When the problem arose concerning the administration of the benevolent ministry for widows, the disciples made it clear that their priority was to focus on the ministry of the Word and being devoted to prayer (Acts 6:4). This moves the priority from the organizational realm (developing and running programs) to the spiritual (carefully seeking God's will through prayer and transforming people through biblical proclamation).

The writer of Hebrews further emphasizes this perspective when he states that the leadership of the church should "keep watch over you as men who must give an account" (Heb. 13:17). This statement both clarifies our role as leaders and gives us a warning about our accountability to God in how we lead. The phrase "keep watch over you" portrays the imagery of a shepherd who is vigilantly keeping guard over the flock under his care, lest some danger threaten the sheep. The Greek word translated "keep watch" is used only three other times in the New Testament, and in each case it occurs in the context of prayer (Mark 13:33; Luke 21:36; Eph. 6:18). The stress is that the leadership is to be spiritually alert to the threats that might come against the flock, so they must be vigilant in prayer. This parallels the imagery of a watchman given in the Old Testament (Jer. 6:17; Ezek. 3:17; 33:2). (For a fuller discussion of the importance and characteristics of a watchman, see chapter 5.) Although providing oversight of the organizational planning and function of the church is part of our role as leaders, it is not central. Central is the spiritual oversight we are to give to the spiritual health of the congregation.

As leaders, we will give an account for the spiritual condition of the congregation. If we have allowed the congregation to become spiritually anemic, destroyed by strife and inappropriate behavior, we will be called into account by the living God. As Homer Kent Jr. points out in his comments on Hebrews 13:17, "A shepherd must remain awake and alert to care for their feeblest sheep, so these pastors were likewise exercising great care. Their task was actually a stewardship for which they must someday give an account at the judgment seat of Christ. These words serve as a solemn reminder to the leaders of the awesome responsibility which is theirs."[2] However, lest we be mistaken, this responsibility is not just for pastors, but for all those in leadership, for the focus is not on the pastoral gift but on the responsibility of those who serve in the position of elder.

✳   ✳   ✳

After discussing their roles for several weeks, Pete raised the question, "What is a biblical leader?" Because of his background as a business owner, Pete recognized that before

the church leaders could develop a clear understanding of
their role, they needed to have a definition of a leader that
was thoroughly biblical. Everything he had read on leadership for business focused on vision, goals, and strategies.
However, when he read Hebrews 13:17, 1 Timothy 4:11–16,
and 1 Peter 5:2–4, they seemed to have a much different
focus. As the board discussed this at the next meeting, they
all agreed. While organization and strategies are important,
biblical leadership goes far deeper. In response they came
up with the following definition: *"A biblical leader is a person
called by God to serve the church by providing a godly example,
by overseeing the church's spiritual health, and by supervising the
ministry of the congregation in order to lead people in spiritual
transformation."*

✳   ✳   ✳

Leadership Is Based on Empowerment Rather Than Abilities

As we look at the task and responsibility of leadership, it is easy
for us to become intimidated, thinking that we are not qualified
for such a role. We look at the responsibility and see ourselves as
woefully inadequate for the task. Indeed, in many ways we are
incompetent. The problem is that we look upon our abilities and
talent rather than upon supernatural empowerment. Like Moses
(Exod. 3:11), we question God's (or the congregation's) wisdom
in placing us in leadership. We do not see ourselves as spiritual
enough or smart enough or gifted enough. However, God reminded Moses, "Who gave man his mouth? Who makes him deaf
or mute? Who gives him sight or makes him blind? Is it not I, the
LORD? Now go; I will help you speak and will teach you what to
say" (Exod. 4:11–12). Our confidence for effective leadership does
not come from ourselves and our abilities, but from God's work
within us and through us. God expresses displeasure, even anger,
at Moses, not because Moses doubted his own ability, but because
he doubted God's empowerment and enablement (v. 14). Likewise,
the disciples became effective leaders within the early church, not

because of their innate abilities, but because of the empowering work by the Holy Spirit. In Acts 1:8, Christ, in giving his final charge to the disciples, gives the foundation for their effectiveness: Before they will become witnesses, they will first be empowered. The order is both historic (pointing to the historical event of Pentecost) and fundamental. Empowerment always precedes calling and activity. God equips us to do what he has called us to do. To doubt his empowerment is an affront to God as it calls into question his very being (cf. Exod. 4:11–14).

Leadership Is Service Rather Than Power and Authority

The contemporary view of leadership focuses on power and authority. We equate leadership with the power to make decisions and the authority to implement those decisions. In this model, the responsibility of the congregation is to accept our authority and follow our leadership. However, as we examine Scripture, we discover that the emphasis for biblical leadership is not on the exercise of authority and power but on the responsibility to serve.

When the disciples became embroiled in a conflict concerning who would have the highest positions of leadership in the kingdom, Christ responded by gathering them together and pointing out, "You know that the rulers of the Gentiles lord it over them, and their high officials exercise authority over them. Not so with you. Instead, whoever wants to become great among you must be your servant, and whoever wants to be first must be your slave—just as the Son of Man did not come to be served, but to serve, and to give his life as a ransom for many" (Matt. 20:25–28).

To press home this lesson, in the next event Christ gives a living picture of what it means to be a servant. When confronted with two blind men, whom the crowds thought to be obnoxious, Jesus stopped and asked, "What do you want me to do for you?" (Matt. 20:32). When he asked that question, he knew what they desired— they desired to have their sight. He asked the question to show that servant leadership involves compassion and the willingness to sacrifice our time and energy to minister to the needs of people. Leadership is to ask the people we serve, "What do you want me to do for you?" Biblical leadership is not about the church serving our agenda and plans, but about those of us in leadership serving the congregation in helping them fulfill their ministry.

※　※　※

Ken raised a concern he often felt about the dangers of misuse of authority, "Too many times I have seen church leaders who become dictators—not listening to the congregation and forcing their agenda upon the people. But I have also seen church boards who have provided no leadership at all. They just do whatever the people want, even if it contradicts Scripture. How do we find a balance between them?"

Dave responded, "Let's look at a couple of passages that I think help give us perspective on this. In Hebrews 13:17 we find that leadership does involve the exercise of authority."

Ken agreed as Dave read the verse.

Dave continued, "But we also find in Matthew 20:25–28 that leadership involves servant leadership. Our authority resides in the authority of Scripture. We must uphold what it teaches. But our focus must always be on being a servant. Leadership is not getting people to do what we want, it is assisting them in accomplishing their God-given roles within the church. While there is no easy answer to this tension, we must constantly depend upon the Holy Spirit for guidance in appropriately applying these two principles."

※　※　※

Leadership Is Focused on Transformation Rather Than on Maintenance

Often our approach to leadership and to the ministry of the church focuses on how we can maintain the present structures and programs of the church. The perception is based on the past activities of the church. This past then becomes the basis by which we define a healthy church. We believe that as long as the church has a Sunday school program that is traditionally separated into age groups, a Sunday morning worship service, Sunday evening Bible study, and a midweek prayer meeting, then the church is faithfully accomplishing its mission. However, what we often overlook is that the task of the church is not to maintain certain programs but to lead the congregation in personal and corporate transformation. The purpose of the church is to be used by God to bring people into a personal and life-changing relationship with Christ. This life-changing process is not just superficial but penetrates to the very core of our being. It deals with the inner character, motives, values, and attitudes of the individual. It is this goal we must constantly keep as the focus of our ministry. The success of leadership is not determined by how smoothly the church is running or the programs that it maintains, but by how effectively it leads people into transformation. This is what Paul was referring to when he wrote, "We proclaim him, admonishing and teaching everyone with all wisdom, so that we may present everyone perfect in Christ. To this end I labor, struggling with all his energy, which so powerfully works in me" (Col. 1:28–29). Too often we replace internal, substantive change (i.e., changes related to our character and values) with external, superficial change (change of programs and growth in numbers).

When we approach the opportunity to be on the board and be involved in the leadership of the church, it is easy for us to lose sight of the empowerment and sufficiency of God. We must recognize that with both ourselves and the church, God has provided all that we need to be effective in ministry. The question is not a question of resources or abilities, but of our willingness to allow God to supernaturally work in our lives. Too often we abrogate our responsibility of leadership by failing to recognize God's empowerment and by passing that responsibility on to the pastor or others within the church. The church board is more than a maintenance committee who is responsible to care for the church building. The church board is to be a group of spiritual leaders in the church who guide the church in spiritual transformation. The question is not whether God has called us to this responsibility, or if he has equipped us for this task, but whether we are willing to embrace this charge in our service for God.

ONE

The Biblical Offices of Leadership

What does it mean to be a board member? What are the duties that we are to perform? Perhaps nothing strikes more fear into the heart of a potential candidate for the board than these questions. There always remains something mysterious about the church board that places it on a different plane than any other committee or team within the church or within the community. Part of the fear stems from our preconceived ideas of what it means to be a church board member. When we think of the board, we think (and rightly so) of those individuals who consistently demonstrate spiritual maturity. Rather than being a young novice in the faith, we see the board member as someone who exemplifies what a Christian is to be. The board is more than an organizational entity, governing the programs of the church; it is a spiritual institute designed by God to oversee the spiritual health of the congregation. It is this spiritual nature of the board that makes us feel uneasy. No matter how many years we have been a follower of Christ and involved in the church, we never see ourselves as being "spiritually qualified." Furthermore, the responsibility of overseeing the spiritual health of the church seems confusing and overwhelming. This is especially true within the small church, where a person is often placed in the position without any prior training or instruction. For many people in the small church, being on the board involves "on-the-job training."

However, the bulk of our confusion and fear about being a board member come not from the significance of the responsibility but from our failure to understand the nature, purpose, and calling of the board. When we properly understand the nature of the board, we realize that it is not a position to be feared but one that we can confidently fulfill as we recognize God's work through us.

The New Testament Terms for Leaders

Understanding the nature of the church board begins with a grasp of the biblical office itself. If we are to be effective in positions of leadership, we must understand what God has called us to do and be. The writers of the New Testament utilized a number of different terms to refer to those who were to be the spiritual leaders of the church. While these words overlap in their meaning and significance, each carries a nuance that provides a different look at the nature of the position.

✳ ✳ ✳

John was confused. He had served on the board for a number of years. As he read the Bible he noticed that the term used most to refer to those in leadership was the term *elder*. Yet when he looked at the description of what an elder was to do, it seemed to describe the role of the pastor. He never saw himself as a spiritual leader in the church. Yet people often came to him for advice when they were facing struggles in their lives. One day John called Pastor Dave to find out what the role of the board was and how it differed from the role of the pastor. What he found out both surprised and frightened him. As he talked with the pastor and as he examined the Bible, he discovered that the role of the elder did not just apply to the work of the pastor but also applied to his own involvement on the church board. Yet for all the apprehension he felt, he was also excited. For the first time since he was voted onto the board sixteen years ago, he realized the importance of his task. He realized that he truly could make a difference in the lives of people.

✳ ✳ ✳

Elder

The most common word for a church leader in the New Testament is the term *elder*, which is a translation of the Greek word *presbuteros*. It was from this word that the word *presbyter* is derived in English. The term originally referred to an elderly man. It was then used of those who, because of their age, were members of various guilds and village officials. In the Christian era the two meanings blended together so that there was little distinction between the designation of age and the title of a member of governing bodies.[1] An elder was more than just an older person, mature in age; he was an older person who was spiritually mature. Elders were individuals who had been followers of Christ for some time and could serve as models and leaders for the church.

As the term is applied to leaders within the early church, it emphasizes the spiritual maturity of the individuals, which was demonstrated by their moral character and consistency of conduct.[2] The term was first used in the New Testament of those who were the established governing council of the church in Acts 14:23. On this occasion we discover Paul and Barnabas establishing churches in Lystra, Iconium, and Antioch. What should catch our attention was that before leaving these churches and moving on in their church-planting endeavors, Paul and Barnabas did not appoint a pastor but appointed elders (plural) in each of the churches. This became the standard practice whenever they planted a new church (Titus 1:5). These individuals were the governing authority within the church, responsible to oversee the spiritual care and maturation of the people (Heb. 13:17). Furthermore, there were within the ranks of these individuals both those who devoted themselves full-time to the task (i.e., our modern concept of the pastor) and those who were volunteers (1 Tim. 5:17). Thus the term *elder* was used to emphasize the dignity and authority of the individuals overseeing the church and the spiritual experience and understanding they were to possess.

Overseer

The second term used in reference to the leadership of the church was *overseer* (in the Greek *episkopos*, from which we derive the word *episcopal*), or *bishop*. Paul utilizes the term in 1 Timothy 3:1: "If anyone sets his heart on being an overseer, he desires a noble task." While the term *elder* focuses upon the qualifications of the position, the term *overseer* emphasizes the function of church leaders. This is seen especially in Acts 20:28, where the church leaders are reminded, "Keep watch over yourselves and all the flock of which the Holy Spirit has made you *overseers* [the term *episkopos*]." The Greeks used this term to refer to a protector and one who gave oversight. In the Greek translation of the Old Testament, the verb form of this term was used for the loving way God watched over his people and cared for them (Ruth 1:6; Ps. 80:14; Zeph. 2:7).[3] Within the church, this term focused upon the function the leadership was to have in overseeing the overall ministry and spiritual health of the congregation.

Pastor

The third term, *pastor* (Greek: *poimen*), is used of both specifically gifted individuals and the function of leaders in the church. The term is used in reference to a specifically gifted individual in Ephesians 4:11, where Paul states that God gave "some to be . . . pastors and teachers." However, Peter uses the term to refer to the function of the elders in 1 Peter 5:1–2: "To the elders among you . . . be shepherds [pastors] of God's flock that is under your care, serving as overseers." The term, which is normally used today to refer to one individual within the church, was used in the New Testament as central to our understanding of the "elders" and "overseers." As John MacArthur points out, "The term *elder* emphasizes who the man is. *Bishop* speaks of what he does. And *pastor* ('shepherd') deals with how he ministers."[4] This does not mean that our modern position of a "pastor" who is serving full-time in ministry is unbiblical. Even in the New Testament we find that there were those who were devoted to full-time ministry (1 Tim. 5:17). These were specifically gifted to be teachers within the church (1 Cor. 12:28–29). However, the term does point out that pastoral care is not just the responsibility of the "minister" but the responsibility of the whole board.

To be a shepherd invokes the imagery of a one who provides care, protection, nourishment, and guidance for the flock. Like the word for overseer, or bishop, the focus of this term *shepherd* is upon the function the leader is to perform. The leader is to protect and care for the spiritual needs of the congregation. The leader is responsible to make sure the spiritually immature are being nurtured and discipled. The elders are to oversee the care given to those who are going through physically, emotionally, or spiritually difficult times. They are to provide care to those who are faltering in their faith.

Deacon

The fourth term for church leaders we find in the New Testament is *deacon*. The position of deacon was first established in Acts 6:1–7. In the development and outgrowth of the organizational structures and programs of the early church, it soon became apparent that the organizational needs were conflicting with the spiritual role of the leadership. In order to maintain a focus upon the spiritual needs and growth of the congregation, the early church elders appointed deacons to care for the church's organizational needs. While many of the *qualifications* of the deacons corresponded to those of the elders, there was a difference in their *function*. The primary role of the elders was spiritual care and teaching, while the deacons were responsible for the "material ministries of the church, specifically distribution of relief to the poor."[5]

As is evident in the study of these four terms, the focus of leadership in the New Testament is upon the spiritual function of the leaders, especially those who are called to be elders within the church. They are not just to direct the organizational functions of the church but also to oversee the overall health of the congregation. It is important to realize that whatever terms we use to refer to a leader are not nearly as important as the function of that leader's position. Within the small church a number of terms may be used to describe the governing body of the congregation (for example, deacons, elders, trustees, church counsel, board, etc.). The task of this governing agency is to provide the spiritual oversight and care of the congregation. The terms may change, but the function does not.

The Office of the Board and the Gift of Pastor

Often, within the small church, the mistaken idea has been that the board is responsible for the physical and organizational needs of the church and the pastor is responsible for the spiritual needs. This, however, fails to understand the overall role and responsibility of both the board and the pastor and the distinction between the two. As has been shown previously, there are overlapping meanings and function. However, Scripture does point to a distinction between the individual gifted to be a pastor and the individuals chosen to be on the board. When we miss this distinction, we feel inadequate and unqualified to serve on the board because we do not think we are gifted for such a role. As a result, some turn down the opportunity to serve on the board, even though they manifest spiritual maturity and wisdom. Or if we do agree to serve, we often focus solely upon the organizational function because we do not think we are gifted or qualified to provide spiritual oversight. However, if we understand the distinction between a spiritual gift and the office of leadership, then we can serve effectively and can confidently recognize that God has equipped us to serve.

First, concerning the distinction, we need to recognize that gifts are bestowed sovereignly by God while the offices are conferred by God through the local congregation. Concerning the spiritual gifts, Scripture reveals that it is God who bestows the gifts. In outlining the spiritual gifts, Paul points out that God the Holy Spirit is the one who determines which gift each individual will receive (1 Cor. 12:11). These are not arbitrarily assigned, but given based upon his sovereign guidance of the church as he equips and calls the church to accomplish specific purposes. In writing to the church at Ephesus, Paul mentions that God has given the church certain individuals who possess the gift of pastor/teacher (Eph. 4:11). These individuals are divinely enabled with special abilities to assist people in becoming fully mature and effective in ministry. On the other hand, being placed in a position of leadership over the church involves both divine appointment and congregational recognition (Acts 6:5–6). In other words, one is not a leader within the church until appointed by the congregation.

A second distinction is that gifts are sovereignly given to all believers, regardless of spiritual qualifications, while offices are to be filled according to specified standards of spiritual maturity. Nowhere in Scripture is spiritual maturity a requirement for receiving or exercising a spiritual gift. Rather, the moment one receives Christ and thus also the Holy Spirit, the person is equipped by God with a specific gift to be utilized to the benefit of the whole congregation (1 Cor. 12:11; 1 Peter 4:10). However, to be an elder, one has to be spiritually mature. For example, the apostle Paul, upon his conversion, received the gift of teaching and preaching. Immediately he began to exercise this gift within the ministry of the church (Acts 9:20). However, it was not until after an extended time of intense discipleship and after serving under the tutelage of Barnabas that Paul actually became a leader within the church (Acts 11:25–29).

Consequently, the focus of leadership is upon neither ability nor giftedness, but upon spiritual maturity and growth. We may fear becoming a board member because we do not possess certain gifts and abilities. We may feel inadequate because we do not perceive ourselves as "natural" leaders. However, Scripture places no such qualification upon those who oversee the church. Instead, we are to be individuals who are firm in our faith, godly in our conduct, and pure in our motives.

Third, there is a distinction between the role of the pastor and board in relationship to the mission and ministry of the church. While both are responsible for the oversight of the congregation, there is a difference in their function. As pointed out by Aubrey Malphurs, the responsibility of the board is primarily that of establishing the mission of the church and monitoring its accomplishments, while the pastor is responsible for the daily achievement of the missions. It is the role of the pastor to recruit and train people to accomplish the mission and to aid in helping them utilize the best possible methods. The board, on the other hand, is responsible for identifying, promoting, and monitoring the mission and vision.[6]

Plurality of Leadership

Throughout the New Testament the norm was for each church to be led by a team of leaders, rather than one specific individual. In each case where a new church was started, we find that a team of leaders was appointed to govern the church. Luke records in Acts 14:23 that Paul and Barnabas followed this practice, "Paul and Barnabas appointed elders for them in each church." So also Paul instructed Titus to "appoint elders in every town" (Titus 1:5). Nor should it escape our notice that on every occasion when the writers of the New Testament referred to the governing body of the church, they did so in the plural (see Acts 20:17; Phil. 1:1; 1 Tim. 5:17; Heb. 13:17). The only two exceptions to this plural use are in 1 Timothy 3:2 and Titus 1:5–7, where the singular term is used as a generic reference to the individuals who make up the office.[7]

This plurality involves mutual authority and responsibility. While board members may *function* differently within the board and congregation, they possess the same *authority*. We find in Hebrews 13:17 that the congregation is responsible to "obey [its] leaders and submit to their authority." Furthermore, in the same verse we discover that every one of the leaders has the same responsibility. "They keep watch over you as men who must give an account." As already pointed out, this stands in stark contrast to many small churches, where the pastor is seen as the "spiritual leader" and the board views themselves as the "organizational leaders." However, Hebrews 13:17 points out that God will hold all the elders responsible for the spiritual health of the congregation, not just the pastor.

This is not to say that there is absolute equality in function. As Paul points out to Timothy, there are different functions within the leadership: "The elders who direct the affairs of the church well are worthy of double honor, especially those whose work is preaching and teaching" (1 Tim. 5:17). While all the elders are responsible to provide spiritual oversight, leadership, and supervision for the congregation and ministries of the church, certain individuals are assigned the function of preaching and teaching. These are to be given special honor, which would involve the twin benefits of respect and financial remuneration.[8] Within the board, the members will function differently as they exercise the different spiritual gifts they have received. This difference in function may involve different realms of authority and different levels of influence within the congregation. For example, the one who functions as a preacher and teacher will have greater influence, not by position, but by function.

✳   ✳   ✳

Pastor Dave was discouraged. He had been serving as the pastor for eight years. He had enjoyed his ministry and enjoyed the people within the church. The ministry was going well, and the church was spiritually healthy. Yet, even though he was pleased with the direction the church was going, he felt burned out. Ministry had become a drudgery rather than a joy, as he struggled to keep up with all the demands of the congregation. That night, as he sat in his easy chair, he realized that he needed help. The task of ministering to the needs of people was exceeding what he could do. But where could help come from? The church could not afford to hire even a part-time associate. For the first time in his ministry, he felt like quitting. Dave called Ken to share his feelings. Ken was surprised. For the past several months they had been talking about how they could be more effective as a board. But as he talked with Dave, Ken realized they were not helping take the load off of Dave's shoulders. While they wanted to be spiritual leaders, they were not becoming spiritual servants who ministered to the needs of people. After promising to bring this up at the next board meeting, Ken hung up the phone. As he did so, he realized that ministry was never intended to be a one-man show. He suddenly realized how alone pastors often feel in ministry. It must be like what Elijah experienced in 1 Kings 19:14–18. In response to his discouragement, God provided him an assistant to help (v. 16). Ken recognized that if the church was to be healthy, then both the pastor and the board must work together to minister to the needs of people. This would not only strengthen the ministry of the church but also result in a better retention of pastors. As Ken thought back over his years on the board, it dawned on him that most of the pastors had resigned, not because of problems in the church, but because of being burned out. The small church can easily overwork the pastor because there is no one to offer assistance and support. At the next board meeting, Ken was going to make this the top priority of the meeting.

✳   ✳   ✳

Board-Pastor Relationship

The health of the church begins with the pastor and the board having a positive relationship. Too often the board and pastor develop an adversarial relationship, with the board being suspicious of the pastor. This especially can be true when a previous pastor was forced to resign because of inappropriate behavior. Consequently, we can develop a perspective that the role of the board is to "keep the pastor in check." The result is that the ministry of the pastor becomes hamstrung as the board seeks to control the activities of the pastor and maintain the status quo rather than support the pastor in leading the church toward spiritual transformation. Consequently, without the support of the board, the pastor becomes ineffective. Soon the pastor gets frustrated and leaves. The cycle then is repeated with the church suffering as the pastoral ministry becomes a revolving door that further results in mistrust of the pastor. In order to break this cycle, it is important that the board understand its responsibilities in relationship to the pastor.

First, the board is responsible to support the pastor. Before the board can be effective leaders, they must first be effective followers. This does not mean that they give unquestioned approval to everything the pastor says or does. This is both unbiblical and irresponsible. However, it does mean that the board must recognize that the pastor is placed within the church by divine appointment and they are to respond to the leadership the pastor provides. Supporting the pastor involves accepting the teaching and instruction of the pastor. It requires that we allow the pastor to guide the church in giving direction to the daily ministries of the congregation. We are to accept and trust the leadership God has provided for us and to allow God to teach us through the pastor's ministry.

Second, the board is responsible to protect the pastor. Too often the pastor is subjected to criticism by those who desire to control, manipulate, and even destroy the pastor's influence and ministry. These are individuals who are not teachable and do not desire to be led, so they resist the pastor when he tries to do so. Tragically, these individuals usually are allowed to remain in the church, constantly criticizing the pastor and undermining any changes the pastor seeks to make. However, Paul gives a severe warning in 1 Timothy 5:19–20, "Do not entertain an accusation against an elder unless it is brought by two or three witnesses. Those who sin are to be rebuked publicly, so that the others may take warning." To attack the leadership that God has provided is equivalent to attacking the leadership of God. David recognized the danger of undermining the leadership God has appointed when he had the opportunity to destroy Saul. When Abishai wanted to kill Saul, David responded, "Don't destroy him! Who can lay a hand on the LORD's anointed and be guiltless?" (1 Sam. 26:9). The board should not stand by and allow people to publicly criticize the pastor and force the pastor to defend himself.[9] Instead, they should publicly support the pastor and defend his ministry and authority.

Third, the board is responsible to care for the pastor. Who pastors the pastor? Tragically, the answer to this question quite often is no one. The result is that many pastors leave ministry because of burnout and stress. Too often the church places unrealistic expectations upon the pastor. Consequently, the pastor is overworked, which adversely affects his family and his own emotional and physical well-being. To prevent this, the board needs to accept responsibility to care for their pastor. This begins with the board making sure that the pastor has adequate financial resources (see chapter 11). Sadly, many pastors of small churches live under financial stress because the board fails to recognize its biblical responsibility to provide for their needs (1 Tim. 5:17). However, providing care for the pastor goes beyond financial remuneration. It also involves caring for the emotional and spiritual needs of the pastor by providing for his spiritual growth through conferences and seminars. Protecting him from burnout begins by having realistic expectations and making sure that he takes his days off to be with his family.

Fourth, the board is responsible to care for the pastor's family. Ministry often has a devastating effect on the family. People criticize the pastor's wife and place demanding, unrealistic, and petty expectations on her. She is always to have a perfect home and be frugal in all areas of finances. (In one church, the wife was criticized for using too much electricity in the parsonage.) The result is that she becomes discouraged, feeling criticized and alienated from the congregation. Tragically, many spouses of pastors feel overworked, unappreciated, and isolated. The same thing happens to the pastor's children. They are expected to be spiritually perfect. If their behavior is in any way unacceptable, they are told that they are to "shape up" because "they are the pastor's kids." Such unrealistic pressures lead to depression and rebellion. According to one study, 80 percent of pastors stated that the ministry has had a negative impact upon their family.[10] Such statistics are shocking and tragic. They challenge the board to make sure that the family of the pastor is protected and cared for in ministry. The role of the board is to protect the pastor's family from petty and unrealistic expectations of people. They should expect nothing more from the pastor's family than they would expect of their own family.

Last, the board is responsible to provide oversight of the pastor. As board members we should always be supportive of the pastor, but we must also recognize that we are to provide loving oversight of the pastor's leadership. The board provides oversight of the pastor's performance by developing policies that clearly communicate his responsibilities. As Malphurs points out, "The idea here isn't to control him or keep him in check but to care for and minister to his soul."[11] This involves providing accountability for where the pastor leads the church and what he teaches from the pulpit, as well as for his actions and behavior. Through mutual, loving accountability we should ask the hard questions regarding his personal life, even as we allow him to ask the hard questions regarding our own behavior, attitudes, and actions.

❋ ❋ ❋

Last Sunday the church had their annual meeting. As the chairman of the board, Ken was concerned for the pastor. During the meeting, a couple of key members in the church directed some strong criticism at the pastor. Mr. and Mrs. Jones were dissatisfied with the fact that the pastor would not perform the wedding of their daughter, who was a Christian but was marrying an unbeliever. Ken knew that the position of the pastor was right, but he felt pressure to side with the disgruntled members because their farm was just down the road from his home. If he sided with the pastor, he risked losing their friendship. Yet if he sided with them, he knew he would be violating Scripture. Ken called Steve that evening to get his advice. He knew that Steve was good friends of these members. As Ken shared his feeling, Steve reminded him of the conversations they had at the recent board meetings. Being in leadership in the small church involves the challenge of maintaining spiritual integrity and upholding biblical truth. While there are no easy answers in dealing with tensions within the church, as leaders they must recognize that they are ultimately accountable to God for obedience to Scripture. A church will never experience God's blessing if it compromises spiritual integrity for personal expediency. As they talked about the issue, both Ken and Steve realized that they had failed to be spiritual leaders when they had allowed the Joneses to be critical of the pastor for what they both knew to be right. Ken and Steve decided they needed to go to the Joneses and affirm the teaching of Scripture. Furthermore, they needed to apologize to Pastor Dave for failing to stand behind him on the issue.

✳ ✳ ✳

The Appointment of the Board

In the small church, a person often is placed on the church board based upon past activity within the church. If the family has a long history within the church and a member of the family has held the position in the past, then it becomes an unwritten expectation that the position belongs to the family. When one family member no longer can serve, the position is passed on to another member of the same family. Often too a person is placed on the board because there "is no one else to fill the job."

Even when the right qualifications are sought after, the small church may struggle to find individuals who are not only qualified to serve but also willing to serve. For many small churches, the annual selection of the board is a struggle just to find willing people. Consequently, the selection is based more on "getting a warm body" to fill the slot than it is on following biblical guidelines.

To be spiritually healthy, the small church needs to recognize the biblical process for the selection of leaders. An examination of the New Testament finds that leaders were not selected based upon bloodlines, or the fulfillment of organizational (or constitutional) requirements; rather, the selection was based upon a spiritual process governed by God and recognized by the church.

First, we discover that before we are placed on the board, we must manifest a willingness and desire to serve on the board. While some may think the desire to be an elder is a sign of arrogance and pride, Paul states that it is commendable: "If anyone sets his heart on being an overseer, he desires a noble task" (1 Tim. 3:1). Peter likewise requires a willingness to serve before one is to be placed in the position, "Be shepherds of God's flock . . . not because you must, but because you are willing, as God wants you to be" (1 Peter 5:2). It is important to realize that the desire for this task is not a desire for power but for influence. This should be the desire of all believers. As followers of Christ, it should be our constant desire to use our gifts, abilities, time, and energy to influence others in their relationship with Christ (Heb. 10:24–25).

Second, to be a church leader we must be motivated by service. Our willingness to be on the board should come not from a desire to be in control, but from the intense passion to serve others. We are to be "eager to serve; not lording it over those entrusted to you, but being examples to the flock" (1 Peter 5:2–3). Before we serve on the board, we must ask ourselves, "Why do I want to be on the board?" This question is not meant to discourage us from serving but to cause us to examine our motives to ensure that they are based upon the desire to serve. If we serve for the wrong reasons, we will have a clouded perspective. Our concern will no longer be for the health of the congregation and the glory of Christ but for our own personal agenda and power. When this happens the board will inevitably fracture and become divided by opposing strategies.

Third, we must meet the qualifications of one who is spiritually mature. While more will be said about this in the next chapter, it is important to realize that God evaluates the character of the leader and not the performance. Mature leaders are not only ones who manifest the spiritual qualities described in the next chapter, they are also those who recognize that ultimately the church belongs to God and we are merely following his leadership (Eph. 5:23; 1 Peter 5:2). The ultimate task of the board is not to set the agenda for the church but to discern and follow God's will and direction.

Fourth, we need to realize God's appointment. Ultimately, if the church is following the biblical procedure for selecting its leadership, God is the one who determines who will be on the board (Acts 20:28). If the church appoints people based upon family relationships or organizational requirements, they will eventually entrust the wrong leaders. Before the church selects the leadership, they should carefully examine each candidate according to the biblical qualifications and then prayerfully seek God's direction. When it has done so, then both the church and the leaders can be confident that God has directed the selection process.

Finally, the individual must be appointed by the church. While there has been some debate in terms of this principle, Scripture does suggest that in the early church there was public recognition of the individuals by the congregation (Acts 6:3). If the congregation does not accept the person appointed, then the person will not be able to function as a spiritual overseer. This is true whether the person is appointed by a congregational vote or appointed by the governing board.

Regarding the actual length of service on the board, Scripture remains silent. Consequently, individual church polity and practice will serve as the guide. However, there are several issues to take into consideration. First, the length of service should be long enough so that at no given point is the whole board up for selection. By offsetting the selection year, the board is provided continuity even when new members are brought on. For example, a church may have a four-year term with one-fourth of the board up for reelection each year. Second, it is recommended that there be a specific length of term assigned, with the person being able to serve more than one term. While some churches place a person on the board to serve in that position for as long as they are members of the church, this is not recommended. Having a specific length of service enables the individual to take a break when needed. Typically in a small church, once a person is on the board, that person is reselected to the position for a number of terms. Often these are individuals who are actively involved in a number of different ministries. There are times when they need to take a break from ministry to be rejuvenated emotionally and spiritually. Furthermore, there may be occasions when a person is no longer fit to serve and is unwilling to step down. This provides a way to gracefully remove the individual with minimal impact on the person and the congregation. The pastor, however, should always be given an indefinite term of ministry.

Every church utilizes different terms to describe the governing body given the responsibility of providing oversight of the church. Far more important than the title is the function. Some churches may call them deacons, others trustees, and still others elders. While we may call ourselves by different terms, it is crucial that we see that our biblical responsibility is outlined by the term *elder* in Scripture. As elders, it is our responsibility to oversee the spiritual health of the congregation. To be a board member is not to fill an organizational slot. It involves much more than that. To be a board member means that we are responsible for spiritually caring for the congregation. It is not merely the pastor's job. The pastor may be the one who provides the teaching, preaching, and counseling function of the board, but it is the whole board's responsibility to care for the congregation. As the appointed leaders within the church, we must recognize that we are appointed by God to be spiritual leaders of the church.

TWO

Character:

The Foundation of Ministry

What do we look for when we look for someone to serve on the board? In many small churches, struggling to find enough individuals to fill the various ministry needs within the church, the job requirements for a board member may look something like this: *Necessary requirements*: A warm body. *Preferred requirements*: Regular attendance (i.e., comes to church regularly on Christmas, Easter, and Communion Sunday—after all we need someone to pass out the Communion elements), previously involved in some ministry of the church (like being an usher), related to someone else in the church (have to keep it in the family), not a newcomer (depending on the church, this may mean a person who has come two Sundays or someone who has been in the church for thirty years or more), and significant financial contributor (the more a person gives, the more likely the person will be appointed). *Ideal requirements*: Likes the pastor and is liked by the pastor.

While the small church often struggles to maintain its leadership positions, it needs to recognize that Scripture places rigid requirements upon those who would serve on the board. In filling the position, the congregation often looks at the position from an organizational point of view and appoints individuals who will fulfill the organizational requirements of the church. However, Scripture looks at the position from the spiritual standpoint. Rather than examining the organizational contribution and requirements, Scripture emphasizes the spiritual foundation. With the focus on the spiritual rather than the organizational, the emphasis is placed on our character rather than our performance and the modeling of Christian living rather than decision making.

Leaders Serve as Living Models

When Paul was writing to the early leaders of the church, he made it clear that central to their role and purpose was providing an example for others to follow (1 Tim. 4:12; Titus 2:7). Paul did not write to Timothy about leading in organizational decisions, taking care of the facilities, or even establishing and overseeing the programs of the church. Instead, he challenged Timothy to be an example. The word translated "example" is the term from which we derive our English word *type*. It refers to the imprint an object leaves behind when pressed against another, such as an impression of a seal upon melted wax.[1] The picture Paul presented by using this term is that we are a model that is to make an impression upon others because we ourselves have been shaped by Christ.[2]

An important task of leadership is to give reality to faith by providing a living model for people. We are the living picture of what it means to be a disciple of Christ and how we are to live daily in relationship to Christ. The congregation is to see in us what they are to become. The adage that a picture is worth a thousand words expresses the heart of biblical leadership. Our lives form a living picture, serving as a guide to others on how they are to live out their Christian faith. This comes as we follow the living model of Christ (1 Cor. 11:1). This mandate challenges us to be continually asking ourselves as leaders, "If everyone in the church lived like I live, would they be vibrant, growing disciples of Christ?" When our lives do not match the message we claim to follow, then we are going to mislead people and the entire congregation.

In writing to those in ministry, Paul outlines the type of people who can be such models. They are not necessarily individuals of exceptional abilities or achievements. Rather, they are individuals of exceptional character.

✳ ✳ ✳

Pastor Dave began the board meeting with a short devotional from 1 Timothy 3:1–13 on the qualification of an elder and deacon. As he finished, Steve asked the question, "Pastor, what is the most important qualification? If we are the elders that are mentioned in Scripture, I certainly don't feel qualified. It's not just the character issue; it's the whole issue of being a spiritual leader. I just don't feel that I have the ability to lead the church." Pete quickly concurred.

Dave thought for a moment before he replied. "I know that the whole idea of each of you being spiritual leaders is new and seems overwhelming. But let me ask you this, What is the most important contribution that we as leaders make to the church?"

Steve quickly responded, "I think the most important thing we do is make sure the church is growing spiritually and being transformed to be like Christ."

"That's right!" replied the pastor. "But how do we do that?"

"That's just it, Pastor. I'm not sure. I know we are to do more than make sure the programs are running smoothly. We have been talking about leadership, but to be honest, I'm not really sure that I am a leader," Steve answered.

"Steve, when you hire a teenager to help you during harvest, how do you teach him to drive the combine? Do you just give him the manual and then tell him to go start driving it?"

Steve laughed. "Not on your life. I am not going to turn over a $250,000 combine to a kid who is not dry behind the ears yet without first showing him how to run it. Usually I spend half a day showing him how to operate the machine by having him ride with me while I drive. Then I will have him drive for the rest of the day, and I watch him to make sure he understands what I showed him."

"Exactly!" Dave exclaimed. "And that is the same type of leadership that is most needed from us. The most important aspect of leadership is not what we do or even the decisions we make. It is how we model the Christian life before others. The most important contribution we give to the church is our holiness. Being an example is by far the most important responsibility we have as leaders. Whether we realize it or not, people are watching our lives. The question is not whether we will be an example, but what type of example we will be. Will we point people to Christ and holiness by our lives, or will we distort people's perspective and lead them astray? The benefit of the small church is that people rub shoulders with us on a daily basis. They know us personally. They know how we live, not only on Sunday but also throughout the rest of the week. Steve, you understand that showing someone how to operate a machine is the best way to teach the person how to operate it. The same is true in the church. The most important thing we do for people is to show them how to live the Christian life. That is why Paul places so much emphasis on character. For it is this that becomes the most important role we have as leaders."

※   ※   ※

Leaders Demonstrate a Right Relationship with God

When we read the qualifications for leaders set down by Paul in 1 Timothy 3:1–13 and Titus 1:5–9, we often become overwhelmed with our own shortcomings. We examine the list and conclude that we are disqualified for ministry. What we often overlook is that the list of qualifications is not for perfect, super-saints, who have their lives all together. Instead, Paul describes the qualities of a mature Christian, qualities that we should be striving to implement in our lives, regardless of whether or not we are leaders. If we do not feel qualified, instead of shying away from leadership, we should be challenged to make adjustments in our lives so that we are developing these qualities.

* * *

The task of the nominating committee was normally just a formality. They would open in prayer and then go down the list of leadership positions that had to be filled. In each case they would ask the person who had served last year to serve again. Since most people agreed (sometimes after a little persuasion), they would just provide the list to the church. Usually the meeting lasted less then an hour and people spent the rest of the time discussing the latest happenings in the community. But on this occasion it was different. Instead of the meeting being placid, it was becoming heated. The reason was that John was stepping down, leaving the board after thirty-five years of service. Some felt his son, Jim, should naturally be put on the board in his place. However, some on the committee felt that Jim was not yet qualified. Although he had accepted Christ at VBS when he was young, he had walked away from the church during college and only recently had started coming back to church. Since he did not fit the biblical qualifications of a mature Christian, some (including the pastor) did not want to place him on the board. Those who did pointed out that the constitution required four board members, and since he was the only person available, the church should put him on the board anyway. The meeting was moving into the third hour, and the discussion was becoming more heated. Finally, Pastor Dave told the committee that they would discuss it at the next elder meeting and bring a recommendation back to the committee. This seemed to satisfy everyone, and so they ended the meeting with a commitment to make the issue a matter of prayer for the next week.

Dave approached the board meeting with a great deal of apprehension. While the board had been becoming more spiritual in its focus, he was concerned that John would be upset that some were questioning Jim's qualifications. After spending the first half hour in prayer for the needs of the church, Dave brought up the issue of someone to replace John on the board. But before he could say anything, John stated that he had something to say. Dave's apprehension grew.

"Pastor, I have been thinking about this whole issue. Now I know that some think that Jim should replace me on the board; after all, he is the most logical person. But you know, we were talking last meeting about the importance of character and modeling as foundational to leadership. To be honest, as much as I am excited about Jim getting himself right with God, I just don't think he is ready for leadership. As you pointed out, Pastor, being biblically correct is more important than organizational expediency. I was wondering if perhaps I should stay on the board for another term. This would allow you to spend time with Jim, discipling him. Perhaps we could even have him sit in on some of our training discussions to see what it means to be a board member."

Dave breathed a sigh of relief. "John, I appreciate your perspective. To be honest I was thinking the same thing. I am sure the nominating committee will agree with this. I will talk with Jim and start meeting with him once a week to disciple him. I also think it would be good to have him attend our meetings as an observer. This will give us a chance to show him what it means to be a spiritual leader."

※　※　※

Godly Leaders Have a Mature Grasp of Doctrine

One of the first, and perhaps most important, qualifications of board members is that they faithfully uphold the theological foundation of the church. Paul writes to Titus, "He must hold firmly to the trustworthy message as it has been taught" (Titus 1:9). This trustworthy message was the faith of the Bible, which found expression in the doctrinal teachings of the church.

In contrast to the lackadaisical and haphazard approach that the modern church has taken to theology and doctrine, the early church viewed doctrine as the very expression of the soul of one's belief in God. Theology may be defined as "a right understanding of who God is and what he does and how we are to respond to him." It is this understanding of God that forms the backbone of the Christian church. Without a biblical theology as the basis for the church, it is reduced to a social organization that operates programs rather than a spiritual organism that challenges the hearts and minds of people with biblical truth. Our theology, rather than our programs and strategies, is what will determine the future health of the church.

First, we need to have a correct understanding of right theology. This is the one qualification that moves from the moral requirements to a theological requirement. The focus of Titus 1:9 is that we are to understand and uphold the core doctrines of Scripture. However, developing clear theological teaching is not merely for doctrinal correctness; it is the basis on which we encourage people within the church. What we believe about God becomes the basis for spiritual, emotional, and psychological health. While we may not have all the answers for the difficulties and problems people face in life, we can provide encouragement for them by sharing biblical truth.

We need a right understanding of doctrine because of the prevalence of false teaching and teachers who will enter the church and bring theological distortion (Acts 20:29–30). If the leadership is anemic in doctrinal truth, then the church will become easy prey for theological error. This does not mean that we must demonstrate a Bible college or seminary-level understanding of doctrine. But it does mean that we have an understanding of the foundational truths of Scripture so that we can identify, confront, and correct doctrinal error (Titus 1:9). If we are theologically illiterate, then error can easily creep into the church unchecked.

Second, we are to model a transformational theology. In the pursuit of doctrinal knowledge, we cannot allow it to become merely an intellectual exercise whereby our knowledge of doctrine has little implication for our lives. Instead, doctrine must be the springboard from which we dive into practical Christian living. In 1 Timothy 1:8–10 Paul indicates that moral and spiritual depravity stems from a rejection of and lack of application of sound doctrine. Theology is not genuine theology until it is lived theology. Theology is our understanding of God and our understanding of how he works. This understanding then determines how we are to live before the living God. This is why the first step toward spiritual apostasy is the abandonment of doctrinal truth (2 Tim. 4:3). As leaders we must continually demonstrate the reality of our theology. People must see in us the difference our theology makes in our attitudes and actions both within the church and in our daily lives.

Godly Leaders Demonstrate Teaching Ability

Church leaders should be able to teach. This does not necessarily mean that we must have the gift of teaching. Nor does it mean that we must be able to teach an adult Sunday school class. When Paul states the requirement that the elder must be "able to teach" (1 Tim. 3:2), he had more in mind than just publicly communicating the Word of God. The ability to teach relates to our ability to instruct others and refute false teachers. Paul expands upon this in his writing to Titus, where he states that the elder needs to "encourage others by sound doctrine and refute those who oppose it" (1:9).

Teaching relates to our understanding of the truth and the ability to explain that truth to others. While the focus may include a formal classroom situation, the idea is much broader than this. It includes informal interaction as well. While we may not be gifted or called to teach a Sunday school class, we need to be able to explain the Scriptures to others so that they can grow spiritually. This requires that we have a firm understanding of Scripture so that we "correctly [handle] the word of truth" (2 Tim. 2:15) and refute false doctrine when it arises (Titus 1:9). While we may lack the communication skills necessary to teach in a classroom setting or preach from the pulpit, we need to be able to articulate the meaning of Scripture to people. Teaching is much more than just formal instruction; it encompasses informal instruction as well. As we look in the pages of Scripture, we find that a number of individuals God used to significantly influence and lead the church demonstrated not only a variety of personalities but a diverse number of gifts as well. Barnabas had the gift of mercy and compassion, while Paul had the gift of apostleship. It is obedience to God that is central to leadership.

✻ ✻ ✻

Ken was ready to resign from the board. Recently the pastor, representing the nominating committee, had approached him about teaching the adult Sunday school class. Ken was a mature Christian who had a consistent walk. People readily recognized his insight and maturity. But the one thing Ken feared most was getting up in front of people. Consequently, he always felt insecure about being on the board; after all, the leader is to be "apt to teach." He knew he could not teach the class, so he decided he should resign from the board. He gave the pastor a call.

"Dave, you know that I like being on the board, but I just cannot get in front of people. The last time I tried it, I became such a bundle of nerves that I actually broke down in tears. I guess I need to resign from the board since I cannot teach."

Dave was quiet for a moment, and then he answered, "Ken, I have a great deal of respect for you, and I value your spiritual insight. That is why I asked you to teach. I understand if you don't feel comfortable in front of people. That's OK, and that does not disqualify you from the board. You may not realize it, but you are one of the best teachers we have in the church. You don't do it in a classroom, but I have observed you at Joe's Cafe sharing the Bible with people who are going through difficult struggles. You know, Ken, that is just as much teaching as teaching in a classroom. Don't worry about the Sunday school class. I will find someone else who is more comfortable being up front."

Ken was relieved, "Thanks, Pastor. I guess you won't get me off the board yet," he said, as Dave laughed. "By the way, Pastor, I again want to tell you how much I have enjoyed the discussions we have been having on the board. For the first time in the years I have been serving on the board, I feel that we are really doing something that will have a significant impact. Keep up the good work."

❃   ❃   ❃

Godly Leaders Demonstrate Spiritual Integrity

Paul likewise points out that the leader must be one who is "upright [and] holy" (Titus 1:8). The first of these terms, *upright*, refers to one who is morally upright and righteous. It speaks of one who conforms to the moral law of God and fulfills the will of God. Likewise, *holy* refers to one who is in harmony with the moral laws God has established in the universe. To be a leader in the church, we must live in accordance with God's ethical, moral, and spiritual code of conduct, which is an expression of his own character and being. Spiritual integrity is consistency between what we believe about God and how we act before God. This consistency springs forth, not because of congregational expectations and pressures to conform to external standards, but because it is an expression of our own character as we have been transformed by the person of Christ. When we possess and manifest spiritual integrity, we respond in all situations in a way that is in harmony with the character of God. As leaders within the church, we must strive to make every decision and activity within the church correspond to the nature and person of God. We are to properly reflect Christ in all we do as a congregation.

Godly Leaders Are Faithful Stewards

To be a leader before God, one must be approved by God. (cf. 2 Tim 2:15). The term *blameless* (Titus 1:6, 7) is derived from the idea of one who is not called into account or question.[3] The reason for this is because we are stewards of God's ministry (v. 7). We need to recognize that God holds us accountable for our performance as leaders. As we serve, we are always to remember that we are ultimately accountable to God rather than just the congregation. One of the dangers within the small church is that we can become relationally driven to the point that decisions are based, not on what is biblically correct, but on what is politically expedient. We can be governed by the desire to please others rather than to please God. It is easy to allow political expediency (how I can please people) or personal agendas (what I want) to govern decisions rather than the will of God. In leadership, there may be times when decisions must be made that will be unpopular but necessary because of the biblical instruction. While it is important in the small church to be relationally sensitive, we must always remain biblically driven.

Being biblically driven requires consistency in our lifestyle so that no one can accuse us of misusing our authority for personal advantage. We are to be "above reproach" (1 Tim. 3:2). In other words, we exercise our responsibilities in such a way that people recognize our character and cannot malign us with a charge of inappropriate action. Concerning character and spiritual integrity, John Harris writes, "The personal authenticity of the minister . . . is the greatest strength of any congregation. The inauthenticity of the clergy is the greatest weakness of organized religion."[4] This is even more true regarding the church board. A church with strong spiritual leadership on the board can survive many difficult challenges, but it cannot survive when the board becomes dominated by sinful, self-serving individuals.

Godly Leaders Demonstrate Spiritual Maturity and Growth

According to 1 Timothy 3:6, to be qualified as a leader, one must not be a recent or immature convert. The term used is the word from which we derive the English term *neophyte,* which refers to one who is a novice. It literally means "newly planted," thus referring to one who is a new convert to the faith. However, the focus is more upon spiritual maturity than the age of the person or the amount of time the person has been a Christian. Some individuals are still newly planted in the faith, even though they have been Christians for some time and have been involved in the church (see 1 Cor. 3:2; Heb. 5:11–14).

This qualification serves to correct some common mistakes in the small church. The first mistake is to equate length of attendance with spiritual maturity. One of the hazards of the small church is that we are reluctant to give positions of leadership to people who have not been attending the church for a considerable length of time. Board positions are often given to individuals based upon their length of involvement in the church rather than spiritual maturity. "Newcomers" (which may be defined as anyone who has come in the last five to ten years) are not given a position on the board, even though they have demonstrated significant spiritual maturity and wisdom. On the other side of the coin, we can also be mistaken when we assume that a person who has been a long-time attendee is spiritually mature.

A second mistake this qualification corrects is that of placing people on the board as a way of getting them involved. In the small church, people are sometimes appointed to serve on the board in the hope that it will motivate them to become more active in the church. For example, when the annual election is held, Tom is nominated because "he does not come very often and maybe this will get him to come more faithfully." While it is often helpful to involve people in ministry in order to encourage them to become more engaged in the church, the board (or any leadership position) should never be seen as one of these ministries. The church should place on the board only those who have demonstrated spiritual maturity.

Wisdom to lead comes only from spiritual maturity. As James Means points out, "Maturity is necessary if a leader is to react properly to criticism, manage time carefully, be disciplined in work habits, behave appropriately and with common sense in a variety of situations, counsel with godly wisdom, be self-controlled, be gentle, be not quarrelsome, and so forth."[5]

Godly Leaders Manifest a Passion for What Is Good

As God's representative leaders, we must be passionate about righteousness. It is our intense longing to manifest what is honorable and good that must drive every decision. We are to promote good in all areas of life.[6] This means not only within the church, but within the community as well. This may involve working with others outside the church to promote the protection of the unborn. It may involve working with other social agencies in order to provide physical assistance to those in need. We are not to have a narrow vision of ministry where we look only upon what our own church is doing. Rather, we are to have a comprehensive view of ministry and promote good throughout the whole community.

Leaders Demonstrate a Right Relationship with Others

Godly character is manifested not only in our attitude and relationship with God, but also in our interaction with others. One of the hallmarks of a transformed life is an intense and unconditional love for others (John 13:35). The love we are to have is to be radically different from the attitudes of the world. We are not just to overlook the faults of others; we are to have a genuine concern for the welfare of even those who consider themselves our enemies (Luke 6:27–36). To be qualified for the position of a leader requires that we maintain this higher standard in our personal relationships.

Godly Leaders Should Be Respected by Others

To be respectable (1 Tim. 3:2) requires that we maintain positive relationships with others so that they cannot speak negatively about us. It refers to one who relates well to the world in which he lives. We maintain orderliness so that we are not criticized for our lack of organization. As leaders we are to maintain the organization of the church in order to assure that everything is done "in a fitting and orderly way" (1 Cor. 14:40). This means that we make sure that we follow the guidelines set forth in the constitution of the church. It means that we establish policies to guide people in their respective ministries and that we hold people accountable to follow those policies. This is especially critical in the areas of how the church handles its finances and how the church protects children from potential abuse.

Godly Leaders Are Congenial

As our society has become increasingly fast-paced and deper-sonalized, people long for meaningful interpersonal relationships. One of the strengths of the small church is that it is a place where people can form close personal relationships with mutual encour-agement and accountability. As leaders within the church, we are to take the initiative in developing these relationships (1 Tim. 3:2; Titus 1:8).

However, just as a strength of the small church is the interper-sonal relationships enjoyed by people, one of the weaknesses is that it can remain aloof to new people who come into the church. Thus, we need to be intentional in building relationships with these people as well. Before and after the service, we should be searching for new faces to welcome. We should be willing to invite them into our homes and "adopt" them into the church family. Bill Kemp warns,

> Small congregations, in subtle and subconscious ways, maintain a welcoming posture toward those who are "like us," but often have little latitude with regard to those of a different class or culture. They go out of their way to wel-come an individual who shows up from a different race or economic strata than their own, but inviting that person into the intimate circle of the congregation's membership and fellowship life is a different matter.[7]

As leaders, it is our responsibility to make sure that new people are grafted into the fellowship of the church (for an example see Barnabas's actions in Acts 9:26–30 and 11:25–26).

Godly Leaders Manifest Skill in Conflict Resolution

Conflict is a part of life and a part of leadership. To be a leader means that we are constantly confronting people with personal, spiritual, and organizational change. Change inevitably leads to conflict as the old contends with the desired new. An effective leader is one who does not respond to conflict with further hostility but rather strives to lovingly and properly resolve the conflict. A quarrelsome individual is one who sees conflict as a threat and challenge and responds to it as such. Paul states that we are not to be "quarrelsome" (1 Tim. 3:3). To serve, we should manifest humility rather than aggression, being willing to sacrifice personal rights and desires for the benefit of others. We are to be gentle, and when challenged, we are to respond with grace and compassion rather than with hostility and aggression. This does not mean that we pursue peace at all cost but that we seek to resolve issues quickly and appropriately in a way honoring to God. A biblical leader is slow to criticize and does not respond with anger even when mistreated by others. This is especially true with respect to the pastor. Congregations often become critical of pastors because of unrealistic expectations that they place upon them. As leaders we are responsible to support and encourage the pastor and his wife.

Godly Leaders Maintain a Good Reputation with the Unsaved

We are to relate positively not only to people in the church but with people outside the church as well (1 Tim. 3:7). This involves allowing the character of Christ to govern our business practices and recreational activities. In business, we seek to honor God first and foremost rather than pursue success and financial gain. In recreation, the things we enjoy, the places we go, the activities we are involved in are tempered and governed by our relationship with God (Eccl. 8:15; 12:13–14). We conduct ourselves in such a way that people will acknowledge our character, even if they reject our faith (1 Peter 2:12, 15). We are like the disciples in Acts 4, who were despised by the Sanhedrin because of their faith, yet the religious leaders "when they saw the courage of Peter and John and realized that they were unschooled, ordinary men, they were astonished and they took note that these men had been with Jesus" (Acts 4:13). We are qualified to serve as elders when our faith governs every activity, both within the church and within the community. As White points out, "There is something blameworthy in a man's character if the consensus of outside opinion be unfavorable to him; no matter how much he may be admired and respected by his own party."[8]

Godly Leaders Remain Humble

In writing to Titus, Paul disqualifies one from service who is "overbearing" (Titus 1:7). The term refers to one who is stubborn and self-willed, one who is self-pleasing. As leaders we are not to be inflexible in our opinions, demanding our own way. We do not use our position in order to accomplish personal agendas. Instead, we are willing to respect and listen to other viewpoints and perspectives. Leadership involves authority. Humility involves servanthood. A humble leader is one who exercises authority in a way that best serves the needs and interests of others rather than themselves. Our goal is not our own recognition, nor are we concerned about elevating our reputation. Instead, we strive to please God and see his will accomplished within the congregation.

Godly Leaders Demonstrate Honesty with Finances

A preoccupation with money brings corrupt motives and fraudulent activities (1 Tim. 6:10). Consequently, we need to have a proper perspective on money. Instead of seeking the pursuit of money at all cost (1 Tim. 3:8; Titus 1:7), we are to recognize that money is a tool to be used for the glory of God. The focus is not on the possession of material things, or on wealth itself, but on our attitude and perspective on our possessions and wealth. A person who sees wealth as a means of attaining satisfaction and security inevitably will compromise biblical integrity to attain it. Instead, we are to place our trust in God's daily provision, recognizing that our present satisfaction in life and our future security are not determined by what we possess but by the watchful God who cares for our needs. When we fail to have a proper perspective regarding our own material wealth, we will be misguided in our decisions regarding the ministry and finances of the church.

Leaders Demonstrate Godly Character in Relationship to Their Family

Stated bluntly, no one should be a leader who is not first a spiritual leader in the home. A person who aspires to serve on the board of the church must first be a servant-leader within the home, modeling godly servanthood regarding the family. We recognize that family comes before vocation and the needs of the family before personal pursuits.

Godly Leaders Are Spiritual Leaders in the Home

There is an epidemic of spiritual passivity among men. Many, many men are more concerned about the health of their portfolio than they are about the spiritual health of their family. They are content to let their wives (who are to be commended for their faithfulness) to take the spiritual leadership rather than taking upon themselves the responsibility of raising their children in Christ. When men fail to take the spiritual leadership in the home, they seriously handicap their children's potential for spiritual maturity. When the child senses the father's passivity, they regard Christianity as unessential, no matter what the parents might say. As Josh McDowell states, "You can con a con, you can fool a fool, but you can't kid a kid."[9] We can fool our congregation into thinking we are spiritual, we can hide behind organizational wisdom, we can wear suits on Sunday to appear devout, but we cannot fool our children regarding our faith. If we do not live it at home, they will not follow our footsteps to church. Consequently, Paul requires that church leaders be individuals who are leaders at home (1 Tim. 3:4; Titus 1:6). This means that we model Christ before our family and lead them in worship and fellowship.

Godly Leaders Are Committed to Their Spouse

Much debate has centered on the command that a leader be the "husband of but one wife" (1 Tim. 3:2).[10] Not withstanding, the focus of the verse is upon the character quality manifested by the individual. To be effective in leadership, we need to be consistent in our moral integrity and faithful to our relational covenant. A leader must not have a "wondering eye" but be committed to his wife. This goes beyond sexual purity. To be committed to one's wife involves emotional faithfulness as well. It involves placing a priority upon one's relationship with one's spouse. Many individuals who would never consider committing sexual adultery have committed emotional adultery. Their mistress is not a person, but a job, a career, a hobby or anything that has replaced their loyalty and commitment to their spouse's well-being. Leaders serve as examples to others concerning the importance of not only integrity in the marriage bed, but also faithfulness to the marriage vow of loving their spouse and serving their spouse's emotional, physical, and spiritual needs (Eph. 5:25–33).

Godly Leaders Are Committed to Training Their Children

It is significant that Paul emphasizes the importance of the leaders' relationship with their children as a prerequisite for serving (1 Tim. 3:4–5; Titus 1:6). This statement highlights not only the parents' training of the children, but also the children's attitude toward their parents. Ministry should never be an excuse for neglecting our relationship with our children. It is also noteworthy that this is one of the few qualifications that Paul expands upon, thus further calling attention to its importance. We must maintain order within the home, exercising authority in a loving and godly way. "It must be done in such a manner that the father's *firmness* makes it *advisable* for a child to obey, that his *wisdom* makes it *natural* for a child to obey, and that his *love* makes it a *pleasure* for a child to obey."[11] Too often, the focus in selecting leaders is upon performance and accomplishments in the business or church realm, rather than in the home.

Tragically, many leaders in the church have broken relationships with their children. They are bitter and angry at their child because he or she made decisions that not only embarrassed the parent but also violated biblical principles. However, rather than responding in anger and bitterness, we are to respond with forgiveness and grace. While we do not excuse or condone sin, we do demonstrate love to our children no matter how much they may have hurt us. By doing so, we are demonstrating the type of forgiveness that God has demonstrated to us.

Leaders Demonstrate Godly Character in Relationship to Themselves

Not only does the leader maintain right relationships with God, with others, and with his family, but he also maintains a right perspective on himself. If we desire to serve within the church, we need to recognize our responsibility to control our own natural desires and feelings so that we are governed by the truth of Scripture rather than by cultural norms and expectations or by personal feelings. Within the small church there is often a set of cultural standards that govern people's behavior. As long as a person adheres to these expectations, they are "acceptable." These may be expressed in the way we dress (always dress up on Sunday, no hats in the sanctuary), the activities we are involved in (do not play cards or go to movies), or manner in which we conduct our worship service (hymns with a piano or organ, but no drums). To be a leader, we must look beyond these and recognize that biblical truth—not our cultural setting—is the basis of decisions and conduct.

Godly Leaders Maintain Control of Natural Appetites

The term translated as "disciplined" (Titus 1:8) has the idea of one who exercises personal restraint. While the phrase has reference to sensual desires, it also encompasses much more. It includes all one's desires that lead to sin (James 1:13–14). Paul manifested this attribute of discipline in his own life. In 1 Corinthians 9:27 he states, "I beat my body and make it my slave so that after I have preached to others, I myself will not be disqualified for the prize." As leaders we need to restrain our natural desires toward self-centeredness, laziness, sexual temptations, gluttony, and other "habits" that distract or hinder our work for Christ. As leaders we must show restraint in all areas of life, so that our identity and self-worth are found in God and our satisfaction and joy in life flows from our relationship with God. We should not be dominated or controlled by any other activity or force.

Godly Leaders Are Controlled by the Holy Spirit

A leader is not given over to drunkenness (1 Tim. 3:3; Titus 1:7) but rather is temperate (1 Tim. 3:2). The foundation of this prohibition is the command to be controlled by the Holy Spirit (Eph. 5:18). When an individual is under the influence of alcohol, it is controlling the individual and governing the actions of the person. Instead, we are to be controlled only by the Holy Spirit, living in submission to him and allowing his will to be accomplished in us. We lead effectively when we are directed by the will and purpose of God. We are not to be governed by anything else. The word *temperate* describes "a mental self-control that rules out all forms of excesses."[12] Within the small church, we are not to be controlled by tradition or popularity. Tradition plays an important and vital role within the small church, as it provides continuity and relational connection between generations. However, the danger is that the tradition can control decisions and govern the ministry of the church. When this happens, we are not to be afraid to stand up and break with tradition because we strive to follow God's direction.

Godly Leaders Are Careful Thinkers

The term *self-controlled* (1 Tim. 3:2; Titus 1:8) means to be "of sound mind, rational and prudent." The focus is on the ability of the person to carefully evaluate all options before making a decision. As leaders, we should not be rash in our judgments, jumping to conclusions about plans, ideas, or people without carefully thinking through the issues and seeking to know all the facts. We should not immediately reject an idea because "it has not been done that way" or because "it did not work before." Nor do we accept an idea simply because "one of the experts said it would work." We do not follow fads but carefully examine each issue based upon the foundation of Scripture and the understanding of the cultural setting.

The godly leader is someone who not only carefully examines issues but also is serious about spiritual truth. We understand the gravity of the spiritual world and the importance of the ministry. We have the ability to see things from God's perspective. We recognize we are to act Christianly because we think Christianly. Because of this we know how to set priorities in our own lives and in the ministry of the church.[13]

Godly Leaders Are Patient with Others

A patient person is one who is considerate, gracious, and gentle. Such character qualities are required of those who desire to serve (Titus 1:7), for these are qualities that God exhibits. To be patient involves a willingness to overlook and forgive the faults of others. As board members we often will have information regarding the problems and struggles confronting individuals within the congregation. This is especially true in the small church, where we know everyone, including their past failures and present struggles. The danger is that this information can cloud our perspective and treatment of them. A leader does not look at the wrong people have done, nor does a leader condemn people because of their present struggles; rather a good leader looks at the good of people and considers their potential in Christ. When we manifest this quality, we are not easily upset by the criticism of others (Eccl. 7:21–22). When we are in leadership, we will be criticized. At times the criticism is justified, and we are responsible to seek forgiveness and change in response. Often it will be unjustified. Rather than becoming bitter, vindictive, and defensive, we are to be ready to forgive even if the person has not shown any repentance.

Godly Leaders Are Motivated by Service

Paul writes that the leader is not to be "a lover of money" (1 Tim. 3:3). In other words, our motivation for ministry and involvement in the church is not to be based upon what we get out of it. Instead, we are to be motivated by our love for God and our desire to serve others. When we have a love for money, it can cloud our perspective so that we make decisions based not on what is best for God's kingdom but on what is best for the bank account. Ministry involves sacrifice. It not only requires the sacrifice of our time, but also the sacrifice of our financial resources. As leaders we are to have a proper perspective on money. We are to recognize that it is a tool to be used for God's glory rather than something merely for our own enjoyment. To be godly leaders, we need to set the standard by being good stewards of our personal finances and manifesting a willingness to sacrifice our resources for the needs and good of others. We are not to be tightfisted, nor are we to be judgmental of those within the church who are experiencing financial difficulties. Instead, we should be willing to give and give generously and sacrificially to those in need.

✳   ✳   ✳

Before the annual meeting, Mary asked Fred if he would like to be nominated to the board. His father had been a prominent leader in the church, and so it was expected that he also serve. Some of his friends also wanted him to serve because they wanted certain changes made, and they felt that if he was on the board they could get their agenda pushed through. However, as Fred thought and prayed about it, he realized that these were not legitimate reasons to accept the nomination. As he looked at 1 Peter 5:1–4, he realized that it was not the church that chose the leaders but God, and as a result he must be a servant of God and of the church. Leadership is not about position and manipulation to attain one's agenda; it is about serving people. While he desired to serve God, he knew he was not yet ready for such a role. That night he called Mary and thanked her for thinking of him, but he turned down the nomination offer.

✳   ✳   ✳

At the center of leadership is character. We can possess all the natural leadership abilities that would make us a success in the secular realm, but if we lack godly character we will never be effective for God. Conversely, we may not be outstanding leaders from the world's perspective, yet if we possess godly character we will be effective leaders in the church. The most effective leaders are not the ones who can dream of lofty goals or develop efficient programs. They are not the ones who can speak eloquently or reveal keen insight in problem-solving techniques. They are not the vocal individuals who can push their ideas through. Within the church, the most effective leaders are those who possess a deep love for Christ, possess a thorough understanding of Scripture, and can apply that understanding to the issues confronting the church. We are effective leaders when we follow Christ wholeheartedly and are shaped by his character in such a way that God shapes others through us. As leaders we must recognize that the spiritual health of the church is directly related to our own spiritual growth. If we are not growing in our relationship with Christ, then the church will become spiritually stagnant. Both individually and corporately as a board we must always be examining our character, motives, and actions to make sure that we are exemplifying the character of Christ.

THREE

The Priority of Leadership

Bill was typical of many new board members. At the annual meeting, his father, Sam, who had served for thirty years, announced that it was time for him to step down. While there were several men who were qualified, it seemed natural for the congregation to replace Sam with his son. While Bill had grown up in the church and been involved all his life, he suddenly realized that he did not know what the board was supposed to do. He understood the biblical qualifications for being a leader, and he knew the board took care of the church building. However, Bill had always felt the board was to do much more than decide who was going to fix the plumbing. Bill wanted to fulfill the biblical responsibilities. But as he thought about it, he realized that he was unclear what those responsibilities were.

Like Bill, we often are unclear about the role and responsibilities of the board. Because there is often only one "governing board" within the small church, the focus shifts to the physical maintenance of the church. However, Scripture emphasizes the spiritual nature of the board. Being a board member involves both substance (character) and responsibility (action). However, the task we are to perform is not just organizational (taking care of the facilities, making decisions about programs, etc.). Tragically, within small churches, the job description looks more like that of a maintenance technician than it does a spiritual leader of a spiritual organism.

The calling to be on the board is a calling to guide the church toward spiritual growth and the fulfillment of its mission. To be a leader is to be responsible for the spiritual well-being of the congregation (Heb. 13:17). This moves leadership from an organizational context to a spiritual context.

When Paul gave his final address to the leadership in the church in Ephesus (Acts 20:28–35), he focused upon the spiritual priorities of the board. While there are many demands placed upon the board, the board should never neglect the priorities that God has given. Instead, we need to keep them as the focus of our meeting.

✳ ✳ ✳

Pastor Dave was excited about the direction the board had been going in the last six months. For the first time since he began serving the church, he began to sense that the leadership wanted to grow and become biblical leaders. But something still was not quite right. In last night's board meeting, Steve raised a critical question, one that Dave was not prepared to answer. While Steve was excited about becoming a spiritual leader, he was still not clear what the priorities of the board should be. While he agreed that character was important and foundational, what were the priorities the board was to focus upon? That morning as Dave read the Bible during his personal devotions, he was struck by what Paul challenged the elders at Ephesus with in Acts 20. As he read the passage, he realized that Paul was giving the church leaders the priorities they were to focus upon. This was the answer to Steve's question. Dave kind of laughed to himself. It always amazed him how his time in personal reading of Scripture always seemed to provide him answers to issues he was facing in his own life. As he reread the passage, he knew that he would have something to share at next month's board meeting.

✳ ✳ ✳

The Board Is to Recognize Their Accountability to God

Paul reminds the church leaders that they are placed within leadership, not by the decision of the congregation, but by the will and purpose of God. This points not only to the importance of our responsibility, but also to our accountability before God. Paul reminds the leadership, "Keep watch over . . . all the flock, of which the Holy Spirit has made you overseers" (Acts 20:28). The concept set forth by Paul is that we leaders are the ones who are put in a position of giving oversight of the congregation. However, this does not come from our own volition or choosing but by the decision of God. Critical to understanding our role as leaders is the recognition that the church does not belong to us or even the congregation, but it belongs to God. In the New Testament we find a number of terms and metaphors that emphasize the headship of Christ over the church. He is the Head (Eph. 5:23), he is the Chief Shepherd (1 Peter 5:4), he is the Cornerstone (Eph. 2:20), and he is the Bridegroom (Rev. 18:23). We, on the other hand, are undershepherds, who will give an accounting of how we have cared for the flock (1 Peter 5:4; Heb. 13:17). While given responsibility to oversee the congregation and "shepherd the flock," it is always to be done with the recognition that we are undershepherds who are accountable to the Chief Shepherd.

Critical in understanding our role and responsibility of leadership is the understanding of the stewardship we are given. In Titus 1:7 we are described as stewards of God (NASB). A steward was a person who was given responsibility for the affairs of a household. However, he was not given absolute freedom to do as he pleased. Rather, he was responsible to fulfill the wishes of the master of the house. We cannot lead the church as we please; rather, we are to lead in submission to Christ. Consequently, leadership begins with being a follower. Before we can effectively lead the church, we first must be a follower of Christ; otherwise, we will lead the church astray. Paul reminds us of this pattern when he states that the church should follow his example as he follows Christ (1 Cor. 11:1).

The Board Is to Continually Examine Their Personal Relationship with Christ

Being a steward begins not with our relationship to the congregation but with our personal relationship with God. We are to "keep watch over [ourselves]" (Acts 20:28). The emphasis of the verse is upon the importance of continually paying attention to and being concerned about our own spiritual health. Maintaining a right relationship with God is not a momentary decision but a lifelong pursuit requiring continual vigilance. The basis of this is the deep awareness of our propensity toward sin. As the hymn writer, Robert Robinson, aptly wrote in his great hymn, "Come, Thou Fount of Every Blessing,"

> O to grace how great a debtor
> Daily I'm constrained to be!
> Let thy goodness, like a fetter,
> Bind my wandering heart to Thee:
> Prone to wander, Lord, I feel it,
> Prone to leave the God I love;
> Here's my heart, O take and seal it;
> Seal it for Thy courts above.

The diligence with which we keep watch over our own spiritual health stems from our awareness that we are prone to wander and that every individual, no matter how spiritually mature, is one moment away from straying off the path of godliness. To be an effective leader, we must first realize our own spiritual frailty. Our position as leaders heightens the danger, because the enemy's strategy is to attack and destroy the leadership. Consequently, when we serve as leaders, we need to be even more vigilant.

Paying close attention to our spiritual health begins with an ongoing relationship with God through prayer and the study of God's Word. This is more than an emotional state of happiness in which we feel good about our lives and our circumstances. Often we confuse spiritual well-being with psychological wholeness. While it is true that our psychological and emotional health will flow from our spiritual health, it does not follow that spiritual health will be indicated by psychological and emotional tranquility. We become mature and maintain a level of spiritual vibrancy through a life of obedience, even when emotionally our lives are in turmoil. Christ states that obedience to his commands is the test of authenticity of our relationship with God (John 14:15).

Paying close attention to our spiritual vitality involves submission to Christ in all aspects of life. Our primary task is to tenaciously pursue the will of God. It is easy for us to fall into the pattern of going after our own agenda. Like Israel during the political upheaval of Isaiah's day, we make our plans before we consult God, to which God responds, "'Woe to the obstinate children,' declares the LORD, 'to those who carry out plans that are not mine, forming an alliance, but not by my Spirit, heaping sin upon sin'" (Isa. 30:1). We make our plans and then ask God to bless them, rather than prayerfully seeking God's will and striving to fulfill it. What is true in our personal lives is equally true in the church. The danger for the church is that we can develop our strategies and plans without consideration of God. Thus, to effectively lead the church, we need to manifest an attitude of submission within our personal lives. It means that we are continually seeking to grow in our attitudes, character, conduct, and thoughts, changing our will and thinking to conform to the will of God.

Being spiritually healthy necessitates positive relationships with others. Central to the expression of our faith are interpersonal relationships. To be a follower of Christ, transformed by his nature and being, is to be radically influenced in our attitudes and actions toward others. Spiritually healthy individuals have developed skills in conflict resolution. They can see beyond the fault and focus upon ministering to the person. They can readily forgive the wrongs of others and manifest love even to those who have hurt them. A spiritually healthy individual realizes the importance of accountable relationships and the value and importance of community. We live in an individualistic culture, where the emphasis is on self-sufficiency. But this violates the tenets of Scripture, where the stress is upon mutual support and interdependency. To be a disciple of Christ is to be in community. To be a leader within the church, one needs to be an active part of that community.

The Board Is to Provide for
the Spiritual Care of the Congregation

Another priority Paul mandates relates to the spiritual care of the congregation. Maintaining the spiritual health of the congregation begins with the recognition of the necessity of spiritual care. Paul exhorts the leaders to keep watch over the congregation (Acts 20:28). First, this involves caring for the health of the congregation. Just as leaders are to maintain vigilance over their personal spiritual health, so also they are to be aware of the spiritual condition of the congregation. The importance of this task is summarized by John MacArthur: "God has given the leadership, care, and feeding of His Flock to the Elders . . . the very flock for which He paid His own blood. This is a grave and high responsibility . . . demanding dedication to study and spirituality for the purpose of perfecting the saints, which, in turn, glorifies Christ."[1] Much more will be said about what this involves in subsequent chapters. What is important to realize at this point is that Paul's command shifts the focus from the organizational function to the spiritual function of leadership.

Second, spiritual care involves the care of each individual within the church. Being a spiritual leader requires that we be spiritual leaders for the whole church and that we oversee the spiritual well-being of every person within the congregation. When exhorting the elders at Ephesus to fulfill their responsibility, Paul challenged them to keep watch over *all* the flock (Acts 20:28). This places upon the shoulders of the leadership the task of serving everyone and providing care for all people within the congregation. Giving this care requires that we remain sensitive to the spiritual needs of people, even when they are different from the rest of the church community.

The more isolated the church and community, the more it will tend to be uniform in its perspective and culture. As a result, when new people enter the community and church, they often bring ideas and views that are not only different but also may violate some of the viewpoints of people within the church. For example, a new person who moves from an urban area may bring perspectives on the environment that is at odds with the farm community. A person who is a vegetarian may find himself at odds with the culture and values of a ranching community. As a result of such differences, people in the church may be reluctant to accept new people into the fellowship. While it is never spoken or intentional, there may exist a subtle atmosphere that the new person is an outsider. They are labeled as newcomers, and the label remains even after they have attended the church for a number of years. As a result they are not given any prominent positions within the church. The task of the leadership is to recognize that we are not to segregate people based upon cultural, social, or philosophical differences. Rather we are to embrace them within the fellowship and value their differences. The responsibility we have as a board is to make sure that they are not only accepted into the church fellowship, but also that their spiritual gifts are utilized by the church for the mutual growth of one another.

The Board Is to Live in Dependency upon God

Another priority that Paul assigns the board in Acts 20:32 is that they are to entrust themselves to God. In the phrase, "Now I commit you to God," Paul is stating that the foundation for their lives and the exercise of their oversight of the church is to be done in the context of submission to and dependency on God. He was entrusting them into the care of God. Central to the task of leadership is the priority of living in dependency upon God, recognizing that in all that we do we must seek the guidance and direction of God and trust in his leadership. We are to recognize that he is the one who supplies all things we need for both life and ministry. When we serve in a position of leadership in the church, we continually face the limitations of our own abilities, resources, and wisdom. In fact, central to effective leadership is the recognition of our incompetence to lead. If Paul's statement is true that we can do all things through him who gives us strength (Phil. 4:13), it is equally true that we can do nothing apart from his strength. We often lament the lack of resources in the small church. When faced with difficulties in the church and challenges in ministry, we decry our lack of training and the lack of skills and abilities. As a result we often feel shortchanged in our service. If only, or so we reason, we had more training and greater abilities, we would be more effective in serving God and building the church. What we fail to recognize is that it is in our incompetencies that we learn dependency upon God. It is his strength, not ours, that makes us competent. Our aptitudes and proficiency for ministry come from the presence of the Holy Spirit.

First, we must be dependent upon God for the strength for ministry. Ministry is never easy. There are times when it will tax our emotional and spiritual strength, leaving us physically exhausted and spiritually and emotionally empty. When we are called by God to be leaders within the church, we must recognize that there will be times that the exercise of our leadership will require us to make hard decisions requiring strength and courage. Everywhere Paul went there were detractors who challenged his authority and credibility (see 1 Cor. 4:1–5). Even though there were those who rejected Paul, he was not hesitant to address very painful issues confronting the church. The reason he did so was not because he was overly enamored with his position as an apostle, rather it stemmed from his understanding of God's call upon his life. He was called by God to serve Christ in the church; therefore he was accountable to God for how he served.

Second, we must be dependent upon God for wisdom in ministry. Ministry continually confronts us with issues that will challenge our wisdom. There are many times when we are faced with problems for which we have no answers. It may be the crisis of a marriage that is falling apart and the couple comes to us for help. It may be a decision about building a new sanctuary. It may be the moral failure of a key leader in the church that devastates the whole congregation. It may be the steady decline in membership, even though we have sought to do everything possible to attract new people. The list goes on. In the face of such insurmountable problems, we find ourselves at a loss as to how we should respond. Yet Paul again reminds us that the basis of ministry is not our wisdom and abilities but God's (1 Cor. 2:1–5). Our confidence for action in the midst of confusion does not come from our education, training, or knowledge; it comes from the awareness that God will give us the wisdom needed to respond to the situation in a way that corresponds to his will (Matt. 10:19–20; James 1:5).

Third, we must be dependent upon God for results in ministry. As leaders in the small church, we can easily become discouraged because all our efforts seem to accomplish little. We become discouraged as we see the steady migration of people out of the community as they pursue better-paying jobs. With their departure we lose key leaders in the church with no one else to fill their shoes. In rural areas experiencing a migration of people into the community, we become discouraged when we cannot attract these newcomers into the church. Instead, they travel outside the community to attend churches that "have more to offer." In suburban areas, we are disheartened by the lack of growth in our church while the church down the road is continually expanding. In the midst of this, we must remember that in Scripture the focus is continually on faithfulness in ministry rather than results (Matt. 25:14–30). God never places upon our shoulders the responsibility for growth; rather he places upon our shoulders the responsibility to remain faithful in the proclamation of the gospel. This does not mean that we do not seek to improve our ministry and remain culturally sensitive. We are to be relevant and adaptive to our cultural surroundings (1 Cor. 9:19–23). What it does mean is that as we remain faithful striving to follow his direction and guidance, God will work through us to accomplish his purpose. Consequently, in the end it is not we who receive the credit nor do our methodologies (Luke 17:7–10), but God receives the glory (1 Cor. 2:5; 3:7).

✳   ✳   ✳

John was discouraged as another midweek children's program concluded. Along with serving on the board, John also served as the director for the children's program the church ran every Wednesday night. John was normally upbeat, so Pastor Dave could tell that something was bothering him.

Pastor Dave approached John cautiously, "Hi, John. How are things going? Looks like we had a good group tonight."

John dejectedly expressed his frustrations. "I don't know! This year we wanted to really focus on outreach. We have been working really hard to get new kids coming. However, it seems as though all we have are the same kids every week. Don't get me wrong. I am glad for the kids that do come, but I guess I was just hoping we would see new kids this year."

Pastor Dave thought back to his morning study as he prepared the devotional for next week's board meeting, "You know, John, at last month's board meeting we were talking about the priorities of the board. I have been working on that for the last several weeks. Let me share with you something I learned from Acts 20:32. When Paul was leaving the elders of Ephesus, he committed them to God. In other words he reminded the leaders that they were to be dependent upon God in all things. This is true for our ministry and the results of our ministry as well. Sometimes we forget that our job is not to 'get results.' That is God's responsibility. Our task is to be faithful."

As John walked away, Dave could tell he was thinking about what he just said, and Dave knew that at the next board meeting, John would affirm what he was going to tell them.

❇ ❇ ❇

The Board Is to Be Committed to Scripture

Along with the priority of dependency is the priority of Scripture. Often we become so focused on the programs available and the methodology we implement in the church that we forget that Scripture is what brings transformational change in the lives of people and in the community. When Paul tells the leadership in Ephesus that he is committing them to the "word of his grace" (Acts 20:32), he is not just giving them a passing exhortation. Rather, he is providing for them the foundation for effective ministry, as he goes on to point out that it is God's Word "which can build you up and give you an inheritance among all those who are sanctified." In other words, it is the Scriptures that remain pivotal for spiritual growth.

Being committed to Scripture begins when we allow Scripture to govern our lives. As leaders in the church, we must be individuals of the Word. That is, we must make the Word of God central to our thoughts so that we think biblically in all aspects of life. Often we regard the Scriptures to be something for the pastor to study.

He is the one who is to be in the Bible. Our diet of the Word of God consists of what the pastor tells us on Sunday. However, as the leadership in the book of Acts exemplified, the study of the Word is to be central. It is not something only for the professional pastor to remain dedicated to. In order to lead others to spiritual transformation, we must be transformed. To point others to the Bible, we must be dedicated to the study of God's Word (1 Tim. 4:13–16; 2 Tim. 2:15).

Second, if we are committed to Scripture, then it must govern our leadership. The challenge of leadership is the challenge of remaining biblical in all that we do. This includes how we operate the church. In order to be effective, the church must be biblically governed and biblically focused. When decisions are made it is easy to allow our culture and personal preferences to determine the decisions rather than Scripture. It is our responsibility to view every decision in the church through the lens of Scripture. This means that we are continually going back to the Bible to determine what biblical principles apply to the present situation. To do this we must not only know the Bible, but we also must know the theology Scripture teaches. If we desire to have Scripture governing our church and our decisions, we must also develop a biblical understanding of God and his works. We need to understand theology and be students of theology. As Paul points out to Timothy, it is this pursuit of doctrine that will save both ourselves and the people we serve (1 Tim. 4:16). An understanding of sound doctrine is not only essential for effective leadership in the church, but it is also necessary to prevent the infiltration of error into the church.

Third, if we are committed to Scripture, then it must remain central to our teaching. The church stands or falls upon its teaching. Without biblical teaching, the church will lose its moral compass. The priority of the leadership is to make sure that the Scriptures remain predominant in the ministry of the church. In writing to Timothy and Titus, Paul continually points to the centrality of the teaching of the Scriptures to the role of leadership (see 1 Tim. 4:13–16; 2 Tim. 1:13; 2:14–15; 4:2; Titus 1:9; 2:1). We are to be immersed in the Word of God, so that as we talk with people and discuss the situations and issues they are confronting, we can provide biblically sound answers. To be able to teach others refers to an ability to "explain Christian doctrine and to refute or oppose error."[2]

✳   ✳   ✳

After Pastor Dave shared the priorities that Paul gave the leaders in Acts 20, Steve moved on to the first order of business. Betty had called and was upset because one of the teens had worn a baseball cap to church and did not remove it when the service started. She was demanding that the church contact his parents and reprimand the student.

Ken agreed, "Everyone knows that a man is to take off his hat when he enters the church as a sign of respect. I saw it too and I would have said something, but they left before I could."

Before Pastor Dave could say anything, Pete entered the fray. "Wait a minute. Before we fly off the handle, I think we need to think this through a little bit. Pastor Dave just shared how we need to be committed to Scripture to govern our decisions. Before we do anything, we better first look at what Scripture has to say. I think Pastor Dave is right, we must let Scripture, not culture, determine what we do." Reluctantly, Ken nodded.

For the next hour they talked about what Scripture teaches about clothing and worship. After much discussion they decided that it was far better to have the teen in church, even with a hat on, than to alienate the teens because of cultural expectations. After all, didn't Christ accept people who did not conform to the cultural norms?

Pastor Dave was pleased as he drove home. While he still had to give Betty a call and explain to her the position of the board, he felt that the board had really sought to allow

Scripture to govern their decision. That was something that had not always happened in the past.

It is easy for us to become distracted by the insignificant in ministry. If we are not intentional in our focus, we will become sidetracked by issues that have little bearing on the overall vitality of the church. As leaders we must be deliberate. We must maintain a firm focus upon the priorities that God has established for us in ministry. Otherwise we will be busy doing many things but accomplishing little of eternal value.

FOUR

The Responsibility of Prayer

A typical board meeting goes something like this. The pastor or several of the board members open in a brief time of prayer, usually lasting from five to ten minutes. After the opening prayer, the treasurer gives a financial report. Since the small church always struggles with having sufficient funds to cover expenses, considerable time is devoted to where the money should be spent, what bills and expenditures should be given greater priority, and how the church can raise more funds for next month's budget. After the budget is discussed, the board discusses any of the maintenance issues (such as roof repair, etc.) facing the church and how the church should raise the funds to fix the problem. After this discussion, everyone is asked if they know of any problems or concerns people in the church have. If there are any, then the board will discuss the issues and decide what needs to be done. After this discussion, the pastor brings up any new ideas or programs he desires to implement. If it does not cost much and it does not require much time from other people, the board gives their approval. Then the meeting is closed with a brief prayer and everyone spends the next half-hour sitting around the table discussing the latest price of wheat or lumber or some community activity.

As we look in the pages of Scripture, we find a completely different picture of how the early church leaders spent their time. In Acts, when the church was just beginning its formation, the leadership did not allow itself to become bogged down in organizational issues, even though there would have been immense organizational challenges as the baby church sought to sort out and arrange all its various ministries. Instead, the leadership assigned these tasks to others in order that they might give their "attention to prayer and the ministry of the word" (Acts 6:4). They saw their responsibility to be one of prayer and the search for biblical truth in order to guide the church toward spiritual maturity and discipleship.

※　※　※

Before the board meeting started, the men sat around bantering about the usual topics of sports, hunting, and the latest market trends. However, Pete, usually the most talkative, was strangely quiet. Finally, Steve noticed. "Hey Pete, why are you so quiet today?"

"Oh, I don't know," Pete responded. "I guess I was just thinking about a conversation I had last night. I talked with Fred last night, and he was sharing how his son was starting to run with the wrong crowd and was starting to drink. He was heartbroken as he talked. I guest I am just troubled. For the last six months we have been talking about how we are to be more spiritual leaders within the church, yet we are losing our teens to the world. I know that Paul and Betty really have been trying to work with our youth and have done a great job, but it doesn't seem to be having an effect. We have talked about this in the past and tried to make changes, but nothing seems to be working. I guess I am just discouraged. I don't know what else we can do."

Pastor Dave answered back, "Pete, I am glad you have brought this up because I too am troubled by what has happened. I think we need to do something differently."

"But what?" asked Pete.

Dave continued, "Recently I've been reading from Acts. As you can imagine, when the early church first started, they had an enormous amount of details to work on. The church had been growing exponentially daily. As a result they had to minister to a great number of needs. While the Bible does not tell us a great deal about the various ministries they needed to get started, we do know they had them because in Acts 6 we find that there was a problem with the ministry they had formed to care for the widows."

"Yeah, didn't we study that earlier?" interjected Steve. "Wasn't that where the whole ministry of the deacons got started?"

"That's right. But the one thing I think we should notice is why they appointed the deacons to handle the administration of that ministry." Dave opened his Bible to Acts 6. "We see this in verses 3–4." Dave read the verses. "As you can see, they gave the task to the deacons so that they could devote themselves to 'prayer and the ministry of the word.' We get so focused on the organizational aspect of spiritual leadership that sometimes we overlook the most obvious, and that is the importance of prayer."

"I agree," Pete replied. "Instead of worry about another program, maybe we need to be spending more time in prayer for our youth."

John, usually the quiet one, spoke up. "Not only do we need to pray for the spiritual well-being of the youth, but we need to pray for the whole congregation as well. Maybe we should spend less time talking about the church business and more time praying about the church needs. After all, didn't you point out in our study of the priorities of the board that we need to be more dependent upon God?"

Dave smiled, "I'm glad you remembered. Prayer is the way we express our dependency upon God. I would like to suggest that from now on we spend at least the first half hour of our board meeting praying for the needs of people in the church."

"I think that would be a great idea," Ken exclaimed. "However, to be honest, Pastor, I am not sure how to really pray for people. Could you do one of your studies again and come back and do some training for us on how to pray for the needs of people?"

"Sure. I would be glad to," Dave agreed. Once again he had an assignment.

✳   ✳   ✳

Prayer: The Neglected Responsibility

A perusal of the books on leadership today reveals an absence of the priority of prayer. The focus of leadership today is upon vision development and organizational planning. While these are certainly valuable and critical, prayer remains strangely absent. Thus the question we must ask ourselves as leaders is, "Why is prayer the neglected work of the leadership?" While there are a number of reasons why this is so, there are four that undermine our recognition of the importance of prayer.

Prayer Is Neglected Because We Are Self-sufficient

In James 4:13–17, James makes the point that we are to live with the constant awareness of our need for God and his sovereignty at work in our lives. We must live each moment with the attitude of submission to Christ, so that we are completely and utterly dependent upon Christ. This stands in stark contrast to our society today, which places a high value on self-sufficiency. As a result we go through much of our day with little consideration of God. We are continually being taught that we can be what we want to be and do what we want to do. Often in rural society, this value of self-sufficiency also dovetails with the value of self-reliance. We believe that those who cannot take care of themselves are weak and those who rely on others are feeble and spineless. The problem is that we bring this same view into the church and into our relationship with God. We see ourselves as self-sufficient and self-reliant and thus not needing to ask for help from others or even from God. God is someone to whom we turn only when everything else has failed. Consequently, while we would never openly say this, we often approach ministry in the church the same way. We can handle most things, and only when things get really desperate do we pray. However, Paul reminds us that prayer and our dependency on God should characterize our attitude in all things. When Paul states that we should "pray continually" (1 Thess. 5:17), he is stating that every moment we should be living in complete recognition of our absolute dependency upon God.

This is not only true of life; it is true of the ministry of the church. If our desire is to be spiritual leaders who lead the church toward spiritual maturity, we must recognize that this task is beyond us. We cannot transform anyone, and we cannot lead anyone toward maturity. Rather, it is the work of the Holy Spirit. However, this does not mean that we sit on the sidelines watching God do all the work, while we become spectators in ministry. We must recognize that as God works in the lives of people, he utilizes us in the process. God desires to use us as leaders to be the means through which he works to lead his people. Consequently, since it is his work through us, we must continually pray for his guidance, empowerment, and enablement.

Prayer Is Neglected Because We Are Focused upon Organizational Operations

A second reason we often neglect prayer in our function as leaders of the church is because we have become focused upon the organizational aspects of the church rather than the spiritual. We view the church as an organization to run rather than a spiritual organism that is to be led spiritually. If the church is spiritual rather than organizational, then, as Paul points out in Ephesians 6:12, our struggle is spiritual and victory is accomplished only through spiritual means. Because it is spiritual, prayer becomes the focal point through which we face the battle (v. 18). When the church is viewed organizationally rather than spiritually, vision, strategic planning, and program development become more important than prayer. This is not to say that vision and planning is unimportant and unneeded. They are crucial to effectiveness, but they are secondary to prayer and dependence on God.

The church is the living body of Christ. While it has organization and organizational structure, it is not an organization. It is a living organism of which we are a part and our local church is its visible manifestation. While the church has a physical building and physical people, it is ultimately spiritual in nature. The church is both visible and invisible; it is both local and universal. It is a spiritual body, to which we belong, with Christ as the Head. Just as the nervous system is the means by which our body communicates with our head and receives directions from it, so prayer is the means by which the spiritual body of Christ communicates with the Head, which is Christ himself. When our body no longer can communicate with the head, it becomes paralyzed and immobile. So also when the church body no longer communicates with Christ, it becomes paralyzed and ineffective, existing but not moving.

Prayer Is Neglected Because We Do Not Pray Individually

A third reason we do not focus upon prayer as leaders in the church is because prayer is absent from our individual lives. When prayer is not central to our daily lives, prayer will not be central to our church lives. When we do not see the importance of depending upon God in every aspect of our daily existence, we will not see the importance of depending upon God for our church's existence. All too often we operate our farms, conduct our business, and raise our children with little prayer. We purchase a combine, buy and sell timber, and hire and fire employees without once asking God for his wisdom and direction. In Romans 12:1–2 we are reminded that the Christian life is to be lived daily, not just on Sundays. Our existence is to be governed by the daily pursuit of God's will. We are not loggers, farmers, factory workers, or business owners who happen to be Christians; rather, we are Christians who happen to be a loggers, farmers, factory workers, or business owners. Consequently, we are to live in continual relationship with God, where prayer and communication with God remains central to our lives. Every aspect and activity in life, whether it is our work, our home life, or our leisure, is to be done in the context of our relationship with God and our desire to serve and live for him (Col. 3:23–24). This does not mean that we are to walk around with our hands piously folded in prayer, living life with the somberness of a monk. Rather, it means that we live and enjoy life as a gift from God (Eccl. 2:24; 3:13), recognizing that everything we do, everything we have, and everything we are is to be viewed in the context of our relationship with God and the pursuit of his will and purpose for our lives. Prayer is the means by which we not only communicate with God but also live in dependency on him.

Prayer Is Neglected Because We Do Not Live by Faith

No one would deny that we are saved by faith. When we accepted Christ as our Savior, we recognized that we were unable to save ourselves from the grip and judgment of sin. We understood that only the sovereign, gracious work of a merciful God could redeem us from the death sentence we faced. As a result of this recognition, we humbly and desperately sought the face of God in repentance and submission to him. What we often fail to recognize, at least on a daily, practical level, is that not only are we saved by faith, but we are also called to live by faith (see Rom. 1:17; 2 Cor. 5:7; Gal. 2:20; 3:11). In other words, the same trust and dependency upon God that characterized our cry for God's work in salvation is to govern our daily activities in life. Daily we are to recognize our need for God's activity and grace operating in our lives. Without this work, our lives would be lost, just as our salvation would be impossible.

This faith governing our life is not merely a trust and confidence that "in all things God works for the good of those who love him, who have been called according to his purpose" (Rom. 8:28). Faith is transformational, resulting in obedience to God in all things. Genuine faith is active and results in a change of attitude and action, not only spiritually in relationship with God, but also in our relationship with others (James 2:14–26). Because of our confidence and trust in God, we have a different attitude toward others. Since God is the supplier of all our needs, we are not fearful of sharing what we have with others who are in need (vv. 15–16). We do not fear the future but rather place obedience above financial security (v. 25).

Prayer is the means by which our faith finds expression in our relationship with God. Without prayer, faith remains anemic and frail, confessed but not lived. When we pray, we are doing more than talking with God; we are acknowledging our need for God to act and our trust that he will act. Concerning prayer, Charles Hodge writes, "A prayerless man is of necessity and thoroughly irreligious. There can be no life without activity. As the body is dead when it ceases to act, so the soul that goes not forth in its actions toward God, that lives as though there were no God, is spiritually dead."[1] This is equally true of the church. When prayer is no longer central to the church, we have lost the very life that makes us the unique body of Christ. When we do not pray, we stop being the church and we become a social club, a place for people to meet, encourage one another, and have fun together, but a place that is no longer in vital relationship with God. Prayer is both an expression of faith and the avenue by which God transforms and works within the church.

In the small church, with our limited resources, we can easily become fearful of the future and stingy with the resources in the present. Instead of taking risks and trusting God to provide for the future, we become timid and hesitant. We no longer believe that God will sufficiently supply all our needs. We begin to hoard our resources, fearful that we might lose them in the end. We become fearful of risks. We become fiscally conservative, believing that the future financial security of our church is found in the savings we have in the bank rather than the supply of an infinite God. Rather than this being an expression of fiscal responsibility, it becomes an indication of our lack of faith. When we pray we recognize we are to take risks, to daily place the future of the church in the hands of the living God (Heb. 11).

The Necessity of Prayer

Prayer is not a sideline for leadership but stands at the heart of everything we do. The spiritual health of the congregation begins with the leadership praying for the congregation. If the leadership is not devoted to prayer, then the congregation will remain spiritually anemic.

Prayer Is to Undergird All Decisions

Again, Paul writes that we are "to pray continually" (1 Thess. 5:17). The emphasis is that this is not optional but commanded and is to be the continual practice of the Christian rather than an occasional event. This focus is further emphasized with the word *continually*. The term is used only three other times in the New Testament, and in each case it refers to continuous prayer, especially on behalf of others (see Rom. 1:9; 1 Thess. 1:3; 2:13). This refers to an attitude in which we live the totality of our life in constant awareness of our need for God and for his wisdom and direction. John MacArthur summarizes: "To pray unceasingly is to live life as if you were looking through the mind and heart of God. It doesn't mean walking around mumbling with your eyes closed all the time. Prayer is living life in a God-conscious way."[2] Whenever we are confronted with issues and decisions within the church, our first response should be to pray, whether it is for the need of a new roof on the church, the need for Sunday school teachers, a conflict in the congregation, or the spiritual struggles people are facing within the congregation.

Prayer Is a Requirement for Leadership

Charles Hummel writes, "We usually think of murder, adultery, or theft as among the worst. But the root of all sin is self-sufficiency—independence from God. When we fail to wait prayerfully for God's guidance and strength we are saying, with our actions, if not our lips, that we do not need Him."[3] The challenge we face in leadership is a battle between our desire for self-sufficiency and the need for complete dependence upon God. Too often it is much easier to run the business of the church without recognizing our need for God.

At board meetings we pray that God will guide our decisions, but we conduct the rest of the meeting without much consideration of what God would have those decisions to be. Nevertheless, if we are to be effective in leadership, we need to make prayer a priority in all that we do. When we fail to do so, it is a sin that undermines our leadership (1 Sam. 12:23).

Prayer Is Necessary to Follow God's Direction

As leaders we are to seek the will of God. One of the symptoms of a prayerless church is a lack of clear direction in ministry. In the small church we constantly face the challenge of maintaining the existing ministry of the church. We struggle with limited financial resources. We often fail to see any substantial change in the growth and influence of the church in the community. As a result the focus of the church becomes maintenance rather than growth. Instead of having a forward perspective that continually challenges us to advance the church, we become preoccupied with the present and the past. We no longer seek God's direction for ministry.

In contrast, Scripture points out that the purpose of the church is to build the kingdom of God by striving to proclaim the gospel to the unsaved and to instruct believers for the purpose of spiritual transformation. Central to the fulfillment of this task is the pursuit of God's will for the church. Just as God has a distinct purpose and will for each person, so also God has a distinct purpose and plan for each church. This includes how we are to use the resources he has provided us, whom he has equipped us to reach, and what programs would best suit the needs of the church. Ministry is not done in a spiritual vacuum; rather, it is lived in the daily life of the people of the congregation. We minister in a specific setting with specific needs. As leaders we need to pray for God's direction in order that we might discern those needs and discern which needs he desires us to meet.

Prayer Is the Basis for Influence

The purpose of leadership is not to run a program or organization but to lead people in spiritual transformation. Because ministry is ultimately spiritual, it requires spiritual means to accomplish spiritual ends. At the heart of this is prayer. Throughout the Scriptures we find that there are two ways God effectively brings about change in the lives of people. The first is through the proclamation of Scripture. The second is through the prayers of his people. It is no wonder that we find the leaders in the early church devoting their time and efforts to "prayer and the ministry of the word" (Acts 6:4). The ability to lead the church and effectively influence the church comes not through the development of programs nor through the development of specific strategies, it comes through the avenue of prayer. A board that prays is a board that will have an impact in the life and vibrancy of the congregation.

Prayer Is Necessary to Maintain Perspective

It is easy to lose perspective in leadership. We face the constant expectations and pressures of people in the congregation. The church is designed to be a spiritual hospital where people can find help as they struggle to live in a right relationship with God. When we enter the church, we do not do so free from the devastation and distortion of sin. As a result, people are critical when they should be loving, they are selfish and self-centered when they should be giving, they are critical and judgmental when they should be forgiving. People often accuse the church of being hypocritical, and it is. There is not a single person (ourselves included) who is perfectly living out the faith that we so passionately profess. As a result, it is easy for us to become discouraged in ministry. In one survey of pastors, 58 percent stated that they felt their ministry was futile.[4] This is often equally true of our attitude when serving on the board. We freely volunteer our time and sacrifice our energies only to have people second-guess and criticize the decisions we make. They accuse us of wrong when we have sought to do our best. It is no wonder that people are often reluctant to serve on the board. Without prayer it is easy to lose perspective. It is easy to become discouraged by the politics of the church rather than see the importance of what we do. Prayer is what enables us to see the hand of God at work through us and in the church.

Prayer Is Necessary to Maintain Unity

When Christ states that people will be able to identify our connection with Christ by our mutual love for one another (John 13:35), he places unity at the core of the vitality of the church. A church embroiled in controversy is a church that not only loses the vibrancy of its witness but also maligns the nature and person of Christ. We must recognize that how we conduct the business of the church and how we relate to one another becomes our testimony about the person of Christ. The church is the visible representation of Christ in a world that no longer sees Christ.

Christ set the pattern for us in his High Priestly Prayer in John 17, where he prays for all believers, "that all of them may be one, Father, just as you are in me and I am in you" (v. 21). The unity we have within the church becomes a witness to the unity between the Father and the Son, even as Christ goes on to pray, "May they also be in us so that the world may believe that you have sent me. I have given them the glory that you gave me, that they may be one as we are one: I in them and you in me. May they be brought to complete unity to let the world know that you sent me" (vv. 21–23).

This is especially true of the small church. The strength of the small church is the unity that exists within the congregation. It functions as a family rather than a business. Consequently, it draws people in search of personal connection in a disconnected and impersonal world. In many rural areas, the church becomes the cornerstone of the whole community. It plays a critical role in the psychological and sociological makeup of both the congregation and the whole community. People look to the church for comfort in times of tragedy. They look to the church for help in times of economic upheaval. When the church is unified, it has an impact in the whole community that often far exceeds the size of its congregation.

Tragically, the church often becomes riddled with conflict as people disagree over programs, agendas, and philosophies. However, most of the conflicts that fracture the church are not due to doctrinal differences but personal and philosophical differences. Since we are created in the image of God, we are created with individuality and a unique personality. This results in different perspectives, opinions, and desires. These differences can result in conflict as our opinions differ from others within the church. As a result, prayer becomes central to maintaining the unity of the church, for it is prayer that aligns our will with the will of God. Prayer is the means by which God moves in our lives to rise above our petty differences and focus our attention on the direction that God has given.

As leaders we are to be continually praying for unity within the church. We need to pray before decisions are made so that we are following God's purpose, not our own personal agendas. We are to pray for programs and ministries so that the focus is on serving Christ. When differences arise, instead of forging ahead regardless of strong opposition, we need to stop and pray. When issues arise that can potentially divide the church, our first response should be spending time in concentrated prayer.

❋　❋　❋

For the first time the board spent the first thirty minutes of the meeting in prayer. Surprisingly the time went by very quickly. It seemed as if they just got started when Pastor Dave ended their time of prayer.

After taking a quick break for everyone to get a cup of coffee and cookies that Ken's wife had made, Dave began the discussion on prayer. "As I did the study this last month on prayer, the one thing I discovered is that we could spend hours studying prayer and still not cover every facet."

"Ugh, please don't," joked Pete. "I have to get up early to go to work." Everyone laughed.

"Let me just summarize the highlights. After all, we don't want Pete to miss getting his sleep; otherwise he might fall asleep at church." Everyone again laughed because they knew that Pete worked long hours and so he often struggled to stay awake during the service.

Dave continued, "As we think about prayer and leadership, we find that there are four key issues that we are to pray for. The first is that we are to pray for the needs of the people." Dave wrote the word "PEOPLE" on the whiteboard. "Throughout both the Old and New Testaments, we find the leaders of God's people praying for the needs people had." He had them look up Genesis 20:17, Exodus 17:4 and 21:7, 1 Samuel 12:23, John 17, and James 5:14.

"Second, we are to pray for guidance and direction for the church. When Nehemiah was faced with the daunting task of rebuilding Jerusalem, the first thing he did was pray. As we seek to develop the ministry of the church, we need to make sure that we are praying for God's direction and guidance so that we are doing his will." Dave wrote "DIRECTION" on the board.

"Third, we find that Jesus himself prayed for the church. He not only prayed for our spiritual needs, but he particularly prayed for the love and unity of the church." He had Steve read John 17:20–23. Then he continued, "As we know, Satan is continually seeking to destroy the harmony of the church. We need to be praying that the church, while dealing with different issues, always is governed by love and unity." He wrote "UNITY" on the board.

"Fourth, as we find in James 1:5, we need to pray for wisdom." Again Steve read the passage. Dave further explained, "When we are making decisions, are we making decisions based upon our own wisdom, or are we seeking God's wisdom? Too often we make decisions based upon past history or our personal opinions rather than really seeking the wisdom of God." He wrote the word "WISDOM" on the board.

"This does not cover everything the Bible teaches about prayer, but I believe that as leaders this needs to be the primary focus of our prayers."

They then stopped and spent another half hour in prayer, praying for the issues that Dave had pointed out.

✳   ✳   ✳

The Content of Prayer

As we examine the prayers of Paul in the New Testament, we discover a pattern for the focus and content of prayer. Often when we pray, our prayers tend to be general and superficial rather than specific and transformational in focus.

We Are to Pray for the Spiritual Well-being of People

When Paul prayed for people, his focus went beyond the superficial needs that often capture our attention. He prayed for the condition of people's relationships with Christ (see Eph. 1:15–23; Phil. 1:3–11; Col. 1:3–14; 2 Thess. 1:3–12). As we carefully examine these prayers, we discover that the primary focus of Paul's petition was spiritual and transformational. In other words, the entreaty of Paul was that the church would grow spiritually and be transformed into the image of Christ.

As leaders we are called by God to spend considerable time praying for the growth of the people within the church. This was not just the pattern of Paul; it was the pattern established by Christ in his High Priestly Prayer in John 17. Here again we find the focus, not upon the superficial, but upon the internal change as we become united with Christ. As the spiritual leaders of the church, we should examine how we spend our time in board meetings. Is a significant amount of our time spent in prayer and the pursuit of God's transformational work in our lives and the lives of the people God has called us to serve, or do we spend the majority of our time discussing who is going to fix the leaking roof or repair the sink in the fellowship hall? An effective board is one that recognizes the most important task we have when meeting together is praying for the spiritual needs of the congregation.

We Are to Pray for the Physical and Emotional Needs of People

While the focus of prayer is to be on the spiritual growth of the congregation, this does not mean that we should neglect praying for the physical and emotional problems facing people. In James 5:14 and 3 John 2, we find that the leadership of the church was responsible to pray for the physical needs of people. When people are faced with lingering illnesses, we should pray for their physical healing.

There has been much debate about James 5:14 concerning the significance of anointing the person with oil. Some have seen this as "the outward sign of the inward power of prayer, or, more likely, a sacramental vehicle of divine power."[5] More likely is the view that James is referring to the medicinal practice of using oil to foster rapid healing (see Mark 6:13; Luke 10:34).[6] The point is that prayer is not a replacement for common medical practices but is to be used in conjunction with them. Nevertheless, as the structure of the sentence reveals, the emphasis is not upon the medical practice but upon prayer. The basis for this is the fact that ultimately all healing comes from the hand of God, whether that healing is accomplished through a miraculous act or through medical practices. Since God is the one in control of our lives, he is the one who is in control of our spiritual and physical well-being. Just as the board is to pray for the spiritual health of the congregation, so also we are to pray for their physical health as well.

❊　❊　❊

After spending time in prayer, Pastor Dave led the board in a short devotional in which he read the prayers of Paul that are recorded in the letters Paul wrote. Afterward, Dave wrote the words *PRAYING FOR PEOPLE* on the board.

"Last meeting we talked about what we are to pray for as leaders in general. Tonight I want to continue that discussion but look specifically at how we can be more effective in praying for people. As we look at the prayers that Paul recorded, what are some of the things you notice?" Dave asked the board.

"The one thing I notice is that Paul focused on the spiritual needs of people rather than just the physical needs. I notice that oftentimes when we spend time in prayer, we are focused only on the physical needs," Steve answered.

"Good observation," continued Dave. "What are some of the requests that Paul made?"

"What struck me was that Paul prayed in Ephesians that the people would know God better. And then in 1:18 he prays that they might have a right perspective of God's redemptive plan in their lives," responded Ken. Dave wrote the words KNOWLEDGE OF GOD and PERSPECTIVE on the board.

"As you mentioned last meeting, Paul also prayed for the love and unity of the church in Philippians 1:9," John interjected. Dave wrote down the word "UNITY." "Then in verses 10–11 he prays that they will have spiritual discernment regarding right priorities of life," John continued. "Last, he prays that they will be blameless and pure and have the fruit of righteousness in their lives. To me, what he is praying for is that they will demonstrate godly character in all their attitudes and actions."

"Good," Dave encouraged. He then wrote down the words SPIRITUAL DISCERNMENT and GODLINESS. "Is there anything else you observe in what Paul prayed?"

Steve spoke up, "I also notice that in Colossians 1:9 Paul prayed that they would know and fulfill the will of God for their lives and then he prays for the same thing for the people in Thessalonica."

After writing the words *WILL OF GOD* on the board, Dave asked, "Anything else?"

"In Colossians 1:10 he also prayed that they would live a life worthy of God and that they would be fruitful," said John.

Dave wrote down, *FRUITFUL LIFE*. "We could continue, but I think you are getting the idea. As we can see, when we pray for people, there is so much more to pray for than just their physical needs. When we pray for people this should be our focus," he said as he pointed to the list on the board.

Everyone agreed. Again, they stopped to spend time praying for people in the church. This time the prayers went beyond the physical needs. The focus was upon the spirituality of the people.

❋   ❋   ❋

When we meet as a board, the most important activity we do is to pray for people within the church and for the various ministries of the church. Too often we allow the business of the church to supersede the time spent in prayer. However, when we pray our prayers should focus upon the spiritual needs of people within the congregation. If we are praying appropriately for the congregation, the challenge will not be finding things to pray about. Rather, the challenge will be finding enough time to spend in prayer. The model that Paul gives us concerning his prayers reveals the importance and nature of prayer within the leadership. As a board and as a church, our goal should be that we are known as a "house of prayer" (Matt. 21:13).

FIVE

The Role of a Watchman

Protecting the Church

*I*n Ezekiel 3:17, God calls Ezekiel to be a watchman for the house of Israel. While the concept may seem foreign to us, the term portrayed a familiar concept to Old Testament people. A watchman was one who was stationed on the wall that surrounded the city. Like a modern police officer who is entrusted with the responsibility to "serve and protect," so also these individuals played an important role in the well-being of the community. They were responsible to inform the people of any danger that might be brewing against the community. As such, they were responsible to warn the people of internal dangers that might arise, such as the presence of a thief or the outbreak of a fire that might threaten sleeping families in the night. They were also responsible to keep a sharp look out in the distance to warn of any approaching army that would be bent on plundering and enslaving the city (see 1 Sam. 14:16; 2 Sam. 18:24; 2 Kings 9:17–20). So vital was their responsibility to the well-being of the community that a watchman who failed in his responsibility faced the death penalty.[1]

When we are placed in the position of leadership in the church, we are given the responsibility to protect the congregation, just as the watchman was responsible to protect the city. The writer of Hebrews clearly highlights this when he states, "Obey your leaders and submit to their authority. They keep watch over you as men who must give an account" (13:17). God holds us personally responsible for the oversight of the congregation. If we fail in this responsibility, we face the discipline of God's hand.

Protecting the Church from Dangers Without

Fulfilling our responsibilities as watchmen over the church begins by protecting the church from corruptive outside influences. We live in a world that suffers the damaging effects of sin, and if we are not careful, this corruption will enter the church. This does not mean that everyone in the church is perfect. Rather, that we are to protect people from that which would lead them astray from Christ. Nor does it mean that we are to isolate ourselves from the world. Christ makes it clear that we are to remain in the world to be his witnesses (John 17:15). Protecting the church from doctrinal and moral errors that permeate secular culture is especially critical as we approach the end of God's redemptive history when false teaching will increase (Matt. 24:5, 11).

❈   ❈   ❈

John met Pastor Dave for lunch with a concern that he had had for the youth of the church and the community. Not only did it seem that they lost young people each year to moral and spiritual compromise, but there also was an increasing acceptance of the postmodern view of truth. He had read some about it, but it did not hit home until his own teenage daughter expressed the view that they should not condemn other people for their interpretations of the Bible, even if that interpretation opposed the orthodox doctrines of Scripture handed down through the ages.

Dave promised to talk about it in the next meeting.

The board meeting opened in a typical manner in their new practice of spending considerable time in prayer, especially focusing on the spiritual needs of the congregation.

Then Dave gave an overview of postmodernism's basic tenets.

After he was done, Steve objected. "Pastor, I appreciate what you have to say, but I really don't think that has much bearing on us. We are just a small, rural community, and that kind of talk only encourages it. I think that if we leave well enough alone, then the kids won't be worried about it. As soon as we start talking about it, we raise their interest."

John disagreed, "Steve, I think you have your head in the sand on this issue. Whether we realize it or not, this is how young people think. When I asked the teens about it, they said that this is how everyone thinks. If we are not willing to address it, then who will?"

Steve asked Dave a question. "What do you think we should do?"

Dave thought for a moment, "I agree with John. Whether we realize it or not, this is the perspective that many of the young people have. Furthermore, when they go to college, they will be inundated with this. If we don't prepare them for it, then they can be easily deceived. Remember when we were discussing the qualifications of an elder, that we 'must be able to encourage others by sound doctrine and refute those who oppose it'? We need to equip our youth so that they too can challenge those who say that the Bible is not absolute truth. If we don't, then they will be influenced by that, and their faith will be undermined."

❄ ❄ ❄

Protecting the Church from the Rejection of Truth

The struggle continually facing the church is the battle for truth. From the beginning of creation, Satan has been attempting to undermine, distort, and devalue truth. In Genesis 3, the assault of Satan was not upon the ethical and moral standards of God. Rather it was upon the integrity of the truth of God, "Did God really say, 'You must not eat from any tree in the garden'?" (v. 1). This is no less true today. The philosophy of our culture is that "truth is not something objective, to be understood more and more completely. Truth is what is truth for me, and that may be different than it is for you or others."[2] No longer is truth absolute, found in Scripture and authoritative for all people at all times. Instead, truth becomes relative, determined by each individual based upon their own experiences. The result is that Scripture is no longer the sole and authoritative source of truth; rather, it remains one source among many. This has infiltrated the church in its view of the importance of theology as the foundation of belief. Thus the focus is no longer upon "belief" before "belonging," but first "belonging" and then "believing."[3] In other words, traditionally foundational to our faith was what we believed, which then determined how we lived. In the contemporary view of truth, what we believe is not nearly as important as what we experience. Instead of our doctrine governing our experience, now experience governs our doctrine.

The reason we must maintain vigilance in our focus upon truth is because Christianity is grounded upon absolute truth. However, this truth is not governed by man's ability to determine what truth is; it is based upon the nature of God himself, who has revealed that truth. God is a God of truth (John 14:6); therefore what he has communicated must be true or it would be a violation of his nature (2 Sam. 7:28; Ps. 25:4–5). God then communicated to us so that we might know what is true. Furthermore, he has given us the internal presence of the Holy Spirit to guide us in understanding the truth (John 16:13). As leaders we are responsible to uphold the truth of God's Word both in our statement of faith and in our daily practice. We are to protect the integrity of the message of the Scriptures in the life, decisions, and ministry of the church. We should be constantly bringing the church back to the question of "What does Scripture say?" rather than "What works best?" or even "What do we want?" or "How does it make us feel?"

Protecting the Church from the Compromise of Truth

The second danger that can infiltrate the church is the sin of liberalism. The world in which we live is continually pressuring us to compromise the truth by lowering the moral, ethical, and spiritual standards of Scripture in order to gain acceptance by people. When we deny the foundation of absolute truth, then it will inevitably lead to moral compromise, for there is no longer a basis for determining right and wrong. Moral decisions become a matter of personal choice rather than an adherence to a moral standard. Whereas legalism is the denial of freedom, liberalism is the abuse of freedom. Legalism denies the freedom we have in Christ by demanding the adherence to rules and regulations in order to gain God's favor. Liberalism abuses freedom by promoting behavior that violates obedience to God's Word. Harry Blamires defines the difference between biblical freedom and secular freedom, which results in liberalism:

> The Christian concept of freedom, rooted as it is in the no-tion of total self-surrender within the family of God, and accompanied as it is by a code of disciplines rigorous in their check upon self-indulgence or self-assertive individualism, is a virtually contradictory concept to that humanist notion of freedom as residing in an unfettered autonomous indi-vidualism, which plagues current thinking today.[4]

In other words, Christian freedom is not a license to do as one pleases but the freedom to deny oneself and take up one's cross for Christ.

Secular freedom is the freedom to do whatever one wants; biblical freedom is the freedom to do what is right. Os Guiness points outs how liberalism has influenced the church:

> People who, a generation ago, would have considered it "worldly" to go to the cinema now view films in their own homes that would have been unthinkable to much of the "world" before. Mind you, they still may not go to the cin-ema, but in almost everything else they have changed. Both in and of the world, many evangelicals are now out-doing liberals as the enthusiastic religious modernizers—and compromisers—of today.[5]

Effective leaders protect the church against spiritual and moral compromise. We must uphold without apology the standards of Scripture (not my personal standards or personal views, which plague legalism). Our task is to draw the church back to a biblical morality and ethic. It is to call the church to live out the reality of its faith, not only in the life of the church, but outside the walls of the church as well. We are to challenge people to take their faith into their work environment, into their leisure activities, and into their daily existence. We are to be careful students of Scripture so that we have a clear understanding of what Scripture teach and can avoid the pitfalls of liberalism (that is, the failure to accept the teaching of Scripture) and legalism (that is, reading my personal convictions into the pages of Scripture). We are called to live in the world but not be of the world. Liberalism is living in the world and being of the world. Legalism is attempting to remain apart from the world; instead of living in the world, we seek to live in isolation from the world.

Protecting the Church from the Distortion of Truth

While we accept the authority and the inerrancy of the Scriptures, there is a distortion that often plagues the small church that is far more subtle than liberalism and its rejection of truth. This is the distortion of truth through legalism. In our quest to avoid liberalism, we can fall prey to the insidious error of legalism. Chuck Swindoll describes legalism this way, "Legalism is an attitude, a mentality based on pride. It is an obsessive conformity to the artificial standard for the purpose of exalting oneself. A legalist assumes the place of authority and pushes it to unwarranted extremes."[6] He goes on to state,

> In so many words, legalism says, "I do this or I don't do that, and therefore I am pleasing God." Or "if only I could do this or not do that, I would be pleasing to God." Or perhaps, "These things that I'm doing or not doing are the things I perform to win God's favor." They aren't spelled out in Scripture, you understand. They've been passed down

or they have been dictated to the legalist and have become an obsession to him or her. Legalism is rigid, grim, exacting, and law-like in nature. Pride, which is at the heart of legalism, works in sync with other motivating factors. Like guilt. And fear. And shame. It leads to an emphasis on what should *not* be, and what one should *not* do. It flourishes in the drab context of negativism.[7]

At the very heart of legalism is the elevation of our ability to gain God's approval through our efforts rather than through God's grace. It is ultimately centered upon man and devalues the sufficiency of grace. This often rears its ugly head in the church by people demanding certain types of dress (women in dresses, men in ties), the "right" version of the Bible, or only certain types of music. It undermines grace by trusting in one's ability to fulfill religious requirements rather than in inward transformation and a personal relationship with Christ. It measures righteousness by one's faithfulness in attending church on Sundays, going to prayer meeting on Wednesday, and being involved in the church.

Both legalism and liberalism violate God's Word and violate the grace and sufficiency of Christ in our lives. As leaders in the church, we must continually uphold the freedom we have in Christ. Our relationship with him is based upon grace and grace alone. When confronting the legalists in Galatia, Paul reminded them that "it is for freedom that Christ has set us free" (Gal. 5:1). In other words, we are free from the necessity of gaining God's favor through outward performance. Spirituality is not based on external standards. Instead, it is based on inward transformation that the grace of God accomplishes (5:16–26). Love, rather than rules and regulations, is to govern our attitude toward others (5:6).

To revert back to legalistic standards is to allow ourselves to "be burdened again by a yoke of slavery" (5:1). To effectively lead the church, we must move beyond the petty legalism that can hamstring the church. We must recognize that righteousness is internal, not just external.

Protecting the Church from Dangers Within

Not only does the church face the struggle of dealing with a fallen world manipulated by Satan and bent on the church's corruption, but it also faces issues that arise from within that threaten the spiritual health of the church. When giving his final address to the leadership in Ephesus, Paul warns them, "After I leave, savage wolves will come in among you and will not spare the flock. Even from your own number men will arise and distort the truth in order to draw away disciples after them. So be on your guard!" (Acts 20:29–31). These individuals will be concerned only for their own agenda and the pursuit of their own popularity. The difficulty in dealing with these individuals is that they are often very subtle in their false teaching. They appear to be spiritual, they say all the right things and do the right things, but in the end they present a self-serving gospel.

Protecting the Church from Control Freaks

Within the small church there is often an individual or family or group of individuals who have a very strong influence on the decisions and direction of the church. In most cases, these are godly individuals who desire to see the church grow and become more effective. In some cases, however, these individuals become controlling and dominating. Rather than give guidance and direction, they dictate direction and control the whole congregation. Nothing is done without their approval. Decisions that are made must be approved by them. These individuals undermine the ministry and leadership of the pastor, and when the pastor seeks to move the church in a direction that they disapprove of, they will sabotage the ministry of the pastor. The pastor must either submit to their wishes or be run out of the church. The difference between these individuals and the normal power brokers in the church is that the normal power brokers, while influential, are still open to the ideas of others. While they have significant input in the decisions of the church, they do not demand that people follow their opinions. The controlling individual, on the other hand, is one who does not allow for anyone to disagree and quickly silences any differing opinions, even the opinions of the board.

When a person begins to control the church, it is the responsibility of the board to lovingly confront the individual and, if necessary, proceed with church discipline in order to remove the person from ministry and from any position of leadership. The reason we must do so is because these individuals are no longer concerned about the health of the church; they are concerned only about their own agenda. They refuse to recognize that ultimately the church belongs to Christ and he is the Head of the church. While they use spiritual terminology (saying things like, "God told me that this is what the church should do"), they are not responsive to the Spirit. Rather,

POWER BROKERS VERSUS CONTROL FREAKS	
Power Brokers	**Control Freaks**
1. Gain influence because of godly maturity	1. Gain influence by manipulation
2. Desire to hear the opinions and ideas of others	2. Refuse to allow others to share their ideas
3. Can support the ideas of others even when they disagree	3. Undermine other people's ideas when they disagree
4. Desire to follow God	4. Desire to have people follow them
5. Humble and teachable	5. Arrogant and unteachable
6. Slow to anger, respond with love and grace when others disagree	6. Quick-tempered, easily angered with any who disagree
7. Allow others to share their ideas	7. Silence others when they desire to share their ideas
8. See the pastor as a spiritual leader	8. See the pastor as a threat
9. Accepting of others	9. Critical of others
10. Seek the advice of others	10. Refuse the advice of others
11. Legitimate influence	11. Illegitimate leadership
12. Spiritually mature	12. Spiritually immature

they are dogmatic and believe that they have greater spiritual insight than others. Any who disagree with them are seen as unspiritual and carnal. As leaders we must never allow one person to control the church. This is not only unhealthy for the church, but it also violates the very nature of the church as outlined in Scripture.

Our task as leaders is not to assert our own agenda but to prayerfully seek God's agenda. Furthermore, we recognize that God works through the whole church to reveal his will. Because of each person's background, personality, and spiritual giftedness, in any given decision, others may have more spiritual insight than we have. Proverbs reminds us that in many advisors is the nation (or church) kept safe and made strong (Prov. 19:20; 20:18).

Protecting the Church from the Infiltration of Sin

As leaders, it is our responsibility to oversee the spiritual growth of people in the church. While everyone still struggles with sin, when a person becomes ensnared in sin to the point that he or she is unwilling to repent and turn from the sin, then we have a responsibility to lovingly discipline the individual. The purpose of discipline is not to judge the individual or make the person suffer, nor is it to avenge a wrong or demand justice. The purpose is to restore the individual to fellowship and to correct the individual who has strayed from the truth and thus threatened his or her own spiritual well-being.

Discipline Is to Be Motivated by Love

Discipline within the church measures our love for others, for it reveals a willingness to do the difficult task with the goal of restoring a person into fellowship with Christ and the congregation. No form of correction is pleasant. It is stressful for everyone involved. But true correction springs forth from our love for one another. Without the foundation of love, discipline becomes harsh, judgmental, and critical. When this happens our actions will be resented rather than received, causing harm rather than bringing healing. Conducting church discipline is one of the most difficult actions that a board will have to take. It is very painful and stressful. However, we must recognize that the basis and motivation for discipline is not punitive but love. The desire is not to punish the individual but to lovingly restore the individual. In the verses preceding the extended discussion of the process of church discipline in Matthew 18:15–20, Christ gives the parable of the lost sheep (vv. 10–14). The good shepherd is one who is so concerned about the well-being of each sheep that he makes every effort to go out and search for the one that has become lost. Such an attitude is so critical to leadership that God gives a strong indictment against those who fail to lovingly care for those under them (Ezek. 34:1–10). The parable of the lost sheep in Matthew 18:10–14 provides an illustration of the purpose of church discipline. Discipline is the desire and process to restore one who has become derailed in his or her Christian life. Thus it is motivated by love for the person and by the desire to see the person get back on track spiritually.

Discipline Restores the Person's Fellowship with Christ

When people become ensnared in sin, they damage their relationship with Christ. Intimate fellowship with God is broken. The first goal of discipline is to reestablish the communion between God and the person being disciplined. Sin alienates us from God. It hinders our prayer. It corrupts our relationships with others.

In 1 Corinthians 5:1–5, Paul challenges the church to confront an individual who had brazenly become involved in an incestuous relationship. The church was to abandon the person to Satan through excommunication in order that the resultant anguish would cause the person to repent and forsake his sin. James also points out that "if one of you should wander from the truth and someone should bring him back, remember this: Whoever turns a sinner from the error of his way will save him from death and cover over a multitude of sins" (James 5:19–20).

Discipline Restores the Person's Fellowship with the Church

Another purpose of discipline is to restore the person to fellowship with the church. When a person rebels against God, he becomes estranged from the church. Instead of the fellowship being a source of comfort and joy, it becomes a reminder of the person's sin and guilt before God. When we remain in sin, we no longer enjoy being with God's people. We become uncomfortable with and hostile to the leadership. Sin not only destroys our relationship with the church, but it also undermines the ministry we have within the church. When a person is in a state of unrepentant sin, that person is no longer qualified to minister in the church and thus must be removed from ministry or leadership positions in the church until the sin is dealt with. Christ says that when we confront a fellow believer who has wronged us, "If he listens to you, you have won your brother over" (Matt. 18:15). Once the person repents, the individual is to be restored to complete fellowship, lest the rejection causes the person to revert back into sin (2 Cor. 2:7–8). When those under discipline repent of their sin, then they are to be welcomed back into ministry as well. Whereas before they were disqualified from ministry, now once again they can be involved in the work of God.

Discipline Purifies the Body of Christ

Discipline serves to prevent the presence of sin's corrupting influence on the rest of the congregation. When sin is left unchecked within the congregation, it influences the behavior of others and can easily result in the whole community being led astray. Throughout the wilderness wanderings of the Israelites during the Exodus, we see the attitudes and actions of a few affecting the whole group. When one or two individuals rebelled against God and against Moses, his appointed leader, it corrupted the whole nation so that many followed the rebellion (for examples, see Exod. 32:1–33:6; Num. 12:1–16; 13:26–14:45; 16:1–3). When we fail to deal with sin within the church, we are in essence giving our approval to the actions. As leaders our responsibility is to seek to present the church to Christ as the radiant and pure bride that he intended us to be. Our goal is not to build a great organization; it is not to have massive numbers that impress other ecclesiastical leaders. Our goal is to present the church perfect in Christ (Col. 1:28–29). To accomplish this goal we cannot allow sin to remain unchecked. Not only will it destroy the person caught in the sin, but it also will destroy others who may follow that person (1 Cor. 15:33; 2 Tim. 2:16–17). Consequently the church disciplines wayward members in order to prevent their negative influence from affecting other (1 Cor. 5:6–7).

Discipline Protects the Unity of the Church

We conduct church discipline in order to protect the unity of the church and thus keep the church from being fractured by divisions. One of the ploys of Satan to render ineffective the testimony of God's people is to bring divisions and conflicts that weaken the community and thwart their testimony. God takes seriously those who cause division within the church. In 1 Corinthians 3:16–17, Paul states, "Don't you know that you yourselves are God's temple and that God's Spirit lives in you? If anyone destroys God's temple, God will destroy him; for God's temple is sacred, and you are that temple." The context suggests that Paul is referring to the church at Corinth and the temple refers to the congregation. The church is not only the body of Christ; it is now the temple of God. God's presence resides in the congregation. In the context, the destruction that Paul refers to is the devastating effects of division that results in the fracturing of the church into segregated groups that are declaring allegiance to different leaders (vv. 4–5). So serious is the destruction of unity in the sight of God, that God takes deliberate and decisive action to remove the divisive person (v. 17). Those who stir up strife and cause division are to be warned and then excommunicated from the fellowship (Titus 3:10).

Discipline Warns Others of the Dangers of Sin

When the church body corrects an individual, it serves as a warning to all the church members concerning the dangers of sin and the necessity for purity of life. While the goal of discipline is restoration, often the person will refuse to respond, continuing in the rejection of Christ's authority over his or her life and conduct. By publicly rebuking and excommunicating the person, the seriousness of sin is highlighted and the importance of faithful integrity is maintained. In discipline, the whole body of Christ is challenged anew to remain faithful to Christ and to take the presence of sin seriously (1 Tim. 5:20).

* * *

Pastor Dave was just sitting down to watch the NBA play-offs when the phone rang. Reluctantly he got up to answer it. Steve was on the other end of the line, obviously upset.

"Pastor, I don't know if you have heard about it, but Luke and Susan are separated."

Dave was shocked. "No, I didn't even know they were having problems. What happened?" Dave knew that Steve was good friends with Luke and Susan. He was surprised because Luke and Susan had been married for eighteen years and seemed to have a strong marriage. They had been active in the church with Susan being a longtime Sunday school teacher.

"I talked to Luke last night," Steve explained. "He has been having an affair with his secretary at work. Susan is devastated. When I confronted Luke that this was sin, he seemed unconcerned. All he said was that he was not happy in his marriage. I think we need to do something, but I am not sure what."

Dave thought for a moment. "Let me call Ken, and we will set up a board meeting this week so we can talk about this. This is something that we definitely need to deal with. Luke and Susan have been longtime members of the church, and we have an obligation to try to keep them from getting a divorce."

After Steve hung up, Dave silently prayed. Church discipline was the one thing that he hated to do as a pastor, yet it was clear something needed to be done. Even though he went back to watching the game, his mind was not on it. Instead, he was thinking about what he needed to say to the board.

* * *

The Process of Discipline

Christ outlines a four-step process of church discipline in Matthew 18:15–17. This process is designed to protect the reputation of both the church and the individual accused.

Step 1: Personal Confrontation

"If your brother sins against you, go and show him his fault, just between the two of you" (Matt. 18:15). When a person continually practices a specific sin and is not dealing with the problem, then the one who is closest to the individual and/or affected by the actions of the individual is to go to the person and gently confront him. If the individual acknowledges his sin, he is to be forgiven and restored to fellowship, and no further action is required. By keeping it private between two individuals then the reputation of everyone involved is protected, and the church avoids gossip.

Step 2: Group Confrontation

If this private consultation fails to bring repentance and a change of behavior, the second step is to take several individuals (usually the pastor and one or two members of the board) and confront the individual again with the need for repentance. The Old Testament law stipulated that before a person could be convicted of a crime there had to be the testimony of at least two witnesses. Christ affirms this when he states, "But if he will not listen, take one or two others along, so that 'every matter may be established by the testimony of two or three witnesses'" (Matt. 18:16). The reason for this is to protect people from being falsely accused by those who are vindictive and using the discipline process as a personal vendetta against another. It also serves to protect those who are confronting the person from being falsely accused of being critical and vindictive. These witnesses should be those who are aware of the problem and can testify of the individual's sinful behavior. They become a witness not only of the offense, but also of the attempted reconciliation and response, thus protecting both the offended and the offender against wrongful accusations. They should demonstrate wisdom and a willingness to hear both sides of the issue before passing judgment.

Step 3: Congregational Confrontation

The third step is to bring the matter before the whole congregation. The leaders of the church are to carefully examine the accusations to make sure of their accuracy. Once completed, they are then to communicate to the congregation the results of their findings, although they should not go into detail regarding the offense. Although they are to confront the sin, they are still to respect and protect the reputation of the individual. The intent of the confrontation is not to belittle the person in front of his peers but to assure that he has refused to deal with the problem. The goal of the public denouncement is to bring about reconciliation by making the individual aware of the seriousness of the problem. At this point we should "clearly indicate to the congregation that they are to pursue the person aggressively and plead with him to repent before the fourth step becomes necessary."[8]

Step 4: Removal from Membership and Ministry

When all this has failed, the final step is to remove the person from membership and participation in ministry. Christ outlines what this involves when he states that we are to "treat him as you would a pagan or tax collector" (Matt. 18:17). This means that we regard him as we would any other unbeliever. The person is not permitted to be a member (thus the person is removed from membership), is not allowed to participate in any ministry, and is not permitted to partake of Communion. This does not mean that they are excluded from attending church. Like the unbeliever, they are permitted to attend services in the hope that the preaching of Scripture leads them to repentance. However, they are not permitted to have any influence or ministry within the congregation.

❋   ❋   ❋

After Pastor Dave shared with the board what was going on with Luke and Susan, the board spent the next hour praying for them, for their children, and for all those who were being affected by the problems in Luke and Susan's marriage.

They then prayed for wisdom for what they should do as leaders in the church.

When they had finished praying, Dave read the passage on church discipline in Matthew 18. He then opened the discussion, "Men, what are we going to do?"

It was quiet for a time as the men looked at the passage and thought about what it meant. Finally, Ken spoke up. "Well, I guess we don't have much choice. We have to do what God has told us that we need to do. I think Steve has carried out the first step when he confronted Luke. Now we need to go to the next step, which is for several of us to talk with him."

The rest of the men agreed. After some discussion, it was decided that Ken and the pastor would go along with Steve to meet with Luke. Ken agreed to set up the meeting at the church the following Monday. They then closed the meeting in prayer, asking God to give them wisdom to say the right things and for the Holy Spirit to soften Luke's heart.

Not surprising, the meeting they had with Luke did not go well. Luke was defiant. He felt that his life was none of their business, and he placed the blame on Susan.

After hearing him vent his anger for a half hour, Pastor Dave finally interrupted him. "Luke, I understand your frustrations in your marriage. I am sure that Susan has done some things wrong and has not been as supportive as she could have been. But this is not about her. We are here to talk about your actions. We are not here to condemn or judge you. We love you, and we want nothing but the best for you and Susan. But the Bible is clear that what you have done with your secretary is wrong. We are here to help you get back with Susan and get back to a right relationship with God."

Luke did not budge. No matter how much they tried to show

him from Scripture his responsibilities as a husband and the fact that God can bring healing back to the marriage, Luke refused to listen. Even after they informed him that they would have to bring this matter before the congregation, he remained unrepentant.

The next day they informed the rest of the board of Luke's response. They all agreed they had no choice but to inform the congregation that Luke was under church discipline. The following Sunday, Ken informed the church that they would have a special church meeting the next Sunday evening.

At the church meeting, there was little discussion before the meeting. Without going into great detail, Ken informed the congregation that they had met with Luke and that he had refused to repent of sin in his life and was under the discipline of the board. They asked the church to refrain from any gossip. Rather they asked the congregation to pray daily for Luke and for a softening of his heart.

After the congregational meeting, the board met to discuss the next step. After a time of prayer and discussion, it was decided that Pastor Dave and Ken would again meet with Luke to talk about the situation.

After several attempts, Ken was finally able to get in touch with Luke. Luke responded that he did not feel there was anything further to discuss with the board and that he would not meet with them. Ken again told Luke that they loved him and the only reason they were getting involved was because they cared about him and his relationship with Christ.

Because Luke refused to meet again with the board, it was decided that they would send him a certified letter informing him that he was going to be removed from active membership in the church. In the letter they again communicated their love for him and their desire to have Luke come back to the church and be a part of the fellowship of the congregation. They then identified three things that Luke had to do before he could again be a member of the church: (1) He had to acknowledge his sin before God and seek God's forgiveness. (2) He had to meet with Pastor Dave for counseling. (3) He had to ask Susan for forgiveness and seek to be reconciled to her.

※　※　※

The Restoration of the Individual

Following the instruction concerning discipline, Christ gives another parable highlighting the importance of restoration (Matt. 18:21–35). The parable of the unmerciful servant serves to remind us of what our response should be when a person seeks forgiveness. No matter how great the sin or how devastating the effect, when the person comes to repentance, we are to forgive the individual and restore the individual to full fellowship with the church. The particular temptation for the small church is that we can hold the failures of people against them. While giving lip service to restoration, we continue to treat the restored member as a second-class citizen. We subtly remind them of their failures by not allowing them to be involved in any significant ministry. However, true restoration means that we treat the person as if he or she never sinned, though for the sake of the person and congregation there may be occasions when restrictions are necessary. For example, when there has been a case of child abuse it is necessary to protect the children as well as the reputation of the individual by not allowing the person to be involved in ministries that would involve direct contact with children.

※　※　※

It had been six months since the board had sent the letter to Luke. Pastor Dave had seen Luke at the post office and at local high school sporting events. He had tried to be friendly to Luke, but Luke refused to talk to him. So he was surprised when the phone rang one day and Luke was on the line weeping.

"Pastor, I have really screwed up. For the last six months, my life has been a living hell. I can't sleep at night, and no matter what I do I have no enjoyment. I just want to get this taken care of."

Pastor Dave said a quick, silent prayer and then said, "Luke, I am glad you called. For the last six months, I have been praying daily for you. You know, there is nothing that you can do that cannot be covered by the grace of God. He wants nothing more than to forgive you. Remember, it is not where you have been but where you are going that matters. God will forgive you, and he can put the pieces back together."

Pastor Dave spent the next half hour talking with Luke. Luke wanted to get back into a right relationship with God, and he wanted back together with Susan. Dave was honest. "Luke, God can restore your relationship, but it is not going to be easy. It is going to take time to rebuild your relationship with Susan, but it starts with asking God for forgiveness and for strength."

Before they ended their conversation, they prayed together. Luke agreed to meet with Dave once a week for discipleship and counseling. As Dave hung up, he was rejoicing. While it would still be a long road ahead to heal all the wounds, this was the first big step in the right direction. He again praised God for his grace and forgiveness.

* * *

No one ever wants to conduct church discipline. It is one of the most difficult and painful tasks that we must perform as a church board. However, just as it is unloving for a parent to fail to discipline a wayward child, so it is unloving for us to fail to discipline a church member ensnared in sin. This does not mean that we conduct church discipline on every member who sins. Rather it means that we are willing to take what action is necessary to reach a person who becomes trapped by sin and is unable or unwilling to deal with the issues. When we conduct church discipline, it is critical that we follow the procedure outlined in Scripture and that we always demonstrate grace, compassion, and a willingness to restore the individual to fellowship when the person repents of his or her actions.

SIX

The Role of a Shepherd

Caring for the Sheep

*I*n 1 Peter 5:2 we are commanded, "Be shepherds of God's flock that is under your care." The imagery of a shepherd was a vivid picture for Peter's first readers, for it captured the essence of leadership. What does it mean to be a shepherd?

A shepherd is one who makes sure the sheep are well fed (John 21:15–19). A shepherd is also one who provides care for the flock, tending their wounds, treating the sick, and maintaining the overall health of the flock. In Ezekiel 34:1–10, God brings an indictment against the leaders of Israel because they did not care for the flock: "Woe to the shepherds of Israel who only take care of themselves! Should not shepherds take care of the flock? . . . You have not strengthened the weak or healed the sick or bound up the injured. You have not brought back the strays or searched for the lost" (vv. 2, 4). The weak and sick to which he refers are not those physically sick or weak, but those who have become spiritually weak. They have fallen away from walking with God. Although James makes it clear that church leaders also are to provide spiritual care in times of illness and tragedy (James 5:14), more than this, they are to lead the church in a way that leads to spiritual health. They can do this only by making decisions that are determined by spiritual principles.

As shepherds we are to guide the flock. In Psalm 23 we find that God models this by leading us in paths of righteousness. Leading people in spiritual transformation and holiness is what is to undergird our decisions as leaders within the church.

Spiritual Decision Making

We all recognize that leadership involves decisions. At every board meeting we make decisions. Sometimes those decisions are superficial (Who is going to repair the leaking faucet in the kitchen?). At other times the decisions are difficult and affect the whole congregation (Should we go with contemporary worship? Should we conduct church discipline?). If we are not careful, the basis by which we make these decisions can be misguided. While our desire is to be godly leaders who lead the church spiritually, our natural tendency is to become pragmatic (What will get the best results?), or traditional (How have we done it in the past?), or even political (What will the congregation want? What will make the congregation happy?) in our decision making process.

❋　❋　❋

For the past several months the board had struggled with the decision to replace the traditional service with a more contemporary style. While many were for the change, some of the older members were unhappy with the proposal. Ken called Pastor Dave and asked to meet for breakfast to discuss the issue. After they ordered, Ken launched into the discussion. "Pastor, I've been spending a great deal of time thinking about this whole music issue. It seems to me that no matter what we decide we are going to have people upset. I just don't see any solution that will make everyone happy."

"Maybe we're approaching the whole thing from the wrong perspective," countered Dave.

Ken was puzzled. "What do you mean?"

"Well, we've been looking at the whole issue from an organizational and relational standpoint." Ken nodded in agreement, and Dave continued. "Often in the small church when we are faced with issues, we ask the question, 'How will this affect relationships within the church?' Maybe that's the wrong question. If relationships are what drive us, we will compromise to keep everyone happy."

"But aren't relationships important?" countered Ken.

"Sure they are," Dave responded. "But we need to go deeper than that. We need to seek to make decisions that are in line with God's will. Ministry is not about keeping people happy. Our responsibility ultimately is to please God by being obedient to him and doing his will. As leaders, we are not only to make decisions that are organizational and relational. We are also to make spiritual decisions that are governed by spiritual principles."

Ken was intrigued. "That all sounds good, but how do we do that? All of us on the board want to do what God wants. That is easier said than done."

"I agree! In fact I have been struggling with this same issue myself. I have been doing some reading lately that has helped. In this book the author suggested five questions we need to ask in order to make spiritual decisions." Dave wrote the five questions on the napkin:

1. Have we prayed about it?
2. What does Scripture teach us about the issue?
3. How does this relate to the character of God?
4. What counsel can others give?
5. How will this affect our mission of transforming people?

Now Ken was excited. "You're right on! Those are the questions we need to be asking. I would like for us to discuss these very questions next week at the board meeting."

✳ ✳ ✳

Making Spiritual Decisions Involves Prayer

We are to be spiritual leaders who focus upon spiritual decisions, utilizing spiritual principles. This begins with prayer. When a question arises that will affect the congregation, the first step should be to spend a significant amount of time in prayer. When we pray, we are seeking God's direction. Prayer aligns our will with his. We are not just to pray for the needs of people and the needs of the church; we are to pray for God's will to be accomplished in us.

In Nehemiah, we read the account of the rebuilding of Jerusalem. After many years of warfare, defeat, and ruin, the city of Jerusalem was a mound of rubble. When Nehemiah returned to Jerusalem with the goal of rebuilding the city, he not only faced discouragement on the part of the people, but he also faced opposition from those in the surrounding areas. The way Nehemiah led the people in the rebuilding of the city is a case study of effective leadership, and prayer marked all of Nehemiah's activities. Whenever he was faced with a task, decision, or obstacle, his first response was prayer (1:4; 2:4; 4:9). Conversely, in Joshua 9:14–15 we find the Israelites making a treaty without first seeking God. This unwise decision affected generations to come.

If we are to be spiritual leaders, we must use spiritual means, and central to this is prayer. When we are faced with difficult decisions, we need to spend time in prayer. When the congregation is struggling over issues, we need to call the church to prayer, for it is through prayer that we discover the will of God. It is prayer that unites the church in a common submission to Christ so that division does not fracture the fellowship and harm the work of God and the testimony of the church. Consequently, the first question we must ask when making decisions is, *"Have we prayed about this issue as a board and as a church?"*

Making Spiritual Decisions Involves Scripture

Paul writes in 2 Timothy 3:16 that all Scripture is inspired by God so that the people of God may be completely equipped for life and ministry. Often those of us who serve on a small church board feel shortchanged. We feel that we lack the resources, experience, and insight to make spiritual decisions because we have not received any formal training in the Bible or in church leadership. When we are confronted with spiritual decisions, we feel ill equipped to take any decisive action. As a result we delegate those decisions to the pastor, for he has had the training. What we fail to realize is that in the Bible we have all the resources we need to make right decisions. As we examine Scripture, we discover that we have all the available information we need to make wise decisions when it comes to spiritual matters. While the education and input of the pastor is an important part in making sure that we handle the Scriptures correctly (2 Tim. 2:15), we should not think that he has exclusive knowledge and insight. Often we may have the insight into the how the Scriptures would apply to the present circumstance. Education (while beneficial) is not a guarantee of inerrancy. The most critical element in scriptural discernment is the presence and work of the Holy Spirit, who guides us into truth (John 14:26; 16:13) and in understanding God's will and purpose. When faced with a decision or issue, the next questions we need to ask and answer are: *What does the Bible say about this issue? What are the principles in Scripture that pertain to what we need to address?*

As a board we are not to be governed by what is politically expedient in the church; rather, we are to be governed by the pages of Scripture. This means that we may, at times, have to make decisions that are unpopular with the congregation. It means that we obey Scripture no matter what the personal cost will be. When we have carefully applied the wisdom of Scripture to the present context, we can have confidence that we are not only making the right decision but are also in line with the will and purpose of God. As we examine the Scriptures in relation to issues of the church, we become a model for how people should address the problems and difficulties they are facing in their own lives. As Rowland Forman, Jeff Jones, and Bruce Miller point out, "We want to train people to go to the Bible with every issue in their personal lives and church ministries."[1]

Making Spiritual Decisions Reflects the Character of God

The church exists to glorify God in the community, for we are the visible representation of God in the community. Paul writes, "We are therefore Christ's ambassadors, as though God were making his appeal through us" (2 Cor. 5:20). The term "ambassador" refers to one who is a representative of another. When we proclaim the gospel, we are acting as God's representatives. It is important for us to realize that the manner in which the church conducts business, the way it interacts with others, and the testimony it has in a community is a reflection of the person and character of God. All the actions of the church should be an expression of and governed by the nature of God. In the decisions we make and the actions we perform, we should always seek to reflect the character of God in such a way that his reputation is enhanced by what we do as a church.

Tragically, many times churches become embroiled in controversy, conflicts, and division over nontheological issues. More often than not, when a church suffers a split it is over organizational decisions (What program should we use?), or struggles of power and authority (Who makes the decisions?), or personality differences (Which Sunday school material do we prefer?). The result is that the character of God is maligned. We must recognize that how we do business in the church is not only a reflection of our church, but also a reflection upon Christ. Paul writes in 1 Peter 2:12, "Live such good lives among the pagans that, though they accuse you of doing wrong, they may see your good deeds and glorify God on the day he visits us."

As spiritual leaders, we are to lead the church away from the pitfalls of division. We must call the church back to the recognition that we exist to serve and glorify God, not to accomplish our own agenda. We must point people to the fact that the church does not exist to advance our reputation or influence in the community or in the church. We exist to glorify God and advance his reputation and influence in the community and the lives of people. When faced with issues that might damage the reputation of God, we must remain focused upon manifesting his character. Before we make a decision, we should always ask, "How can God be glorified in this, and how will our actions and decisions reflect the nature of God?"

Making Spiritual Decisions Involves the Counsel of Others

When making decisions it is easy to fall into the trap of thinking that we have all the insight needed to make a decision and that we do not need the input of others. However, Proverbs makes it clear that the wise seek the advice of many counselors (Prov. 11:14; 15:22; 24:6). When we seek the counsel of others, we gain greater insight and understanding. Others often have a different perspective that we have not seen or are even blind to because of our own preconceptions. While there are a number of sources from which we can gain advice and counsel, there are six that are readily available. We should seek their advice when we are faced with difficult issues.

First, we can seek assistance from our denomination's or association's regional or national office. Often those who are available, either directors, assistant directors, district representatives, or supervisors, have served in the past as pastors and have experienced similar situations. They also have worked with a number of churches and have most likely been in close contact with churches facing comparable issues. They can help us avoid the mistakes others have made by helping us see the implications of a decision. Second, the faculty of Bible colleges and seminaries can be a source of sound advice, especially if we are dealing with issues that are related to our understanding of Scripture. They can give insight into the biblical text to make sure that we are correct in our understanding. Third, other pastors and church leaders in our denomination or community can provide counsel. They can be especially helpful if they have some knowledge of our church (such as a pastor of a church in a neighboring community) and understanding of our particular setting. Fourth, we can gain advice through research in books, magazine articles, or the Internet. Fifth, we should seek the advice and counsel of our church leaders. As the board we are ultimately the ones responsible for making the decision. However, we can and should seek input from other leaders in the church, especially if we are making decisions that will affect them and their ministry. Last, we should seek the input of the whole congregation. There are times when the person we least expect will be the one who gives the greatest insight into the issue under discussion. Thus the next questions we should ask before making a major decision is, *"Are there others who can give us insight into this issue? What advice do they give?"*

Making Spiritual Decisions Results in the Transformation of People

The ultimate purpose of the church is not to run an efficient organization. In our modern church today, we often mistake organizational efficiency with a spiritual church. Just because things are running smoothly, the work is being done with little or no conflict, and people are happy does not necessarily mean that the church is effective. The measure of effectiveness is spiritual transformation. Paul reminds us of the goal of his ministry when he states, "We proclaim him, admonishing and teaching everyone with all wisdom, so that we may present everyone perfect in Christ. To this end I labor, struggling with all his energy, which so powerfully works in me" (Col. 1:28–29). The call of the church is to lead people in spiritual, moral, and personal transformation. As leaders, we have been given the responsibility to lead people in this renewal (Eph. 4:11–16).

A transformational ministry is one in which people are being trained in biblical theology in such a way that it impacts how they live. The church is not a place for only mature Christians who have it all together spiritually and emotionally. It is a place where the spiritually weak come to be radically changed. This means that ministry can be unpleasant at times, for we are working with broken lives in desperate need of mending. A healthy church is not one where everyone is perfect and living godly. A healthy church is where people who are struggling find encouragement, support, training, and guidance. As we make decisions in the church, this is what is to guide our priorities. In every decision we contemplate, we must ask, *"How will this help us accomplish our mission of transforming people?"*

While every decision we make may not have a direct effect upon the lives of people, the overall goal remains the same. This means that we are governed by what is best for people, not necessarily what is best for the organization. This is especially critical in the small church, where relationships govern activities and decisions. In the small church, the focus is upon each individual within the church. The small church operates under the assumption that the individual is more important than the whole. While a decision may best serve the overall church, if it has a negative impact upon one individual, we do not sacrifice the good of the one for the good of the many. Rather, we strive to keep both in view. God did not come just to redeem the church; he came to redeem individuals. Our goal is to lead the church in such a way that it has a positive effect upon everyone.

✳   ✳   ✳

Before the board meeting, Ken wrote five questions on the whiteboard at the top of five columns:

1. How should we pray?
2. What does Scripture teach?
3. How does this reflect God's character?
4. What advice have others given us?
5. How will this accomplish our mission?

After opening the board meeting in prayer, Ken spent the next ten minutes updating the rest of the board on the conversation he had had with the pastor and the importance of the questions he had placed on the board. For the next two hours, they discussed the questions. As they talked, Ken wrote down their answers in each of the columns. By the end of the meeting the whiteboard was full. Steve organized and wrote down everything that was on the whiteboard.

Issue: How do we develop a worship service that is sensitive to everyone in the church?

1. How should we pray?
    • We need to meet next week to spend a whole evening in prayer.
    • Three issues we need to pray for:
        • Unity
        • Wisdom
        • That we can minister effectively to both the young and old.

2. What does Scripture teach?
   - Worship is not about our experience but God's (Eph. 5:19–20).
   - In Scripture we find a number of different instruments and styles used (Ps. 150; Col. 3:16).
   - Worship is not just about music (Ps. 119; Col. 3:16).
   - We must be focused on the needs of others rather than ourselves (Phil. 2:2–4).

3. How does this reflect God's character?
   - Division because of worship will malign the character of God. WE MUST REMAIN UNITED.
   - We glorify God when we tell others what he has done and who he is. Our church service must communicate something about God.

4. What advice have others given us?
   - People we can get advice from:
     - George, the regional representative for our association.
     - Other pastors.
     - The youth.
     - The elderly.
   - Advice others have given us:
     - Have a balanced service that has both choruses and hymns.

5. How will this accomplish our mission?
   - Benefits of a contemporary service:
     - Appeals to young people.
     - More relevant to unchurched.
     - More opportunity for people to use their talents.
   - Benefits of a traditional service:

- Change would hurt Betty, who has played the organ for years.
- Would encourage the elderly, who often feel disconnected and unwanted by the church.

By the end of the meeting, the board not only had a clearer perspective about the issue and what the pros and cons were, but they also began to see the value and importance of making decisions governed by spiritual principles.

✳ ✳ ✳

Providing Spiritual Care

The second aspect of being a shepherd is providing care for the sheep. In Psalm 23:2 we discover that God, as the Chief Shepherd, leads us in green pastures, symbolic of the care he provides for our needs. In 1 Peter 5:2 we are again reminded that we are to "be shepherds of God's flock that is under [our] care." This is reiterated in Hebrews 13:17, where the church is reminded that leaders "keep watch over you as men who must give an account." The idea of keeping watch is that of being alert, providing care, guarding, and protecting. In other words, our task as church leaders is to care for the church, to oversee the spiritual condition and growth of the congregation. Providing this care involves overseeing the spiritual growth of people and assisting and ministering to people in times of crisis.

Caring for the Spiritual Growth of People

Our responsibility as leaders and as a church is to foster and contribute to the spiritual growth of people, encouraging them in spiritual transformation. God has appointed us to leadership so that the church will "no longer be infants, tossed back and forth by waves, and blown here and there by every wind of teaching and by the cunning and craftiness of men in their deceitful scheming. Instead, speaking the truth in love, we will in all things grow up into him who is the Head, that is, Christ" (Eph. 4:14–15).

We Encourage Spiritual Growth by Being an Example

As we have already seen, we are called to set the example for the church to follow of spiritual maturity and Christlike character (see chapter 2). We are to influence others with our lives as Christ imprints his life upon us (1 Cor. 11:1). When we live in obedience to the Word of God, it leaves a stamp upon our lives as it shapes our faith, our attitude toward others, our speech, and our daily conduct. Our example before others becomes the basis by which we shepherd others. As leaders in the church, we shape the spiritual growth of the congregation by the way we conduct our lives. In the small church we are well known by everyone in the church, including the children. Because of this, our testimony has a powerful influence. People in the congregation know how we live, and they can see if there is a consistency between how we live and what the Scriptures teach. Overseeing spiritual growth begins with the conduct of our own personal lives. We set the benchmark of behavior for the church.

We Encourage Spiritual Growth by Proclaiming the Message of Scripture

Paul writes Timothy, "Until I come, devote yourself to the public reading of Scripture, to preaching and to teaching" (1 Tim. 4:13). In his second letter to Timothy, Paul reiterates this command: "Preach the Word; be prepared in season and out of season: correct, rebuke and encourage—with great patience and careful instruction" (2 Tim. 4:2). Programs and ministries do not transform people. It is the proclamation and application of Scripture that transforms people. Scripture is not a static book of information; it is a dynamic power working in the lives of people (Heb. 4:12). It confronts people and protects them from sin (Ps. 119:9). While the work of the Holy Spirit is the ultimate cause of spiritual growth (Phil. 1:6; 2:12–13), the Bible is the instrument he uses (1 Peter 2:2).

The task of the board is twofold as it relates to the Word of God. First, we are to make sure that the proclamation of Scripture is the priority of every ministry. While we recognize that programs do not in themselves change people, they are the means by which we communicate the Scriptures and thus are a critical part of the ministry of the church. Their ultimate goal must always be to present the Word of God either in word or action. Every program will not necessarily communicate Scripture directly, but it should demonstrate the reality of Scripture and open avenues by which we can communicate God's Word. For example, the ministry of delivering food baskets does not involve the direct communication of Scripture, but our goal is that the people who receive them—and people in the community who hear about them—will be drawn to attend a church service where the gospel message is communicated. Furthermore, when we deliver the food baskets, we are a living testimony of the message of Scripture that God cares for the poor. As leaders, then, we are to evaluate the ministries and programs of the church by asking the fundamental question, *"Is this ministry communicating, either in word or act, the message of Scripture?"*

Second, we are to communicate Scripture in our interaction with others. As already has been pointed out, one of the qualifications of leaders is that they be "able to teach" (1 Tim. 3:2). This does not mean that we must be gifted to teach but that we have a knowledge of Scripture and a willingness and ability to share Scripture with people who are facing difficulties in life. Paul states that when we live as godly examples before others and when we communicate Scripture to others, then we, like Timothy, will "save both [ourselves] and [our] hearers" (1 Tim. 4:16) and thus fulfill our responsibilities as leaders.

Caring for People in Crisis

The church is a spiritual hospital. Christ reminds us, "It is not the healthy who need a doctor, but the sick. But go and learn what this means: 'I desire mercy, not sacrifice.' For I have not come to call the righteous, but sinners" (Matt. 9:12–13). The same may be said for the church. We are not a place where only the spiritually well come; we are a place where people with broken lives come for strength, healing, and encouragement. As a result, we are to minister to people when they are in crisis. Furthermore, this is not just the role of the pastor; this is the responsibility of each of us who are called by God to serve as leaders.

✳ ✳ ✳

Steve was startled by the ringing of the phone. It was 2:00 AM, and he was only half awake when he answered it. Mary was on the line, and she was crying as she talked. "I am sorry to call you like this in the middle of the night, but I didn't know who else to call. Sam (her elderly husband) woke up with severe chest pains. The ambulance has just left to take him to the emergency room. Could you please give me a ride to the hospital?"

Steve was fully awake. "I would be glad to! Give me about fifteen minutes to get ready, and I will be down. Before I hang up, let's pray." Steve prayed for Sam as well as Mary—that they would sense God's hand upon them during this time and that the doctors would be able to effectively treat Sam.

Steve woke up his wife when he turned on the light. After explaining what was going on, she got dressed to go with him. As they drove to Mary's house, Steve felt anxious. This was the pastor's job! But Pastor Dave was on vacation, backpacking in the Idaho wilderness, so there was no way to get in touch with him. Steve felt completely inadequate for this type of ministry. Lately, Pastor Dave had been challenging the board members to be shepherds who ministered to the needs of people. Steve never thought that it would really be needed. As he drove he thought, "It was a lot easier talking about this in the board meeting than it is actually doing it." He and his wife prayed for wisdom as they pulled into Mary's driveway.

✳ ✳ ✳

Spiritual Care During Physical Affliction

James 5:14–15 spells out the responsibility we have as leaders when people are facing physical struggles: "Is any one of you sick?

He should call the elders of the church to pray over him and anoint him with oil in the name of the Lord. And the prayer offered in faith will make the sick person well; the Lord will raise him up. If he has sinned, he will be forgiven." The focus here is on the act of prayer that the elders are to perform. The implication is that this is an individual who is suffering such a serious illness that he cannot go to the elders; rather the elders must come to him. When people are facing serious medical problems that require either hospitalization or confinement in a home (especially in cases where the person has been sent home because there is no longer any medical hope), it is our responsibility to visit the individual, pray with the person, and offer words of encouragement. While we normally see this as the responsibility of the pastor, it does not absolve us of this obligation. James puts it squarely on our shoulders.

We do not need special training or skills to provide significant spiritual ministry to those going through a period of crisis. The best visits are not the ones when we share "great words of wisdom," but when we go and pray with the individual and read an appropriate passage of Scripture (such as Pss. 13; 23; Rom. 8:18–39; 2 Cor. 1:3–11; 4; or just a favorite passage we might have that might be appropriate).[2] The visit does not need to be long. If the person is seriously ill, especially if hospitalized, a typical visit should last no longer than fifteen minutes. It is not the length of time but the fact that we took the time to be there that brings encouragement and comfort.

Spiritual Care During Emotional Trauma

Perhaps even more significant and needed is comfort when people are going through circumstances that bring emotional turmoil into their lives. These situations may include the loss of a loved one, financial pressures, the loss of a job or farm, marriage problems, problems with children, or mental illness. Proverbs 17:17 states, "A friend loves at all times, and a brother is born for adversity" and again in 17:22, "A cheerful heart is good medicine, but a crushed spirit dries up the bones." As leaders within the church, we must recognize the importance of providing spiritual encouragement during times of adversity. Here again we do not need to know all the answers. We do not need to be trained professionals, although we should not hesitate to refer people to those who are. As we provide care, it is important that we do so without being judgmental regarding the situations people face. When we know of someone in the congregation who is going through a very difficult time emotionally, often just being there brings a significant amount of comfort and encouragement. Letting the person know that we care is often what is needed and appreciated the most.

However, a word of caution should be mentioned. Because of the dangers of impropriety, we should never visit alone someone of the opposite sex who is going through a time of emotional crisis. When we visit the homes of people in our congregation, we should take our spouse with us. Not only will they often give greater comfort and perspective than we can provide, but it will make the other people more comfortable. This will protect both our reputation and theirs. Furthermore we should never enter into any extended involvement with someone of the opposite sex who is going through a time of crisis. If the individual needs long-term care and counsel, we should recommend that person to the pastor and/or a trained professional.

❋   ❋   ❋

As Steve and his wife, Alice, drove to the hospital with Mary, they just listened as she described the events of that evening. Through the tears she also talked about the fifty-one years of marriage they had enjoyed together. Steve remembered the words of the pastor, who had told them the most important thing to do to help people was to just listen. So they let her talk when she wanted, and they were silent when she seemed to be lost in her thoughts.

When they arrived at the hospital, they were ushered into the emergency room. Their worst fears were realized when the doctor reported that Sam had experienced a severe heart attack and was in critical condition. The next forty-eight hours would be pivotal for Sam's survival.

Steve again prayed with Mary as they sat in the waiting room. While they waited, Steve called Mary's two sons and explained what had happened. Both would be coming to the hospital as soon as they could catch the next flight. For the next twelve hours, Steve and Alice stayed with Mary, waiting for news from the doctor and the arrival of her family.

※   ※   ※

Spiritual Care During Spiritual Struggles

Since the church is a spiritual hospital, we encounter a number of individuals who are struggling spiritually and in need of assistance. As a board, it is our responsibility to come alongside these individuals to assist them in their spiritual growth. In Romans 15:1–2 Paul challenges the spiritually mature to strengthen and encourage those who are spiritually weak: "We who are strong ought to bear with the failings of the weak and not to please ourselves. Each of us should please his neighbor for his good, to build him up." People who are struggling manifest their struggles in a number of different ways. They may stop coming to church regularly. They may become disruptive and divisive when disagreements arise. They may remain unrepentant of sin. We must remember that caring for these individuals is not just the job of the pastor; it is the responsibility of each one of us on the board. It involves strengthening the immature and spiritually weak by giving encouragement and counsel (Ezek. 34:4). It includes being concerned about and seeking to restore those who have wandered from the truth (Ezek. 34:4–6).

As spiritual leaders we are to be watchful of the spiritual health of the congregation and of the people in the congregation. If the church is unhealthy, it is because the board is unhealthy and has failed in its responsibility. If someone is starting to spiritually wander away from the church by no longer being faithful in attendance, it is not just the responsibility of the pastor, but of each person on the board to contact the person and find out what is causing the absenteeism. If there are issues the person has with the church or individuals within the church, then we need to lovingly and biblically address them. One of the advantages we have in the small church is that we can often know when people are struggling spiritually. The danger is that this knowledge can lead to complacency. Even though we know there are problems, we do nothing because "someone else will take care of it. I'm too busy right now and don't have the time." However, God calls us to do something, and it is our responsibility to take action no matter how busy we are.

✳   ✳   ✳

Although they had several muffins and several cups of coffee the nurses had brought, Steve, Alice, and Mary had eaten nothing else since they had arrived at the hospital. Again Steve remembered what the pastor had told board, "When you are with the family, be sure to minister to their physical needs as well. Often they will not want to leave the hospital, yet they need to eat to keep their strength up."

Around noon, Steve offered to go and get some food. Leaving his wife with Mary, Steve drove to a grocery store and purchased some fruit, drinks, crackers, and cheese. He also stopped and picked up some sandwiches at a restaurant. By the time he got back to the hospital, Mary's oldest son had arrived. Her other son was going to be arriving later in the afternoon. Steve again prayed with Mary and then read Psalm 23.

As they drove home later in the afternoon, Steve realized that ministering to people's needs was not as difficult as he thought. He did not need to have all the answers; all he needed to do was be available for God to use him and to listen and pray. Although he was deeply concerned about Sam, he also had a sense of inner satisfaction because he knew that God had used him to help Mary in her time of crisis.

After they arrived home, Steve and Alice sat at the kitchen table and enjoyed a cup of coffee. They knew that there was still a lot of help that they would have to give. Alice went to the phone and started arranging to have meals prepared for Mary's family during their stay. Steve also knew that he still needed to be available for Mary. In the morning Steve planned on going back to the hospital. In the meantime he called Pete, and Pete agreed to go to the hospital that night to pray and be with the family.

✳   ✳   ✳

Implementing a Shepherding Ministry

How, then, do we fulfill our responsibility as spiritual leaders of the church? While we recognize the importance of the responsibility, we often struggle with how to implement a strategy for providing this care. While there is no specific program that will work in every situation and it is incumbent upon us to develop a strategy that will work best for our situation, this can be the starting point of discussion and development.

Personally Contacting Everyone Within the Congregation

People are not just numbers on the rolls; they are individuals who have unique needs and struggles. The strength and advantage of the small church is that we can deal with people as individuals and we can have a direct ministry in each of their lives. Because of this, the responsibility of the board is to personally contact everyone within the congregation. This can be done by having each person in the church assigned to a board member who is responsible to minister to and provide spiritual care for him or her. This is not a replacement of the role and ministry of the pastor, but it is in addition to it. Having been assigned people in our congregation, it is now our responsibility to periodically contact them to find out how things are going in their lives. This can be done through a personal visit, through a phone call, or by interacting with them when we have occasions to talk with them in an informal setting. Especially in rural areas, we often encounter the people from the church during the week. It may be at the local grocery store, or at a school event, or at the local diner. These are not just social opportunities; they are ministry opportunities as well. As we interact with people, then we are responsible to pray with and for them. We should regularly contact the people under our care for prayer requests so that we can be regularly praying for them as part of our personal devotions.

Following Up with Any Who Are Absent from the Congregation

When people are absent from the church for unknown reasons for more than two consecutive Sundays, the appropriate board members should contact them to let them know that they were missed and to make sure there are no physical, emotional, or spiritual needs that the board needs to pray for or assist in. If there are, then we should plan a time when we can visit them personally and spend time praying with them and encouraging them with Scripture.

When a person or family has been absent for more than four consecutive Sundays, we should personally visit them to find out if there are any problems and to pray with them. Often when people are absent for extended periods, it is an indication of a problem either in their spiritual life or in relationship to the church. In such cases they have begun to "wander," and it is our responsibility to seek them out (Ezek. 34:4). If the people have a conflict with others in the church or with the direction and decisions of the church, then we need to bring the issue to the rest of the board to discuss how we can handle the situation in a godly manner in order to bring them back into fellowship.

Serving Through Crisis Care

When we hear of people under our care who are going through a period of personal crisis, then we should visit and pray with them. As we do so, we should also notify the pastor of the needs of the people so that he might provide further assistance. While we cannot provide the specialized care that some situations may demand, we can be advocates for those in crisis to make sure that those who need further help (such as those with marital problems that require professional counseling) are able to find the right resources to provide such help. This means that we will often work with the pastor in finding the right resources for the people in need.

Serving Through Hospitality

One of the qualifications for board members is that we are to be "hospitable" (1 Tim. 3:2). This means that we have a responsibility to welcome new people and work toward assimilating new people into the life and fellowship of the congregation. As leaders, we are to take the initiative to welcome new people who attend the church and to make an effort to do follow-up contacts with them. If the people have attended the church more than once, we should seek to make a personal visit with them by either visiting them in their home, or inviting them into our home for a time of fellowship. Once they start attending the church, then we need to assist them in discovering where they can use their spiritual gifts in the ministry of the church.

Being on the board is more than taking care of the facilities and organizational business of the church. It involves spiritual leadership that focuses on spiritual care for the congregation and individuals within the congregation. This begins with making decisions that are spiritually driven rather than organizationally driven. Being a shepherd involves providing spiritual, emotional, and physical care for people in need. Too often we leave the responsibility of ministering to the people to the pastor. However, a study of Scripture reveals that it is the responsibility of each board member. As leaders in the church, we are to visit people in need. We are to provide encouragement in times of crisis. We are to be available to help people who are facing struggles, whether those struggles are spiritual, physical, or emotional.

SEVEN

Servant Leadership

Helping Others Succeed in Ministry

It is easy in ministry for the leadership to view the congregation as a tool to use in order to implement the leadership's
plans and make its ministry and leadership effective. However, in
Ephesians 4:10–13 Paul points out that the priority of leadership
is not primarily the exercise of authority; rather, it is the work
of equipping people for effective ministry. Verse 12 defines the
overriding purpose of leadership. We are to work toward enabling
others to be effective in their ministry. The term *prepare* refers to
people being "perfectly, completely fitted out by all those in the
church who are able to transmit the Word."[1] In other words, the
task of leadership is to make sure people are being equipped with
the Word of God so that they can be effective in ministering to
others. The result is that the whole church is "built up until we all
reach unity in the faith and in the knowledge of the Son of God
and become mature, attaining to the whole measure of the fullness
of Christ" (Eph. 4:12–13). In Colossians 1:28–29, Paul reveals that
the primary means by which we achieve this goal is through the
teaching of Scripture.

Equipping people for ministry begins with first equipping them with
the foundation for growth and ministry. Second, we equip people for
ministry by providing them the training necessary for them to maximize the use of their spiritual gifts. Third, we equip people for effective
ministry by providing them with the necessary support and resources
to accomplish the will and purpose of God within the community.

Equipping People with Spiritual Foundations

Healthy churches and effective leaders equip people for ministry by providing the spiritual foundation for ministry. As has already been pointed out, theological training is a critical part of the mission of the church. If we are to effectively accomplish our mission in our ministries, then we need to equip people for spiritual ministry. This involves two essential elements. First, we must equip people theologically; and, second, we must equip them biblically.

Equipping People with a Theological Foundation

It is our responsibility to oversee the teaching of the church to assure that people are being grounded in a right understanding of God. The church needs theological teaching because people do not have a comprehensive biblical worldview. Our understanding of God and how we are to live before him is fragmented at best. While we have an adequate knowledge of God in some areas, we are woefully inadequate in others, which results in theological distortion. For example, during the time of the Puritans, people were deeply aware of the holiness of God but largely failed to understand the love of God. The result was that God was someone to be feared rather than a personal God with whom we can have an intimate relationship. Today, people are often focused on the love of God but fail to understand the holiness of God and the implications of that for their lives. The result is that God becomes a cosmic teddy bear who makes us feel good but does not make demands upon us.

A second reason the church needs theological teaching is because people's views of God are distorted by contemporary views of God. Within the North American culture, success and happiness is measured by the amount of material possessions we have. Pleasure and personal happiness are the highest values. Consequently, we sometimes see God as merely the giver of wealth and possessions, and prosperity theology (with its view that God will bless us materially) governs our perspective. Another cultural perspective, especially in rural areas, is that God helps those who help themselves. Consequently, the focus is on our abilities and efforts rather than relying on God. The success of the farm or family business is determined by our efforts rather than God's grace. As a result we rely upon ourselves more than God.

A third reason we need to teach theology in the church is because we are continually confronted by erroneous views when we witness. Everyone has a theology. Everyone develops a perspective on God that governs his or her belief system. This perspective is often influenced by our culture rather than Scripture. When we witness to people, we encounter views of God that are incorrect. However, rather than studying all the different views of God (from cults to postmodernism), we need to focus upon a right understanding of God as revealed in Scripture so that we can defend what we believe.

A final reason to teach theology is because people can become confused by conflicting theologies. Even among Christians there is a diversity of theological perspectives. While we must always recognize that we will never fully understand all aspects of theology, the diversity of views requires that we study theology in order that we might have a basis for evaluating the teaching of others. Without theological teaching, the church remains spiritually immature, with the result that we are "tossed back and forth by the waves, and blown here and there by every wind of teaching and by the cunning and craftiness of men in their deceitful scheming" (Eph. 4:14).

Equipping the Church Theologically Begins with the Leadership

Before we can develop the theological foundation of the church, as leaders we must build a theological foundation within our own lives. This is not to say that we need to have formal training, but we should have enough understanding of theology to be able to evaluate and develop ministries consistent with sound doctrine. Often when we agree to serve on the board, we have a limited understanding of the doctrines of the church. While we understand the basics (the trinity, salvation by faith, the deity of Christ, etc.), we often lack the knowledge to give an adequate defense of them. Furthermore, we often lack a comprehensive theology that enables us to deal with theological issues that arise within the church (for example, such issues as the nature of spiritual gifts, Calvinism versus Arminianism, the events associated with the second coming of Christ, etc.).

The result of this lack of understanding leads to either dogmatism (anyone who disagrees with me is a heretic) or confusion (I don't know if election is biblical or not). The first results in exclusion (we reject anyone who differs); the other results in error (if we do not know what we believe, we will believe in anything).

To develop our theological understanding, we first need to recognize the importance of it. If we do not believe theology is important, then we will never make it a priority to develop it within our lives. Second, we need to read books on theology to gain a greater foundation. Many books provide an excellent overview of the basic doctrines of the church. These should be a part of our reading. Third, we need to evaluate the decisions and ministries of the church from a theological perspective. It is easy when making decisions to allow our culture and personal preferences to dictate how we vote. Instead, we must always evaluate the issues from the perspective of who God is and how we are to reflect his nature in all aspects of the church. Fourth, we should do research and prepare position papers on current issues confronting the church. Often, conflicts arise within the church over theological issues (such as the mode of baptism, the church's view of spiritual gifts, etc.). When these issues arise, the board should individually and corporately research the issue and develop a position paper that explains the viewpoint of the church. This should then be given to the congregation in order for the board to communicate its position and listen to the input of others within the church.

Equipping the Church Theologically Involves Overseeing the Teaching of the Church

The ultimate task of the church is not to teach people to think rightly about themselves; it is to teach people to think rightly about God. This teaching will occur through the various ministries of the church and is the responsibility of the ministry leaders. Still, it is the responsibility of the board to oversee the theological instruction of the church to make sure that the teaching corresponds to the doctrines of Scripture and the theological position of the church. If someone is teaching a position contrary to the position of the church, the individual should be asked to change his/her instruction or step down from the teaching role. In order to assure the theological instruction of the church, all teachers and leaders within the church should be asked to read the doctrinal position of the church and agree to teach in accordance with that position.

Equipping People with a Biblical Foundation

Ezra came to Jerusalem around the year 457 B.C. The challenge before him was enormous. Approximately eighty years earlier, Zerubbabel had led the first group of people back to Jerusalem, but little headway had been made in restoring Israel politically and religiously. When Ezra arrived with the second group of people, his goal was to restore the spiritual health of the people. While the challenge seemed insurmountable to many, Ezra recognized that God was much greater and the difficulties paled in comparison to the greatness and power of God. When Ezra arrived, he was faced with the question of how to develop a vibrant people of God who lived out the faith they claimed as their own. In Ezra 7:10 we find the priority list Ezra established for equipping the people to be servants of God: "For Ezra had devoted himself to the study and observance of the Law of the Lord, and to teaching its decrees and laws in Israel." For Ezra, the most important task was establishing the foundation of Scripture in the life of Israel. This is equally true for the small church ministry. All ministry is ultimately centered upon the proclamation of Scripture, for it is Scripture, not programs, that results in changed lives (Ps. 119:9–11; Heb. 4:12). This means that we must correctly interpret and apply Scripture (2 Tim. 2:15). It is our task to make sure people are being equipped to correctly understand the Bible. This does not mean that we must be the ones who teach them but that we must be the ones who oversee the teaching of the congregation.

Ezra began the task of establishing a biblical foundation by devoting himself to the study of Scripture. The Hebrew term translated *study* means "to investigate" and refers to the pursuit of the correct understanding of the passage. This means not just the pursuit of the knowledge of Scripture but also the correct interpretation of Scripture, for it is in wrong interpretation that error creeps into the church.[2] Equipping people to study Scripture may involve establishing a class on Bible study methods. It may involve having all the teachers read an introduction on the topic.[3] It may involve providing periodic seminars for the teachers on scriptural interpretation.

Ezra's second priority was to observe the Law. Ezra recognized that the knowledge of Scripture has value only when it is put into practice. When we build upon the foundation of Scripture, it must be based upon obedience. Often in the church today, we have knowledge of Scripture without the application of Scripture. The change of lifestyle must begin with the leadership living out our faith in such a way that people see the difference. As leaders, we are to model obedience. This means that we do not live one way at church and another during the week. How we conduct our business, how and where we spend our leisure time, and how we interact with our family and with others is to be a model of Christian living. This applies not only to our everyday life, but also to how we conduct the ministry of the church. The decisions we make, the priorities we have, and the goals of the church are to be a reflection of our obedience to Scripture.

Third, Ezra sought to communicate the Scriptures to others. Because different individuals and different age groups process information and learn by different means, we need to equip people to communicate the Scriptures in a way that is appropriate and effective for the individuals we desire to reach. For example, a person who teaches an adult Sunday school class will need different communication skills than a person who is teaching four- and five-year-olds. Our responsibility as leaders is to provide training in teaching methods. However, this training should not be limited just to our Sunday school teachers or youth workers but should be available for everyone. A parent or grandparent of four- and five-year-olds needs the training just as much as the Sunday school teacher.

❋　❋　❋

After discussing the music ministry for several months, the church made some significant changes. For a three-month trial period, they intermixed choruses with hymns. After the trial period, the board provided an evaluation form to the congregation in order to get their input on how the changes were being received. Surprisingly, even the older people, who at first had reservations about the changes, enjoyed the new choruses once they learned them. Consequently, the decision was made to adopt a mixture of hymns and choruses. Betty would continue to play for the hymns, while the worship team led the singing of the contemporary songs.

At the next board meeting, everyone was pleased with the outcome. However, as they talked about the progress that was made, John raised a question. "I have enjoyed the worship team's efforts, but there are times when they seem disorganized and disjointed. Is there anything we can do to help them?"

✳ ✳ ✳

Training People for Ministry

Paul challenges us that we are responsible to equip people for "works of service" (Eph. 4:12). This places the responsibility on the leadership to oversee the recruiting and training of people for ministry. Too often we assign responsibilities to people but provide them little or no training and resources. When this happens, people become discouraged because they feel ill equipped for the work of ministry. One of the fears people have is the fear of failure. They feel inadequate, especially for leadership, because they have never received any training. People also become discouraged when they are given a responsibility but lack the resources to carry out that responsibility. It is our duty to avoid these frustrations by making sure that training is available and that people have adequate resources for their task.

Ministry Is the Work of the Whole Congregation

To understand why we need to equip people, we need a healthy and biblical view of ministry. The ministry of the church is not to be the work of a few for the benefit of themselves. Rather it is the work of everyone for the benefit of the whole congregation. When Paul developed a theology of ministry in 1 Corinthians 12, he made it clear that everyone is given a spiritual gift (1 Cor. 12:11). These gifts are not arbitrarily given, nor do we determine what gift we want. We are not offered a spiritual smorgasbord where we pick and choose what we want and where we want to serve. Rather the gifts are determined by the sovereignty of God and are assigned based upon his design for the congregation (v. 18). As a result, "each member belongs to all the others" (Rom. 12:5). Every believer is given a spiritual gift that is critical to the overall health and spiritual ministry of the church. At times in the small church, we base people's involvement on the needs of the church rather than the gifts and abilities of the individuals. As leaders of the church, we need to assist people in discovering the ministry that God has called them to and provide them opportunities to exercise their gifts for the benefit of the whole congregation. If we become restrictive in what we allow people to do, we can hinder the work of God in and through the church. The result is an unhealthy congregation (1 Cor. 12).

Providing People with Training

While spiritual gifts are sovereignly given by God, they can and should be developed (1 Tim. 4:14–15; 1 Peter 4:10–11). For example, individuals who have the gift of teaching can further develop their teaching ability. We are to strive to be the best that we can be for the glory of God. We should not view our gifts as though they were something of little value. We should recognize that the bestowing of a spiritual gift and the call to service are acts of God's grace. Our task as leaders is to come alongside people and help them maximize the exercise of their gifts. One of the ways we do so is by providing the resources so that people can be trained in their area of ministry.

Often in the small church, training goes by the wayside as scarce financial resources limit how much training we can provide. We cannot afford to send people to conferences and seminars, as helpful as they might be. While people are sometimes willing to attend these conferences or seminars at their own expense, more often than not they cannot afford the cost of travel, housing, food, and the seminar. However, a great deal of training can be provided with little or no expense to the church or individual. There are many parachurch organizations, such as Child Evangelism Fellowship, that are willing to come and provide training at little or no cost. Staff members at other churches often are able to come and provide training in their specific fields. For example, the pastor of evangelism in a neighboring city may be able to come and do an evening or all-day Saturday session on evangelizing the community. Even spending time on the phone with a teacher at a Bible college or seminary can provide specialized training in an area that needs to be addressed. What hinders training is not the lack of funds, but our lack of creativity. As leaders, it is our responsibility to make sure that people are given opportunity for training.

※　※　※

After John raised the question about the worship team, Steve agreed, "I have been thinking the same thing. Something needs to be done to make the worship service more organized."

Pastor Dave spoke up. "I agree, but perhaps the problem is more with us than with the worship team."

John was taken aback. "What do you mean?"

"Well," Dave responded, "too often we assign tasks to people and expect them to perform well, but we don't help to equip them for the task. We need to take seriously Paul's challenge in Ephesians that part of the leader's role is to equip others to do the work of ministry."

John again expressed the frustration of the board. "But what can we do? We are just a small church. We don't have the financial resources to hire a staff or send people to seminars."

Everyone but Pastor Dave nodded in agreement.

Pastor Dave smiled at the board's objections. This was something he had often heard in the different small churches he had served. "It is not about finances, but values and importance. There are a number of things we can do to train and equip people that cost little or no money."

John, who oversaw the church finances, liked the sound of that.

Dave continued, "First, we have to model the importance of training. That is why we have been doing this board training material—not only to be better equipped, but also to show others the importance of training. Second, we need to encourage others in their training by working with them to develop a training strategy for their ministry. As a church we need to develop a plan for how we can equip people for ministry. Third, we need to provide the resources people need. One of the problems that has caused the worship team to be disorganized is that they do not have the resources they need. I would like to recommend that we get a projector for them. It will cost a little money, but we can take a special offering to cover it. We can then have the worship leader from First Community Church (a large church in a nearby city) come and do a training session with our worship team. I have already talked to him, and he would be glad to come for free to do so."

※   ※   ※

Providing People with Support and Resources

Along with training people for ministry, we further equip people for ministry by working with them to develop the ministry they are involved in. This means we provide clear goals and objectives as it relates to the overall ministry of the church. Our job is not to be dictators who micromanage every detail of the church. However, the danger is that often we take such a hands-off approach to ministry that we fail to provide any direction for the ministry. This is further compounded in the small church because we tend to be focused on the past rather than the future. Because the small church has a strong sense of tradition, we tend to focus on what has worked well in the past and seek to duplicate it rather than developing clear goals that move us into the future. There are times when this is effective and valuable. The danger is not in looking back; the danger is when we no longer look to the future. While we can learn from the past, we should not live in the past. We need to understand the world in which we are presently living and recognize that it is vastly different from the world in which we grew up. We need to understand our community and culture so that we are able to perceive the ministry to which God has called the church to perform and set the direction for the church.

By giving direction for the whole church, we unify each ministry with a common purpose. Without this common direction, the church can become fractured as each ministry goes its own way and even may conflict with the work of another. Instead of the church working together as a team, it becomes divided as ministries compete with each other for volunteers, finances, and resources. More will be said about this in subsequent chapters, but it is important for the board to recognize that part of equipping people for ministry is providing clear direction for the church, which serves to give direction to each individual part within the church.

The Board Is to Provide Adequate Resources

A ministry will only be as effective as the resources provided. Asking people to develop a youth program without providing financial resources for them to plan and organize events not only will frustrate the team but also will assure its failure. This means that we are to make sure that ministry teams have the financial resources needed to accomplish the responsibilities they have been given. If we do not have the finances, then we need to rethink the way we are currently utilizing our resources or rethink the importance of the ministry. If God has called us to implement a ministry, he will supply all the resources. Our responsibility is to be proper stewards of these resources.

Providing the resources also means that we furnish adequate facilities for the ministry. One of the mistakes small churches make is that we restrict the use of the facilities. Because finances are tight, we become fearful that if the facilities are heavily utilized, it will raise the maintenance expenses for the building, such as the heating and cooling costs. However, by conserving the facilities we hinder the outreach of the church. For example, if we live in a hot climate, not using the air conditioner in order to conserve expenses will keep new people from coming back because the building is uncomfortable. We need to recognize that the facilities are a gift of God to use, not to conserve. We need to place our trust in God for the future.

The Board Is to Provide Spiritual Support

Ministry is demanding and taxes our emotional, physical, and spiritual reservoir. When people become involved in ministry, their faith will be challenged as they enter a spiritual battle against Satan, who desires to nullify their work. They will become emotionally discouraged and drained as they experience the reality of the emotional pain that comes with ministry.

Part of our responsibility as the board is to provide encouragement and support for individuals in ministry. This starts with prayer. As a board we need to spend time praying for and with the people involved in the ministry of the church and praying for the effectiveness of the ministry. Second, we need to provide spiritual support by assisting people with difficult issues that arise. For example, when conflicts arise in a particular ministry of the church, it is the responsibility of the board to seek a resolution to the issues. We support those who are criticized for the decisions they are required to make. We do not allow people to second-guess others in the church, including the pastor. Last, we need to provide spiritual care for people. We need to be sensitive to the spiritual struggles people in the church are facing and come alongside of them to assist them. We need to weep with those who have experienced the pain of ministry. We need to celebrate the victories of people. When they become discouraged because there are no visible results for their effort, we need to offer encouragement by reminding them that we may not see the fruit of our efforts until we stand in the presence of Christ.

✳ ✳ ✳

After purchasing a projector and having the worship team meet with the worship leader at First Community, things were improving. Pastor Dave was pleased with how well things were going. Consequently, he was surprised when Susan, the head of the worship team, called him up on Monday upset and frustrated with the team. After talking with her for an hour, it became apparent that the problem was a clash of philosophy between her and Sally, who played the piano. After praying with her, Dave promised he would bring it up at the board meeting that evening.

That evening he shared with the board the gist of his conversation with Susan.

Steve, who also was a member of the worship committee, gave his perspective: "I agree that we have a problem. There is definitely tension between several members of the worship team. I think there are two reasons. First, we have not provided Susan with the authority to make decisions. Consequently, there is confusion about who is responsible for picking out the music. Second, while Susan does an excellent job, she is easily discouraged. Have we given her any encouragement for the work she has done?"

After spending the next half hour in prayer regarding the issue, the board decided that they needed to implement two actions. First, they needed to sit down with the worship team to clarify the roles and responsibilities of each person on the team. Second, they needed to show greater appreciation to all workers in the church. Each of them agreed to write a note of appreciation each month to someone serving in the church.

✳ ✳ ✳

The Board Is to Provide Organizational Oversight

Supporting people involves loving oversight and accountability. Accountability is not holding a whip over the team like a taskmaster, demanding that they do exactly as we say and achieve the results we desire. Rather, accountability involves loving, supportive oversight so that we can provide assistance when problems arise. When Christ sent out his disciples, he reminded them that they were accountable to God for how they performed their ministry (Matt. 10:28). However, this accountability was not in the area of results but in their faithfulness to be obedient to God and to be good stewards of what he had given them (see Matt. 25:14–30).

There are three areas in particular in which we are to hold people accountable. First, they are accountable for walking in biblical obedience. As ministry leaders they are to exemplify Christ in their lives. Second, we are to challenge them to be faithful to the assigned tasks. If they are failing to fulfill their responsibilities, then we are to come alongside them and help address the issues in their lives that are hindering their ministries. Third, the team is accountable to uphold the values, beliefs, and vision of the church. While each ministry will have its own direction, vision, and goals, it should never conflict with the vision of the church. While people are given freedom in the curriculum, it should never conflict with the theology and values of the church. When it does, the persons involved should be reminded of their agreement to teach what is in agreement with the church. If they refuse, they should be removed; otherwise it will bring division and error into the whole congregation.

Part of our responsibility is to oversee the training of people within the church. Ministry is a skill that is cultivated through training and practice. As a board we can strengthen and expand the ministry of the church by training people to be more effective. This means that we are to provide funds for training as well as set the example by utilizing training opportunities within the church.

EIGHT

Understanding the Purpose
and Mission of the Church

*I*magine a ship without a rudder. What was supposed to be a massive engineering feat designed to move a significant amount of cargo becomes nothing more than a massive bobber in the ocean, driven by the latest winds and destined to become shipwrecked upon some rocky shore. The church was ordained by God to accomplish a purpose. It is that purpose that gives direction and guidance as the church moves upon the ocean of world events. If it lacks this "rudder," the church becomes driven by fads and gimmicks that undermine its purpose. To be effective, the church must be moving in the right direction, steered with the right compass. Without a clear purpose and mission, the church is destined to be shipwrecked upon the rocks of theological and ministerial ambiguity.

Being on the board is more than just fulfilling certain qualifications and making sure that the church facilities are cared for and that the people are happy with the direction of the congregation. We are responsible to supervise the ministry of the church and lead the church in accomplishing its mission. A healthy church has a clearly delineated focus. It understands its purpose for existence and the task that it is to accomplish. This purpose and mission is not determined by denominational leaders or even by the local church. Rather, it is derived from the very pages of the Bible. The task of the leadership is to guide the church in the fulfillment of this mission. To do so we must clearly understand what the purpose and mission of the church is. Then, as leaders, we must be intentional in our focus so that everything the church does works toward achieving its mission. If not, then the church no longer is functioning biblically and no longer has a reason for existence. As a ship fitted with a rudder knifes its way through the ocean currents to reach a desired port, so the church governed by a specific purpose and mission moves to the end that God has ordained.

The Purpose of the Church

Why does the church exist? What is it to accomplish? These two questions are crucial to our perspective of the church. The first question deals with the purpose of the church, and the second deals with the mission of the church. How we answer these questions distinguishes the church from other social and community organizations. The church is not a sanctified Lions club, seeking to build community well-being and identity through "spiritual" means. It is not like the local senior citizens league, which gathers for the purpose of social interaction. The church is a spiritual organism that exists for a spiritual purpose. Our responsibility as leaders is to lead the church by being examples, by developing mission-driven ministries, and by establishing policies and procedures to move the church forward in accomplishing its purpose.

✳ ✳ ✳

The board meeting started with a request from Susan for $500 in order to take the youth to a retreat in a neighboring city. Since this was not in the budget, the board needed to approve it. As they were discussing the matter, Pete raised a question. "Whenever I am faced with an option in my business, I always ask, 'How does this fit into the goals that I have?' If we apply this question to Susan's request, how would we answer it?"

Steve was not convinced. "I'm not sure we need to worry about that question. If we have the money, then let's just give it to her. After all, the youth are important. Furthermore, I am not comfortable with adopting a business approach and making our decisions based upon goals rather than Scripture."

John disagreed. "I don't think this is a business approach. Pastor, doesn't the Bible give us a clear purpose for the church? Too often in the past we have just done things the way they have always been done, without ever asking why. I think if we are going to be biblical, then we should ask why."

"I agree," piped up Pastor Dave. "This is a good time for us to talk about the purpose and mission of the church. We have not spent much time talking about it, yet I believe that we need to. I agree with Steve that we need to give Susan the money. I think the ministry to the youth is important and the retreat would be good for our teens. Remember the hat incident. I think we need to be more concerned about the spiritual condition of our teens than we do about whether they are wearing hats. If they have a deep love for Christ, the issue of the hat will take care of itself. But I also agree with Pete that we need to start thinking about what the purpose and mission of the church is."

In the end, the board approved the money for the youth retreat. They also agreed that they needed to spend time examining Scripture to find out what the purpose of the church is so that when decisions have to be made regarding programs and resources, they have a basis for making those decisions.

❄   ❄   ❄

The Church Is to Glorify God

The Westminster Larger Catechism, developed to teach the foundational tenets of the Christian faith, asks, "What is the chief and highest end of man?" The answer: "Man's chief and highest end is to glorify God, and fully to enjoy him forever." This statement reflects what we find in Isaiah concerning the purpose of humanity: "Bring my sons from afar and my daughters from the ends of the earth—everyone who is called by my name, whom I created for my glory, whom I formed and made" (Isa. 43:6–7). The same could be said for the church. The chief and highest end of the church is to glorify God and to enjoy him forever (2 Thess. 1:12). The task of leadership is to lead the church in the achievement of this end. But how do we accomplish this? Within smaller churches we often leave this question for pastors to answer, rationalizing that they are the ones who are trained in biblical theology and church doctrine. We reason that because we lack any theological training, we are unqualified to lead the church at this level. However, we find in Scripture that we have been given this responsibility, and to abrogate it to another is to fail in our obligation before God (1 Tim. 3:2; Titus 1:9).

We glorify God when his character is revealed in all that we do and when our faith is demonstrated by living in obedience to him. When the decisions and actions within the church result in the maligning of God's character by those outside the church, then we have failed in our responsibility. How, then, do we glorify God? First, we do so by maintaining unity within the church. Tragically, many churches get embroiled in conflict that undermines God's character within the community. How we treat one another reveals the reality of Christ in our lives. Christ points out that the mark of a disciple of Christ is the love that we demonstrate for others (John 13:34–35). This becomes evident as we look beyond differences that might otherwise divide us. Instead, we accept one another in love. When we demonstrate this acceptance we manifest the grace of God to the glory of God (Rom. 15:7–9).

Second, we glorify God when we remain faithful to his Word in all aspects of life. There must be consistency between the faith that we profess on Sunday and the life we live throughout the week. In smaller communities, people not only know us, but they also know our position within the church. They know that we are on the board, and they have expectations about how we are to live in light of our position of leadership. When our life does not measure up to the standards we proclaim, not only will people formulate a negative view of the church, but they will also formulate a negative view of God. As leaders, we must set the example for the church in spiritual consistency.

Third, we glorify God when we handle finances with integrity. In the past several decades, the pages of newspapers and magazines have been filled with embarrassing reports of Christian organizations that have mishandled and, in some cases, embezzled funds. In the vast majority of the cases, the church or religious group started out with the highest ideals of bringing people to Christ. However, this goal was derailed as the church or organization failed to properly manage and oversee the finances of the ministry. Tragically, this not only destroyed their reputations, but it also became a blight upon the whole Christian community. Consequently, we need to develop financial policies and procedures that assure that we handle the finances in an appropriate manner.

Fourth, we glorify God when we become involved in the community. Peter writes, "Live such good lives among the pagans that, though they accuse you of doing wrong, they may see your good deeds and glorify God on the day he visits us"(1 Peter 2:12). These words were written to churches that existed in a hostile environment. As the culture becomes more antagonistic to the gospel, it is all the more critical that the congregation takes the ministry outside the church walls and ministers to the needs of people. Titus reminds us that we are to be "eager to do what is good" (Titus 2:14). The Greek word for *eager* is the term from which we derive the English word *zealot*. It speaks not only of our commitment, but also of our passion. Normally when we think of a zealot, we think of one who is passionate to the point of excess, one who is fanatical in his commitment to a cause. As a church, we are to be so committed to doing good to those outside the church that we are practicing good deeds to a point of excess (Gal. 6:9–10). This is a far cry from many small churches that are self-absorbed in ministry. We become so concerned about not being of the world that we are no longer in the world. We isolate ourselves from the community, doing well at caring for our own needs but doing little to care for the needs of others. Then we wonder why people are not coming to Christ. What draws people to Christ is the testimony of what the people of Christ are doing to minister to others in the community.

Last, we glorify God when we are exercising our spiritual gifts for the advancement of the kingdom of God. Peter writes, "Each one should use whatever gift he has received to serve others, faithfully administering God's grace in its various forms. . . . so that in all things God may be praised through Jesus Christ" (1 Peter 4:10–11). The church is not a cruise vessel, where a few are to wait upon the needs and whims of the majority. Rather, it is a work vessel, where each person is called upon to perform duties and responsibilities based upon spiritual gifts for the well-being of the whole community. As leaders, we are to set the example by utilizing our spiritual gifts in the context of the church. It is not enough that we are merely overseeing the ministry of the church; we are to be actively involved.

✳   ✳   ✳

The first half hour of the board meeting was spent talking about the big buck Ken had shot when driving home from work yesterday. All the events of the day were related, including how upset his wife got when, in his excitement, he forgot to take off his boots and got mud all over the kitchen floor when he walked in. Everyone laughed at this because they knew that this was not the first time.

When the meeting finally turned to church business, Pastor Dave brought up the issue of the purpose and mission of the church. For the next half hour, they bantered back and forth, trying to determine what Scripture taught regarding the purpose and mission of the church.

After much discussion, Pastor Dave realized that this would take more time than any of them had thought. He suggested that they table the issue for now and go away for a weekend retreat to focus just on this issue. Since it was late fall, everyone was slowing down in their work, so getting away for the weekend would not be difficult. But, as Steve suggested, it could not be "during the hunting season," which brought a laugh from everyone.

Pete knew someone who had a hunting cabin they could use. So it was decided that the first weekend after deer season they would leave on Friday night and spend until Sunday afternoon talking about the mission and purpose of the church. Dave would get someone to preach for him on Sunday, and Ken would take care of the food (with the assumption that he would bring some venison steaks for Saturday evening). Everyone looked forward to the weekend, for it would be a time of fun and fellowship, as well as a time when they could get some serious work done.

❋ ❋ ❋

The Church Is to Maintain Theological Integrity

Charles Spurgeon pointed out, "The highest science, the loftiest speculation, the highest philosophy, which can ever engage the attention of the child of God, is the name, the nature, the person, the work, the doings, and the existence of the great God whom he calls his Father."[1] Sadly, this pursuit has been abandoned by much of the church. Instead of viewing theology as central to the church and essential to spiritual health, we devalue it and see it as boring, divisive, and unimportant. Often we approach theology like the stained glass windows of the church. It adds to the overall beauty of the church, but it is not really necessary for the effectiveness of the church. But theology is the church. Without theology, the church loses all reason to exist.

To understand the role of theology within the church, we need to understand what theology is. The term itself comes from the Greek words *theos,* meaning "God," and *logos,* which refers to "discourse, language, or study." In other words, theology is the study of God as he has revealed himself. To study theology is to study who God is, what he does, and how we are to respond to him. It is the pursuit of theological understanding that is to be the focus of the church and the believer. When the church no longer has a doctrinal foundation, it no longer functions as a church, for what we believe about God determines how we live before God.

After describing the characteristics of those who rebel against God, Paul states that their actions are "contrary to the sound doctrine that conforms to the glorious gospel of the blessed God, which he entrusted to me" (1 Tim. 1:10–11). So critical is doctrine and theology that Paul states that the abandonment of theology is the first step in spiritual and moral apostasy: "For the time will come when men will not put up with sound doctrine. Instead, to suit their own desires, they will gather around them a great number of teachers to say what their itching ears want to hear" (2 Tim. 4:3).

One of the central roles of the board and leadership is to protect the theological integrity of the church and teach theological truth to the congregation. More often than not, church boards devote a great deal of attention to the organizational structures of the church but very little attention to the theological foundation of the church. While we follow a church doctrinal statement, we do little to oversee the teaching of sound doctrine in the church.

The board is responsible to be guardians of the theology of the church. Paul writes to Timothy, a leader in the church at Ephesus, "Watch your life and doctrine closely. Persevere in them, because if you do, you will save both yourself and your hearers" (1 Tim. 4:16). One of the most devastating effects of the Fall was the corruption of humanity's view of God. As a result, the people of God are constantly confronted with erroneous views of God. However, corrupted theology comes not only from those outside the church but also from those within the church. Paul warned the Ephesian elders, "I know that after I leave, savage wolves will come in among you and will not spare the flock. Even from your own number men will arise and distort the truth in order to draw away disciples after them" (Acts 20:29–30). Because of this threat, we are to be upholding the theology of the church and making sure that all that is being taught in the church is consistent with biblical truth.

In order to properly protect the congregation from theological error, we as leaders first need to know what we believe and why. We need to have a basic understanding of doctrine and be able to support it from the pages of Scripture. Again, in Titus 1:9 we discover one of the essential qualifications of leadership is that we must "hold firmly to the trustworthy message as it has been taught, so that [we] can encourage others by sound doctrine and refute those who oppose it." Paul states that we need to know our theology for two crucial reasons. First, it is the means by which we bring encouragement to others. When people are going through difficulties and trials, then we are responsible to encourage them by giving a theological perspective to the issues that they are confronting. Second, it is the means by which we confront and correct doctrinal error. This requires that we know what the Scriptures teach about God.

After grounding ourselves in solid doctrine, we are to be constantly evaluating the theological health of the church. In Ephesians 4:11–14 we discover that the purpose of leadership is to prepare people for works of ministry so that the church can reach spiritual maturity (vv. 11–13). One of the essential characteristics of spiritual maturity is doctrinal stability (v. 14). Consequently, in assessing the spiritual health of the church, one of the areas we must examine is the theological health of the church. To do so we must be continually asking these questions: Does the congregation have a basic and accurate understanding of God? Do they understand the redemptive work of God? Is the church grounded in doctrine so that they are not influenced by the latest theological wind that sweeps across the religious landscape? Are decisions based upon a theological and biblical foundation or upon cultural pressures and expectations? Are people developing a worldview that is governed by right theology?

In this process the board must discern between major and minor theological issues. One of the reasons people view theology as divisive is because many churches have become embroiled in conflicts over minor areas of doctrine that subsequently split the church. While it is crucial that we understand and uphold without compromise the basic tenets of the Christian faith (the deity of Christ, the Trinity, the inspiration of Scripture, and salvation by grace through faith alone, to name a few), we also must recognize that there are many areas of theology that we can disagree upon and still remain in fellowship. These are the areas in which there remains some latitude in interpretation due to the lack of clarity on the issues within the church today and the lack of clear, specific teaching in Scripture. We must avoid doctrinal hobbyhorses. While each church can and should maintain its theological identity, we also must recognize that within the greater body of Christ there are others who may differ from our perspective, and yet we can still have fellowship with them as fellow believers in Christ.[2]

✳   ✳   ✳

After dinner the board sat down for their first session to discuss the purpose of the church. They had had a nice drive up to the cabin, seeing along the way eight deer that had escaped another hunting season. After opening the time with prayer, Pastor Dave made two columns on a big sheet of paper he had taped to a wall. In the first he wrote the word *Purpose,* and in the second he wrote *Mission.*

"OK, guys," said Pastor Dave, "before we can go any further, we need to define what we mean by these two words. How would you define the word *purpose?*"

After a time of quiet, Steve was the first to reply. "When I think of purpose I think of the reason for the existence of the church."

"Isn't purpose the result that we are trying to accomplish?" added John.

"Those are good answers, and they are part of what we are talking about," Dave replied. "When we talk about purpose, we answer the question, 'Why does the church exist?' Our purpose determines our mission, which we will talk about tomorrow." Thus under *Purpose* Dave wrote the question, *Why?* "Now, how do we answer this question?"

Ken thought for a moment, then said, "I think the church exists to be a place of fellowship, a place where Christians can get together and help one another grow in Christ. I guess you could summarize it by the word *love.* The church exists to be a place where we can love one another."

"Let's not forget about God," interjected John. "Not only are we to love one another, but we also are to love God. Isn't that what Christ commanded us?"

"That is true," replied Dave. "In Matthew 22:37–39 Christ tells us that the two greatest commandments are to love God and to love one another." Dave wrote the words, *Love God and love others* in the "purpose" column. "When we talk about these, we are really talking about character. As a church we exist to build godly character in the lives of people."

"That's true, but it is not just about love," Pete exclaimed. "I have seen many churches that talk about nothing but love, but they don't teach sound doctrine. Before the church can build godly character, we need to have good theology."

"What about the churches that are so focused on theology that they condemn anyone who thinks differently?" objected John.

"Both of you are right," responded Dave. "We need to have a right belief about God before we can live rightly before him. This is more than just doctrine; this involves the very nature of God. We need to focus on the core doctrines of who God is and recognize that in the minor areas of doctrine we can have some disagreement. Just because we don't always agree doesn't mean that theology should be abandoned. As a church, central to our purpose is teaching people to understand who God is and what he does, which is what theology is all about." So Pastor Dave wrote *maintaining the theology of the church* in the "purpose" column. "This also points to an even more critical reason the church exists," continued Dave. "Ultimately, our purpose is to glorify God. This happens when we have a right understanding about God and we see his character manifested in us, which is character." So Dave wrote *glorify God* in the column and underlined it for emphasis. "While there is more we can add, this is really the core purpose of the church."

✳   ✳   ✳

The Church Is to Develop Godly Character

Theology, if it is genuine theology, is lived theology. It moves from the intellect to the realm of daily life. Genuine theology is translated into character. The church of Ephesus, according to John in Revelation 2:1–7, was a church marked by doctrinal purity, yet they still were in danger of being judged severely by God for they had lost their first love. They no longer loved God or loved people.[3] They were sound in theology but anemic in practice. While doctrinal purity and correct biblical theology are important, they do not affect the spirituality of the church until they dictate practice. Christ provides us with the standard by which we are to live in Matthew 22:37–40: "'Love the Lord your God with all your heart and with all your soul and with all your mind.' This is the first and greatest commandment. And the second is like it: 'Love your neighbor as yourself.' All the Law and the Prophets hang on these two commandments." In other words, love is the foundation for character and action. This love is not the emotional giddiness or experiential feelings that often characterize our view of relationships and spirituality today. Instead, this love is a commitment of the will that results in self-sacrifice and the desire to serve others. It is a love that is grounded in obedience rather than emotions.

Godly Character Involves Loving God

Our character is tied to our relationship with God. To love God is to enter into a covenantal relationship with God, where we live in complete obedience to him (Deut. 15:5; John 14:15). A church that is living out its faith is a church that is walking in obedience, both corporately and individually. To love God is to live in complete dependency upon him so that prayer, rather than self-sufficiency, becomes the hallmark of our relationship. Too often, especially in rural areas, there is a cultural attitude of self-sufficiency. We are to "pull our own weight" and live independent of others. We resent any intrusion by others. Those who need the assistance of others (such as those on welfare) are seen as weak individuals. The result is that we approach our relationship with God with the same attitude. While we recognize that God is over all and we are accountable to him, we see ourselves as self-sufficient. Prayer becomes a sidebar of the church rather than central to the church.

Our position on the board requires that we lead the church in both obedience and dependency upon God. We are to model obedience in our lives and lead the church to manifest it in the affairs of the congregation. The greatest impact we have in the church is not the organizational decisions we make but the example we provide. As mentioned before, we are to provide a living picture of what it means to be a disciple of Christ so that people have a model of what it means to live out our theology. If the goal of leadership is transformation, then the primary means is by showing people how to live.

Godly Character Involves Loving Others

The outgrowth of our love for God is our love for others. In writing of the importance of love, John points out that the failure to love others is evidence of our failure to truly love God. He writes, "Whoever does not love does not know God, because God is love" (1 John 4:8; see also 2:9–11; 3:11, 14; 4:20–21). This love is not the warm fuzzies that we experience when we are with close friends with whom we share mutual interests, respect, and care. It is the type of love that flows from the decision to love people regardless of their treatment of us. Consequently, it is possible (and necessary) to love our enemies (Matt. 5:44). This type of love is unconditional and is expressed regardless of the worthiness of the person and regardless of the person's actions toward us. It does not show favoritism or evaluate people by cultural, social, or ethnic backgrounds (James 2:1–13). When we genuinely love people, we will treat all people the same, whether it be our closest friend or our worst antagonist. This love is not a passive love; it is active, reaching out to minister to the needs of people and seeking to be a source of spiritual, emotional, and physical blessing to them. A healthy church is one that deeply loves people.

A loving church is one that easily forgives others. It is easy in the small church to allow disputes (whether in the church, in the community, or in our own family) to disrupt our fellowship with others. Instead of acting in love, we become resentful and resist fellowship with those who have hurt us. The deeper the hurt, the greater the danger that animosity will supplant love. But Christ points out in the parable of the unmerciful servant (Matt. 18:21–35) that we are obligated to forgive no matter how unjust the pain inflicted, because the wrong we have suffered can never surpass the wrong we committed against Christ. Since he forgave us, we are therefore obligated to forgive others. To fail to do so is to show contempt for the grace of God.

A loving church is one that ministers to the needs of others. Many people in rural areas are facing crises. Rural communities are breaking under the strain of the collapse of the local economy. The poverty rates in many rural areas are some of the highest in the country. Along with the strain has come the collapse of the community's infrastructure as the community declines. Community and social issues such as emotional problems, crime, poverty, addictions, and economic renewal plague smaller communities as well as large urban areas. In order to be effective, a church must do more than just give words of encouragement; it must take action. Christ reminds us that biblical love does not judge those facing hardship; rather, it seeks to serve people by ministering not only to their spiritual needs but also to their emotional and physical needs (Matt. 25:35–40; James 2:14–17; 1 John 3:17–18).

Tragically, the church has remained silent in the presence of those who so desperately need to hear the church's message of hope in the midst of a dying and broken world. In describing the churches' response to alcohol abuse in rural communities, two sociologists lamented, "Rural ministers report that attempts to have prevention programs through the churches are met with resistance by the congregation. In some areas, church members feel that people should not drink at all. Drinking is viewed as an individual moral problem rather than a response to societal pressures. Thus, there are no societal solutions, only individual ones."[4] Rather than engaging our community to provide answers to people's deepest problems, we isolate ourselves in order that we might not become "worldly." As we sit in our white-painted church and padded pews, we wonder why we no longer see people coming to Christ. When Christ states that our testimony hinges on our love (John 13:35), he is talking about love that results in action, not isolation. If we desire to be a loving church, then we must demonstrate love to those outside the church, to those who are the most unlovable and dirty.

A loving church is hospitable. As leaders we are called upon to be hospitable (1 Tim. 3:2). Since the small church is relationally driven, we can easily become cliquish in our treatment toward new people. It is not that we deliberately "give a cold shoulder" to newcomers. It is just that we are so busy visiting with our friends that we overlook the new people who attend. However, hospitality is more than saying "hi" on Sunday morning after church; it is including people in our circle of friends. It is having an open place for them in our lives so that they can feel connected to us and to the church. Loving people means that we strive to incorporate them into the life of the church. A hospitable church is one where people are accepted for who they are, not for what we want them to become. It is easy in the small church to evaluate people by cultural conformity. We make subtle and unconscious evaluations of people based upon our cultural norms (length and style of hair, types of clothing, number of earrings and where they are located, etc.). In demonstrating love, Christ had the capacity to look beyond the cultural differences and see the needs of people (for example, the woman at the well in John 4). When we truly love, we love people regardless of who they are, how they appear, or where they are from. We do not expect people to live like Christians before we will befriend them. Rather, we befriend them so that they will realize their need to enter into a personal relationship with Christ, a relationship that results in inward transformation at the very essence of their being.

A loving church begins with the leadership. As leaders within the church, we must demonstrate the type of love that reveals the genuine nature of God's love. This is most evident in how we respond to people who disagree with our decisions and malign our character during times of tension and conflict. We must set the standard of forgiveness and acceptance. If not, then the church will never become a vibrant, healthy congregation.

The Mission of the Church

While the church is to be grounded in a theology that transforms our life and character, we are also given a task to do. Often people approach the church as though it is a place where we come to relax and be served by the hired staff. We evaluate the church and the pastoral staff by how well they "minister to my needs and the needs of my family." However, when we examine Scripture, we find a completely different picture. We are called into fellowship, not to "have our needs met," but to serve the needs of others through the exercise of our spiritual gifts (1 Peter 4:10). The church is a place where everyone has a responsibility to serve others. The church does not exist to have potluck dinners and coffee hours; it exists to accomplish a threefold mission of reaching people for Christ, teaching them to be his disciples, and equipping them for ministry.

❋   ❋   ❋

After spending the early morning fishing in the privately stocked lake that was on the property, the board members enjoyed a breakfast of deer sausage, eggs, and freshly caught trout. It was a good way for the men to relax and enjoy a time of fun and fellowship together.

Around 10:00 AM, Dave called the men into the living area. "Last night we talked about the purpose of the church and how it answers the question of why the church exists. Today I want us to talk about the mission of the church. When we are talking about the mission, we are focusing on the activity of the church. While 'purpose' answers the question of why we exist, 'mission' answers the question of what we are to do." He wrote *What?* under *Mission* on the board.

Again, Steve was the first to speak. "Isn't the church to help people grow closer to God? Isn't that the main thing we are to do?"

"I agree with Steve," Ken said, "but I don't think we can overlook the Great Commission. To be honest I think that our church has done a good job in teaching people the Bible, but we have not done a good job in reaching out into our community to try to share the gospel with them." Pete nodded in agreement.

"You're right, Ken," Dave responded. "I do agree that one of the biggest weaknesses of most small churches, ours included, is that we do not do a good job in evangelism. We often separate evangelism from discipleship, and it is easy for churches to get focused only on one to the exclusion of the other. But as we look at what Christ states in the Great Commission, we find that both are an integral part of the mission of the church. In fact, you cannot have one without the other. I think we really need to be more focused on evangelism."

"But if we are to do that, we need to train people," objected John. "There are many people in our church who do not know how to share their faith with someone else."

"I agree," answered Dave. "That's why it is important that we recognize the importance of equipping people for ministry."

Dave wrote three words in the "mission" column: *Reach, Teach,* and *Equip.* "As we look at these three tasks, all express an important part of the mission of the church, and they are all interrelated. As we look at the ministry of our church, this is what we have to evaluate. As the leaders of the church, we need to be constantly asking ourselves, 'How is the church doing in each of these three areas?' If we are neglecting any area, then we as leaders need to make the changes in the ministry of the church so that these areas are not overlooked."

The men spent the rest of that day and Sunday morning brainstorming how the church could be more effective in accomplishing its purpose and mission. While they did not come up with a lot of answers, they did come away with three issues they needed to discuss further. First, they needed to develop a strategy for encouraging evangelism in the church. Second, they needed to be more proactive in discipling individuals in the church, especially those who had been longtime attendees. Third, they needed to provide training for the Sunday school teachers.

※　※　※

The Mission of the Church Is to Reach People for Christ

When Christ set forth the mission of the church in Matthew 28:19–20, and then repeated it in Acts 1:7–8, he made it clear that the church exists to proclaim the gospel of Christ to a spiritually dead world. Evangelism must be integrated into all aspects of the ministry of the church so that the church is faithfully and effectively communicating the gospel of Christ, inviting others to enter into a personal relationship with him. This happens when we are communicating the gospel to others in such a way that the person has a better understanding of what it means to accept Christ as their Savior. Without continually refocusing the church on its evangelistic mission, the church can become inwardly focused so that the congregation serves itself and no longer engages the community in which it lives. Our responsibility as leaders is to continually direct the church to pursue the lost.

We must recognize that evangelism is a process, not an event. When we think of evangelism, what most often comes to mind is a person pulling a tract out of his or her pocket, sharing the "four spiritual laws," and concluding with an invitation to accept Christ as Savior. However, evangelism is much more than this. Evangelism is the process of revealing the reality of Christ to others. For some, this may involve the verbal and direct communication of Christ. For others it may involve acts of love and compassion so that the lost see tangible evidence of the reality of Christ's love for them. We are involved in evangelism when we are being used by God to move people closer to Christ. We evangelize people who are antagonistic to the gospel by helping them develop a positive perspective of Christ and the church. We evangelize seekers by sharing the basics of the gospel message and inviting them into a relationship with Christ. Thus, being a witness for Christ encompasses our whole life and our daily interaction with every unbeliever with whom we rub shoulders. It is a team sport, involving the individual as well as the congregation. Dann Spader and Gary Mayes point out that "typically an unbeliever needs to have more than five meaningful contacts with a number of Christians before he or she will begin to trust the message of the gospel."[5] We need to develop a witnessing community that involves both the individual Christian and the whole congregation.

We must make prayer a cornerstone of evangelism. This is true whether it is personal evangelism or a church program designed for outreach. The first step in motivating people for evangelism involves encouraging people to pray specifically for their family, friends, and coworkers. Evangelism is a spiritual process requiring supernatural empowerment. Since it requires spiritual change, it cannot be accomplished through human means or techniques. Yet, God has chosen to use prayer as a basis for his involvement within the affairs of humanity. Prayer needs to be offered on behalf of those we are trying to reach, as well as for those doing the evangelizing. Like the apostle Paul, the believer needs to pray for opportunities for sharing the faith and for boldness in being a witness for Christ (Col. 4:3–4). Prayer is fundamental to success in ministry. We become engaged on the spiritual battlefield for the souls of people through prayer. We can have all our programs in place, our outreach events planned, and our people verbalizing their faith, but it all comes to naught if it is not undergirded with prayer. Prayer prepares the hearer of the gospel message as well as the communicator. Without prayer, there will be no passion for the lost, no power in the testimony, and no presence of God in the message.

The board must set the example for the congregation by culti-vating relationships with the unchurched. After surveying 14,000 church members, the Institute of American Church Growth con-cluded that 75 to 90 percent came to Christ and to the church they attended because of a personal relationship with a friend or relative.[6] Evangelism happens in the context of interpersonal relationships. It happens when we allow God to use us as salt and light within our sphere of influence. We must recognize that our personal mission field begins with our friends and family. But evangelism also must involve being intentional in developing new relationships with people and spending time with them in order to reveal Christ to them in our actions and words.

We must make sure that evangelism is integrated into all aspects of ministry. Building an evangelistic church requires that the congre-gation becomes obsessed with evangelism; otherwise it will always remain a task rather than a mission. Being a witnessing community is not another program but is central to every ministry of the church. Kevin Ruffcorn points out the importance of integrating evangelism into every aspect of ministry when he states, "Evangelism is woven into the fabric of congregational life. It cannot be separated from the fabric without destroying the material because it is not merely a design imprinted on the surface."[7] Without an evangelistic per-spective, every ministry of the church will eventually collapse and become ingrown. Having an awareness of the mission field around the church is vital to the overall health and vitality of the congrega-tion. When we no longer see the lost around us, we stop functioning as a church (John 4:34–38).

We must develop evangelistic programs. Evangelism is not only the task of each individual within the church; it is also the task of the whole congregation. We fulfill our responsibility as individuals when we cultivate friendships and share the reality of Christ with others. We fulfill our responsibility as a congregation when we develop programs and strategies to reach our community for Christ. However, the danger is that our past failures can bring discouragement. Since we have not seen measurable results from past efforts, we conclude that it is a waste of time. However, we must recognize that God does not call us to achieve results; he calls us to faithfulness in proclamation.

The Mission of the Church Is to Disciple People

The focus of what is commonly called the Great Commission (Matt. 28:19–20) is not upon evangelism but upon discipleship. The lone command in the verse is "make disciples." The aim of the church is not merely to make people feel good about themselves or even about God; it is to make them followers of Christ. The healthy church is discipleship driven; it is not as concerned about filling the pews as about transforming people into the character and image of Christ.

Discipleship is a lifelong process of growing in our knowledge of Christ (Phil. 3:10) and walking in obedience to Christ (John 14:15, 21, 23–24). Often we mistake emotionalism (how I feel about God) with genuine discipleship (how I live before God). *We are disciples when we are committed to thinking and living like Christ, allowing Christ to transform us so that we become servants who actively use our gifts for the spiritual growth of others.* Like evangelism, this is not an event; rather, it is a process of spiritual growth.

To be a disciple-making church, we must realize that discipleship takes place at all levels of our spiritual maturity. The person who has been a Christian for a number of years is just as much in need of discipleship as the person who accepted Christ last week and is still trying to understand the basics of the Bible. Those who are new to the faith need to be taught the basics of prayer, obedience, fellowship and service. As we mature, however, we must be taught doctrine,

Bible study skills, and character. The process does not end after the initial eight-week "discipleship program." Churches often do well at developing programs for new believers but neglect the discipleship process for the seasoned Christian. As a result many Christians become stunted in their spiritual growth. They attend church each week and give regularly to the finances of the church, but they never fully maximize their gifts or become spiritual leaders in the church. As leaders within the church we have the responsibility to examine the overall ministry of the church and evaluate our discipleship program. Are we providing a solid foundation for young believers (those new in the faith as well as our children)? Are we training individuals to become future spiritual leaders within the church?

The Mission of the Church Is to Recruit and Equip People for Service

When writing to the church at Ephesus, Paul makes it clear that the primary role of leadership is to train and equip people to serve Christ (Eph. 4:11–13). This mandate is based, first, upon the awareness that God is the one who has equipped people to serve. We are to train others to serve because it is God's will and purpose for their lives. To this end they were created and redeemed (Eph. 2:8–10). Having been equipped by God with a gift, every believer is then empowered by God to serve him effectively. The mandate to train and equip others is also based upon the awareness that everyone's involvement is necessary for the church to be healthy. Spiritual gifts are given to individuals in order to benefit the rest of the body of Christ (1 Cor. 12:7). If people are neglecting to use their gifts, or if the church is not allowing them to use their gifts, the congregation becomes deformed and stunted in its spiritual growth.

How, then, do we equip people for ministry, and what is the role of the board in this process? This is a question that is critical to our responsibility as a board, one to which we must continually devote considerable attention. The process begins by first providing opportunities for people. The task of the church is to release rather than restrict people for ministry. When new people arrive, we need to provide opportunities for them to serve at all levels of the church ministry.

Equipping involves training people in order to help them develop their abilities and spiritual gifts. As already pointed out, training is the process of helping people become more knowledgeable, better skilled, and more effective in the ministries they serve. This instruction involves training related to specific ministry skills, general ministry skills, and spiritual life skills. Training in specific ministry skills is the process of instilling greater expertise and abilities related to specific ministries. It may involve training Sunday school teachers in teaching methods appropriate to various age groups. General ministry skills training focuses on increasing someone's competency in a variety of assignments. For example, the church may provide training for people in how to effectively share their faith with others. Training in spiritual life skills involves communicating basic concepts and principles that equip the person in all areas of ministry as well as their personal Christian experience. Providing a teacher with instruction in the basics of doctrine enables the person to more clearly understand and communication biblical truth. It also better equips the person to understand how the character of God relates to their own personal life.

The purpose of the church is not to maintain a sociological subculture, nor is it to maintain a denominational standard. The ultimate purpose of the church is to glorify God and build his kingdom by assisting people in spiritual transformation. As leaders, it is our responsibility to oversee the spiritual development of the church. The challenge we face is that we can easily mistake outward conformity for inward transformation. As a result we may tend to measure church health by how much everyone is conforming to outward standards. But we are to lead the church to a much deeper level of spiritual growth, one that transforms people at the very core of their identity. This inward transformation will become evident in the actions of people as we seek to evangelize the lost and disciple people. The question we must wrestle with is not, "Are people happy in the church?" Rather, we must be asking the question, "Are we accomplishing God's mission for the church?"

NINE

Teamwork

The Art of Working Together

*E*lijah was discouraged. He had confronted the prophets of Baal on Mount Carmel, but what he initially perceived to be a great victory for God had turned into a tragic defeat in his mind, as the people of Israel responded with indifference to the supernatural demonstration of God. Although the people had given lip service to God, Elijah perceived their apathy. Then he heard that Jezebel vowed to destroy him. Elijah felt alone, abandoned by his people and abandoned by God himself. In the face of such discouragement, he ran into the desert and cried out to God, "I have had enough Lord. . . . Take my life; I am no better than my ancestors. . . . I have been very zealous for the LORD God Almighty. The Israelites have rejected your covenant, broken down your altars, and put your prophets to death with the sword. I am the only one left, and now they are trying to kill me too" (1 Kings 19:4, 14). He was discouraged because he felt he was in the spiritual battle alone.

In response to Elijah's discouragement, God did four things to rejuvenate Elijah. First, he provided physical rest and renewal. Elijah was not only spiritually exhausted, but he was exhausted physically and emotionally as well (1 Kings 19:5–8). Second, God reminded Elijah of his call to ministry (vv. 15–17). Third, God reminded Elijah that the advancement of his cause was not dependent solely on Elijah; God had seven thousand other people doing his work as well (v. 18). Fourth,

God gave Elijah an assistant (Elisha) to help him continue his work (vv. 19–21). Ministry was never meant to be a one-man show. It was designed to be a team sport, where people are working together, each exercising their spiritual gifts for the growth of the body of Christ. The writer of Ecclesiastes recognized the importance of working as a team when he stated, "Two are better than one, because they have a good return for their work: If one falls down, his friend can help him up. But pity the man who falls and has no one to help him up! Also, if two lie down together, they will keep warm. But how can one keep warm alone? Though one may be overpowered, two can defend themselves. A cord of three strands is not quickly broken" (Eccl. 4:9–12).

A church that places the spiritual well-being and care of the church solely in the hands of the pastor is an unhealthy church. At such a church, whenever the pastor brings issues to the board concerning the spiritual care of the church, the board responds by stating, "This is why we hired you." When the pastor invites the board members to join him in visiting people, they feel inadequate to do "ministry."

A central characteristic of a healthy church is when the board recognizes that the pastor is not the only one responsible for the care of the congregation; rather, it is their responsibility as well. Rather than shrink back from the task, they embrace it with enthusiasm and reliance upon the Holy Spirit. One of the critical characteristics of healthy churches is a positive working relationship between the board and the pastor. Instead of being in conflict and viewing one another with suspicion, they work together as a team, each understanding the importance and value of the others. When the pastor and the board have an adversarial relationship, the whole congregation will be adversely affected and the cause of Christ will be hindered. If the leadership is to lead the church toward spiritual health, it is critical that the pastor, the board, and the congregation all work together as a team to advance the cause of Christ.

✳ ✳ ✳

Pastor Dave had an uneasy feeling. He was excited about the way the board had been working at becoming spiritual leaders. The board meetings were far more productive than he had ever experienced before in his ministry. It was a real encouragement to him to see the men strive to be greater servants in the church. Still, there was something missing in the church, but he was just not sure what it was. It wasn't until he went to the high school basketball game that it finally hit him. As he watched the team work together, it suddenly dawned upon him that teamwork was what was missing in the church. It wasn't that there were conflicts or that people were arguing about the ministry of the church. In fact, everything was going well. But he realized that everyone was doing their own thing. While the church was united, it was not working together.

The next day Dave called Ken to share his thoughts. Ken agreed. "You know, Pastor, I have been thinking the same thing lately. I think it needs to start with the leadership. We all get along well on the board, but sometimes I feel that we are not really open and honest because we are afraid of offending one another. At the last board meeting when we were talking about the children's ministry, I had a feeling that Steve was not fully in agreement but he would not share his concerns."

Pastor Dave agreed.

Ken went on, "I think we need to put this on the agenda for the next meeting. Pastor Dave, would you come prepared to share some of the principles about effective teamwork in a church?"

Dave hung up the phone, feeling both excited and challenged. He was excited because he knew this was another key step for the church. He also was challenged, for he needed to come up with some material. The next few weeks would be busy indeed.

❋   ❋   ❋

Defining Team Ministry

A team ministry occurs when the pastor, board, and congregation are working in unison for the spiritual growth and well-being of others, with each understanding their own gifts, roles, and responsibilities while valuing and utilizing the gifts, roles, and responsibilities of others. This begins with the relationship between the pastor and the board as they work together to care for the spiritual needs of the congregation.

Intrinsic in the development of the team relationship between the pastor and the board are four key elements. First, it involves mutual and shared authority. Instead of the pastor and the board being in competition with one another for power and authority, each learns to value and accept the input of the other. The authority given to the board by the congregation does not intimidate the pastor, and the board accepts the pastor as an equal with them. Second, there must be the recognition of mutual responsibility for the oversight of the congregation. Team ministry moves the leadership from the organizational priorities to spiritual responsibilities. They recognize that the spiritual care of the congregation is not just the charge of the pastor, but equally belongs to the board and the whole congregation. Third, team ministry involves organizational oversight. The board is to work with the pastor in the establishment of goals and direction for the church and in the implementation of those goals. Fourth, team ministry involves recognition of the different roles and responsibilities each has within the congregation. While the pastor and the board are both responsible for the oversight of the church, they each have different roles to fulfill as they exercise their spiritual gifts.

Prerequisites for Team Ministry

To build an effective team ministry, the pastor and board need to understand the foundation of mutual cooperation. In order to develop teamwork, we must build upon the right foundation.

Effective Teams Build upon a Biblical Theology of Team Ministry

Working together as a team is not the latest management fad but springs from the heart of the biblical concept of leadership. The sage in Proverbs 11:14 recognized the importance of multiple counselors when he wrote, "For lack of guidance a nation falls, but many advisers make victory sure" (see also 15:22; 24:6). When the early church was founded, it was established under the leadership team of the twelve apostles. In its first missionary venture, they sent out the team of Barnabas and Paul (Acts 13:2), following the pattern already established by Christ (Mark 6:7). When Barnabas and Paul appointed leaders in the churches they established, they appointed multiple leaders (Acts 14:23).

Effective Teams Understand the Nature of Leadership Within the Small Church

An effective team realizes that leadership is not vested by position but by relationships. The pastor is not threatened by the congregation or by the "tribal chiefs." Instead, he strives to work with them and utilize their influence. The team understands that the small church views leadership from a family perspective, where relationships form the basis for all decisions. Rather than the corporate perspective where the organizational health determines the goals, budgets, and programs, the small church evaluates everything from the standpoint of relational health.

Effective Teams Understand the Importance of Mutual Submission

Paul commands all believers to submit to one another (Eph. 5:21). The expression implies that each person within the congregation (and leadership) voluntarily yields to one another in love. Rather than pushing through our agenda, we are willing to set aside our personal desires, needs, and plans for the benefit of the whole and the maintenance of unity within the church. While we can and should have in-depth discussions of the issues, we also must have a strong commitment to uphold the decisions of the board, even when we may not fully agree with those decisions. As leaders, we need to recognize that complete agreement on important issues is at times impossible. The goal in a team meeting is not to get everyone to agree but to make sure that all have the opportunity to express their opinions and that these opinions are honestly considered and evaluated by the group. Then, when the group makes a decision, all members should support that decision verbally and with their actions in helping to implement the decision.[1]

Effective Teams Understand the Importance of Mutual Trust

A hallmark of love is continual trust in the other person (1 Cor. 13:7). Just as God has entrusted the leadership of the church to selected individuals (1 Cor. 4:2), so also we must learn to trust one another. Trust is the "confidence among team members that their peers' intentions are good, and that there is no reason to be protective or careful around the group. In essence, teammates must get comfortable being vulnerable with one another."[2] We need to value others' judgments and opinions, striving to see the best in others rather than seeing the worst. Instead of quickly judging the motives of others, we can learn to have confidence in each other's spiritual integrity. Trust then finds expression in our willingness to listen to one another and to what others are saying. However, listening goes beyond merely understanding the person's words; it seeks to understand how the person's background, history, desires, and needs influence the person's perspective. Listening is the art of understanding, and trust is built when we strive to fully understand the person without passing judgment or hastily condemning the person when we do not understand.

Effective Teams Love the Church

While Ephesians 5:25–33 traditionally has been used as a text on the husband's love for his wife, Paul makes it clear that the primary focus of his discussion is upon Christ's love for the church (v. 32). Effective leaders love the church. They are motivated to serve well as a team, not to get more recognition or influence, but because of their passion to see the church become all that God designed it to be.

Effective Teams Are Built with Spiritually Mature Members

In addressing the qualifications of leadership, Paul places the emphasis upon spiritual maturity (1 Tim. 3:6; Titus 1:5–9). While the secular community looks for leaders who have multiple abilities, keen intellect, and dynamic personalities, the church is to look for leaders who have a deep love for Christ, a passion for truth, and a consistent biblical lifestyle.

Effective Teams Are Built upon a Sense of Community

The church is to be a community of God's people united by our mutual faith in Christ (1 John 1:6–7) and driven by a desire to mutually encourage one another in our spiritual growth (Heb. 10:24–25). The depth of the sense of community becomes the basis for God's blessing upon his people (Ps. 133). As leaders we must set the example. "Church leaders must settle for nothing less than genuine community. When church leaders emphasize the priority of community and consistently model it, their example will shape leaders-in-training and the whole congregation. The level of community in any group will reflect the level of community modeled by the group's core leaders."[3]

Avoiding the Team Killers

While building upon the right foundation for team leadership is critical, it is also important to identify and avoid those things that will destroy an effective team.

Team Killer #1: Pastoral Elitism

Although education and training are critical for effective ministry, the danger is that we can equate training and biblical knowledge with spirituality. If the pastor views the board as untrained and un-educated in spiritual leadership, he can develop the attitude that the board members have less insight into the will of God. Consequently, when the board disagrees with the direction and goals of the pastor, he begins to view the board as carnal. This creates a rift between them that undermines their effectiveness in working together as a team. When the pastor fails to understand and value the board, tensions arise as the pastor concludes that the board is unwilling to change and accept new methods that he deems to be essential to the growth and well-being of the church. For there to be teamwork, it is vital that the pastor learn to value the spiritual insight and sensitivity of the board. (This sense of pastoral elitism can come not only from the pastor but also from the board themselves if they place the pastor on a pedestal.)

Team Killer #2: Lack of Acceptance

Teamwork is destroyed when the board and the congregation see the pastor as an outsider. There are several reasons why they will view the pastor as an outsider. First, when the small church has experienced a rapid turnover of pastoral leadership, the lay leaders begin to develop the mind-set that the pastor will be temporary. Consequently, they do not fully entrust themselves to his leadership for he will soon be gone.

A second reason is the cultural differences that can exist between the pastor and the congregation. When a pastor comes from a different cultural setting (such as coming from the city to the country or from one geographic region to another), he may discover that people are reluctant to accept him into the inner circle of the church. Although they value his spiritual and biblical instruction, they are hesitant to accept any changes because "he does not understand us." They view the pastor as someone who comes in with all kinds of new ideas and programs but lacks sensitivity to the issues and culture of the congregation. They see him as someone who brings in his agenda without listening to their ideas.

In both of these cases, it is critical that the lay leadership takes the lead in setting the example for the congregation in following the pastor's leadership. The board must work to help people learn to accept the new pastor with his cultural differences. On the other hand, it is important for the pastor to seek to understand the specific culture of the area and to manifest a strong commitment to the church.

Team Killer #3: Suspicion

If the congregation has experienced problems in the past with the pastor or the lay leadership, mistrust of new leadership can develop. Instead of rallying around the new individuals in leadership positions and working with them to fulfill the Great Commission, the congregation questions any new idea or change the leadership might propose. When a pastor and board are working within this environment, they need to recognize the importance of gaining trust before attempting to implement new strategies. Furthermore, they need to keep all communication channels open and operate under the assumption that it is better to overcommunicate than under-communicate. If they are not clearly communicating what they are doing and why, people may develop serious doubts and questions about the motives and intent of the leaders.

Team Killer #4: Inflexibility

When the pastor or any individual board member always says "no" to any new idea or proposal, the teamwork within the board breaks down. The board needs individuals who are open to new ideas and are willing to openly evaluate change. Inflexible people refuse to accept any opinion or proposal that is not in full agreement with their personal concept of what should be. Effective teams are not built upon inflexible people but upon those who are accommodating, who evaluate ideas and listen carefully to others before formulating their decisions. They are willing to "agree to disagree" and will support issues and proposals even if they are not in full agreement.

Team Killer #5: Docility

In sharp contrast to the inflexible person is the one who goes with the flow and is always a "yes" person. This is the individual who never expresses his own ideas but always agrees with the pastor and others. This stems from an unhealthy perspective that sees all conflict as destructive and thus fears any disagreement. If a team is open and honest, there will be times of conflict as people bring passionate perspectives to the discussion. Open discussion enables board members to have a broader perspective and to see possible solutions beyond their own. Teamwork is built upon individuals who are not afraid to disagree, who raise objections to issues in order to protect the congregation from poor decisions. While they do not demand that everyone agree and follow their opinions, they are not afraid to express their ideas and give their input.

Productive discussion involves concepts and ideas but avoids personality-focused, mean-spirited attacks. While it has passion, emotions, and even frustration, the focus remains on the issues rather than the individual. As Patrick Lencioni points out, "Teams that engage in productive conflict know that the only purpose is to produce the best possible solution in the shortest period of time. They discuss and resolve issues more quickly and completely than others, and they emerge from heated debates with no residual feelings or collateral damage, but with an eagerness and readiness to take on the next important issue."[4] Aubrey Malphurs likewise argues, "A culture where everyone walks and talks in lockstep with the pastor, chairperson, or benevolent patriarch is spiritually unhealthy. A culture where there's no debate or difference of opinion is spiritually and creatively sterile."[5] A healthy church is one where people are open and honest, not demanding, but willing to share their ideas and listen to the ideas of others.

✳ ✳ ✳

After spending the first thirty minutes praying for the needs of the church, Ken opened the meeting by sharing the conversation he had had with Pastor Dave. Then he asked Pastor Dave to share some principles of teamwork. For the next hour Dave shared what he had learned in his research on teamwork within the church. He shared with them some of the things that could undercut an effective team. Steve and John nodded their agreement. But after Dave had shared the benefits and principles for developing a team ministry, Pete looked puzzled.

"Pastor, I agree with you that this is something we need to further develop within the church," Pete interjected. "But how do we do this? I understand the principles you are sharing, but how do we take it to the next step and make it happen in the church? It seems to me that all the things you have shared from the books are theoretical, but how do we make it practical for us?"

"Those are great questions," responded Dave. "In fact, I have been perplexed by them as well. The one thing we have to realize is that there are no easy answers, for we have to figure out how to apply these principles within the context of our church. One of the reasons the books do not give us all the specific steps is because each church context is so different. They can give us the general principles, but we have to come up with how to apply them in our specific context. Let's spend some time really thinking and praying about this, and let's take the next board meeting and do some brainstorming on how we can apply these principles in our own church."

✳   ✳   ✳

Benefits of Team Ministry

The pastor and board understanding the immense value of working together is foundational to committing to team ministry. Developing a ministry team is not only the cornerstone of effectiveness; it expresses God's desire for the church.

Effective Teams Disarm Potential Conflicts

Unity within the leadership provides the basis for maintaining unity within the church. In the early church, ethnic and cultural tensions threatened to splinter the existing harmony. What kept the early church from disintegrating into factions was the unified position adopted by the leadership (Acts 15:5–21). When the pastor and the board work together to resolve problems and conflicts and to develop a united consensus on problematic issues, it gives the leadership assurance that they are making the right decisions. Furthermore, it gives the congregation confidence in the decision of the board. Consensus grows as the pastor and board develop mutual respect for one another and a willingness to work toward agreeable solutions even when their individual opinions might differ. Unity does not require unanimity on all issues, even those that cause tension. Unity comes as each listens to the opinions of others so that they can set aside their own agendas and ideas and strive for a consensus.

Effective Teams Broaden the Leadership Base

Throughout redemptive history in both the Old and New Testaments, leadership was shared so that burdens were not shouldered by one individual. Following the timely advice of Jethro, Moses chose capable men to assist him in caring for the needs of the people (Exod. 18:13–27). Jesus recruited twelve men to establish the church. Barnabus recruited Paul to assist him in guiding the newly born church in Antioch (Acts 11:22–26). Ministry is a team sport, not to be performed by talented superstars while the rest cheer them on, but conducted by a team who can share the burdens of ministry and mutually encourage and support one another.

Effective Teams Balance Weaknesses and Strengths

Since we still face the effects of our sinful nature, we need others to compensate for our weaknesses and shortcomings. No individual is so multitalented and spiritually strong as to be free from limitations and failures. Because of our failures, we need others to complement us. Strength is found in diversity. The strong-willed, driven Paul needed the compassion and patience of Barnabus, and vice versa (Acts 15:36–41). The stammering Moses needed the eloquence of Aaron (Exod. 6:30–7:2). Even in his perfect state before the Fall, Adam needed the balance of Eve (Gen. 2:20). By working together within the diversity of our personalities, giftedness, backgrounds, and opinions, our weaknesses are overcome and our corporate strengths benefit others. It is our differences that strengthen our ministry as we work together (1 Cor. 12).

Effective Teams Provide Greater Stability Within the Church During Leadership Changes

One of the most difficult periods of the congregation's life is when the pastor leaves for another ministry. However, when the church has developed a strong ministry team with the leadership, where the whole board has been involved in the ministry and direction of the church, the impact of this change is minimized. Joshua was able to take over the leadership of Israel from Moses and rally the people to the difficult task of the conquest because Joshua already had been involved in the care of the people of Israel (Exod. 17:9–14; 24:13; Deut. 1:38). The early church thrived after the ascension of Christ because they had the Spirit-empowered leadership of the disciples to guide them, men who already had been leaders within the movement, who had learned under Christ's ministry (Matt. 10:1–10).

Effective Teams Provide Greater Spiritual Oversight of the Congregation

As leaders we are appointed by the Holy Spirit to be overseers and shepherds of the church. Throughout the New Testament we are constantly warned of the dangers of false teaching and false teachers who will infiltrate the church and oppose the gospel of Christ. Consequently, we are to be united in our vigilance and care of the congregation. The church is stronger when the pastor and board recognize that together they are to oversee and protect the congregation from spiritual error.

Effective Teams Provide Greater Wisdom

The writer of Proverbs states that the wise person recognizes the value of the counsel of others while the fool sees no need for input (Prov. 12:15). The writer of Ecclesiastes recognizes this same truth, when he writes that strength and protection come from working together (Eccl. 4:9–12). While leading the people through the desert, Moses recognized that he would be better equipped to do so if he had his brother-in-law helping him (Num. 10:29–32). Corporate wisdom always exceeds individual wisdom.

✳   ✳   ✳

After the board spent some time in prayer, Pastor Dave opened the meeting by writing the word *TEAMWORK* on the whiteboard. "OK," Dave began, "how can we develop greater teamwork in our church?"

Everyone was silent. "So much for everyone thinking about this last month and coming up with a solution," joked Dave. Everyone laughed.

"Actually, Pastor, I have given it a lot of thought," Steve responded. "You're right; there are no easy answers. The reason is because we are dealing more with an attitude than anything. If we have the right attitudes toward one another, then teamwork will be the natural outworking of it."

"What do you mean?" questioned Pete.

"To me the key attitudes that undergird teamwork are respect, honesty, and humility," Steve explained. "If we respect one another, then we will listen to what each other has to say. If I respect you—and I do—then when you disagree with me, I will weigh your input carefully. Furthermore, we need to be open and honest with one another. If we are not honest in our opinions, then we will not learn from one another and we cannot receive any value from each other's perspective. But this also requires humility on our part so that we do not start thinking that our perspective is always better than any-one else's. So for me, these attitudes are where we must start."

Under the heading of "Teamwork" Pastor Dave wrote the word *ATTITUDE*.

"I agree with you, Steve," Pete replied. "Teamwork grows from the right attitude. It also must be translated into ac-tion. For this to happen we need to teach all our leaders and workers within the church about teamwork. Furthermore, it should be something that we talk about continually. It will take time for this to become part of how we function as a church, so it needs to be constantly reinforced. I think this must begin with us. We need to model teamwork as a board, for if we are not functioning well as a team, then the rest of the congregation will never function as a team."

Everyone nodded in agreement, so Dave wrote the word *ACTION* on the board, and under the word he wrote the statement, *Teach it, reinforce it, and model it.*

John now piped up. "For me, it is easier to see when people are undermining teamwork than it is for me to describe how to develop it. I think if we are going to develop teamwork, then we need to lovingly confront people if they are disrupting the teamwork within the church. When someone is not listening to others and unwilling to allow others to have input, I think we need to address it in a positive way. If we want to have teamwork within the church, then we need to hold people accountable for when they undercut it." Again, everyone nodded.

Dave wrote the word *ACCOUNTABILITY* on the board.

Since it was now getting late in the evening, Ken suggested that they end the meeting for now. They knew that they still had a great deal of work to do to develop a greater sense of teamwork within the church, but they felt that they had made a significant step in the right direction.

❊   ❊   ❊

Developing a Team Ministry

Since the congregation will benefit from a group leading them rather than just the pastor, the pastor needs to seek to develop a team of individuals who will assist in the oversight of the ministry.

Look For and Recruit Team Players

In selecting individuals to formulate a team, the church and pastor must look for "team players." Such individuals are, first, teachable. They are not dogmatic but willing to listen. They recognize that they can and need to learn from others. Second, team players are people who are submissive. Paul writes that we are to submit to one another (Eph. 5:21). This does not mean that team players are "yes" people; rather, it means that they do not come with any personal agendas that they try to force upon others. They are concerned about the needs of others (Phil. 2:4) rather than just their own. Third, team players are people of faith. They are not stingy and are not afraid of risks. They are governed by the Great Commission. They recognize that in Christ all things are possible. While they are prudent, they are not afraid of taking risks, for they recognize that only when we look beyond our limitations do we see the sufficiency of God. Fourth, team players are people who are open to change. While they recognize the value and contribution of the past and the value of tradition, they are not governed by them. They understand that all growth requires change and to be effective in communicating the gospel we must continually be changing our methods while holding fast to our message. Finally, team players possess spiritual wisdom. People look up to them and value their counsel. The danger of the small church is that it can select its leaders because of "tribal connections" rather than spiritual insight. While the "tribal chiefs" often manifest sensitive and godly perception, it is important to realize that it is godly character that legitimatizes leadership rather than bloodlines or past involvement in the church.

The strength of the team is determined by the quality and character of the individuals. Therefore the pastor and congregation must identify and develop individuals who can be a part of that team.

Spend Time with the Leadership Team in Mentoring Relationships

In order to develop a team, the pastor must focus upon building relationships with each person on the team rather than just developing a "training program." Mentoring is more than just meeting together over lunch; it involves imprinting our lives upon the other person. Mentoring involves sacrifice and commitment. It is the process of allowing others to see how we grow in our faith so that they in turn may grow. It involves transparency, a willingness to allow others to see us with all our limitations and faults. It involves showing them how to serve and then guiding them as they begin to serve. Once they have developed proficiencies in service, then we can let them "take the reins" and develop their own ministries.

Provide Training for Lay Leaders in Their Roles

In order for a group of individuals to form a team, they need to understand and be in agreement with the same basic philosophy of ministry and leadership. To achieve this, the pastor must take the initiative to train the leaders. First, we must train the leaders in the art of spiritual leadership. To be a leader in the church is to take responsibility for the spiritual health of the congregation. This involves evaluating the direction and purpose of the church and examining programs to make sure they enable the church to fulfill the mandates of the Great Commission and Great Commandment. Second, we need to train them in organizational leadership, in the principles of effective management, and in how to oversee a ministry. Third, they need training in gifted leadership so that they learn how to utilize their spiritual gifts within the context of the ministry of the church and how to assist others in identifying and using their spiritual gifts. As the pastor works with the board members, they can identify areas they need further training in so they can help people exercise their spiritual gifts.

Encourage Input and Participation

Effective teamwork begins when everyone on the team has opportunity to participate in the discussion and provide their input in the decision-making process. Often people do not gain ownership in the ministry because they feel disconnected from the decisions that were made. Many leaders mistakenly think that their role is to make decisions and gain support from the people. However, Miller and Hall rightly point out, "Team leaders succeed when the team, rather than the team leader, *makes* the decision, because whoever makes the decision *owns* the decision."[6] A team leader is not someone who sets the agenda and the direction for the team; rather, he or she recognizes that each person on the team has an important contribution to make in setting the agenda and direction. Consequently, a good leader seeks the input of everyone on the team so that the team develops a sense of purpose.

Provide Ongoing Support

One of the important roles of the pastor is to provide ministry support for the team as they minister to the whole congregation. Many times questions will arise or problems develop that go beyond the abilities and training of the board member. When these matters arise, the pastor can assist by providing answers or working with the parties involved to resolve the issues. Along with providing ministry support, the pastor also should provide spiritual support for the lay leaders. This may involve accountability to assure that the lay leaders are growing spiritually. It may include spending time with the lay leaders in prayer concerning the issues that are confronting them. If individual board members are dealing with spiritual struggles themselves, they will not be able to effectively minister to the spiritual needs of the congregation. Thus, the pastor should first provide spiritual care for the leadership.

Develop Clearly Defined Roles and Responsibilities

Misunderstandings bring frustration and tension. To have an effective team, each member must have a clear understanding of his or her responsibilities. This begins with the pastor, board, and congregation working together to establish the guidelines that determine what the roles of each will be. The role definitions come from a biblical understanding as well as the traditions of the church and the polity that has governed its organizational structure.

Provide Periodic Mutual Evaluation

When the pastor and board are working together based upon mutual respect and trust, they should periodically evaluate themselves and the congregation. The purpose of the evaluation process is to make sure that the defined roles and responsibilities are being fulfilled and that the church is fulfilling its biblical mission. By providing for periodic evaluations, issues can be addressed before they become major problems. For evaluations to be nonthreatening to people, the pastor must set the example by first allowing the board to examine the pastor's life and ministry. Likewise, the board should honestly self-evaluate its own effectiveness. People will feel less threatened when their ministry is evaluated if they first see the willingness of the leadership to be evaluated.

The health of a church will be influenced by the ability of the church to work together to accomplish the mission of the church. Tragically, many churches flounder in ministry because the pastor and board have an adversarial relationship rather than a positive working relationship, where they are working as a team to effectively lead the church. A church will be healthy and vibrant only when the pastor, board, and congregation understand the roles each have within the church and they support and encourage one another within those roles. Instead of protecting individual turf, they must willingly submit to one another and seek to help one another accomplish the ministry of the church.

TEN

The Board as Change Agents

Within our culture today, we are facing radical shifts in the way people live and think. The advancement of technology has brought incredible changes in how we live, how we conduct business, and how we spend our leisure time. In the past, we spent most of our life in a narrowly defined geographic area. In this small radius, we did all our shopping, conducted all our business, went to church, and spent our vacations. Today, the geographic area in which we live is global. Vacations are spent traveling to exotic places. We conduct our business globally through the Internet. We travel out of the local area to go to church and to do our shopping. Furthermore, what happens on the international scene affects us deeply. If Australia has a drought, the price of wheat is propelled upward. If they have a bumper crop, the price drops substantially. What happens in the Middle East affects the cost of fuel for our cars and tractors and the price of fertilizer. In the previous generation, the farmer paid little attention to such things. Instead, he plowed, planted, and reaped on a continuous cycle that paralleled the year before. Today, the farmer must carefully watch the futures market in order to determine which crop to plant. The tractor, once a simple machine, is now a computerized piece of technology. Application of chemical fertilizers is carefully controlled by computers that calculate the right application based upon the type of chemical, soil composition, and variety of crop. Except for the unchanging message of Scripture, one would be hard-pressed to name one thing in our society that has not been radically affected by the changes that have happened in the last one hundred years.

However, in the onslaught of the rapidly changing society, the small church often has resisted any change. We often find the church today conducting its ministry in the same way it did fifty years ago, singing the same hymns, and following the same order of worship service: Opening prayer, announcements, hymn, congregational prayer, hymn, offering, hymn, sermon, hymn (first verse only), and closing prayer. Nevertheless, as much as we may find change disquieting, the reality is that if we do not change we will not grow. The church ultimately is an agent of change. The purpose of the church is not to maintain the status quo but to lead people into spiritual transformation so that we manifest more and more the character of Christ. This implies that we are not just to make changes on a superficial level (as in the order of the worship service), but we are to make radical changes that alter the very core and essence of our being. What Leonard Sweet states generally is especially true spiritually: "But in the medical world, a clinical definition of death is a body that does not change. Change is life. Stagnation is death. If you don't change, you die. It's that simple. It's that scary."[1] If we do not change as a church, then we have signed our own death certificate, for without change we will die spiritually and organizationally.[2]

❄   ❄   ❄

Before the board meeting, the men were getting their coffee and talking about the changes that had happened in the community in the last ten years. It all started when the local mill shut down and many people were forced to move to other areas for jobs. Today, young people no longer stay in the community but are leaving to go to college and pursue careers in urban areas. Ken, who had lived in the area the longest of anyone on the board, was complaining about the changes that had occurred. "I remember when kids graduated from high school, then they got a job in the mill, married, started a family, bought a home, and became a part of the community. Today they all leave."

Steve joined the conversation. "I agree, the people who are moving into the area now were not raised here. Most of them are from the city, and they have different ideas about how the community affairs should be run and about the use of the land. Frankly, I just can't agree with them. All they want to do is change the way we have been doing things."

Pete smiled, for his family was among the "newcomers" who moved to the area because they wanted to get out of the city. Because of the Internet, he was able to do most of his work from his home. While he had great fellowship with the other board members and had become a close friend, he knew that some of his views were not shared by the group. He joined the conversation. "Steve, I agree that there are some great values in this community. That is why we moved here. But, there are some areas the community needs to improve if we are going to start to attract the type of businesses and jobs that can employ our young people. We need to recognize that the world has changed and we need to make changes as well."

Pastor Dave had heard this conversation many times before, but this time he sensed that there was a teachable moment. "Before you guys come to blows, why don't we at least have our dessert. I would hate to miss out on this great pie that Betty made for us before everyone leaves in a huff." Everyone laughed. While Pete and Steve had had many "heated" discussions on this issue, they were close friends and enjoyed the friendly debate they had over the years. Dave continued, "While you guys eat your pie, let me go ahead and begin our discussion on this very issue. In the last few years we have had a number of new people move into the community, but they are not coming to church. Why is that, and what do we need to do differently to reach them?"

Steve objected, "Why do we need to change? I am all for them coming to church, but if they want to come to church they need to accept the way we do things!"

Ken spoke up. "I disagree. Didn't Paul adapt his methods and message to reach new people? If we don't change the way we do things, then we are no longer going to be relevant to the new people and they are not going to come to church. The end result is that we will slowly die. If we are going to be effective, we do need to change some of the ways we do things. We already did some of that when we changed our style of worship music, but I think there is more that we can do."

"What do you mean?" responded Steve.

"For one, I think we need to do something different for outreach. Every year we have a weeklong evangelistic service. But let's face it: the only people who show up anymore are the church people. If we are going to reach the new people with the gospel, we can't do things the way we have done them in the past."

❋ ❋ ❋

The Methods Must Change, but the Message Must Not

While it is important to realize that how we develop and implement programs within the church must constantly change, the message of the church must never change. The Scriptures do not change, and the demands that God places upon us through the pages of the Bible are just as true and valid as the day they were first penned. The ultimate responsibility of the church of any age is to faithfully proclaim the Scriptures, and the Scriptures make it clear that we cannot alter the message (Rev. 22:18–19). Nor can we interpret Scripture arbitrarily; rather, we are to make sure our interpretation is correct (2 Tim. 2:15). Our interpretation must parallel the original intent of the author (both human and divine).

However, how we do ministry, the programs and methods by which we seek to influence people, can and must change in order to effectively influence people for Christ. In his own ministry, Paul used a number of different methods, depending on the specific setting of the people (1 Cor. 9:19–23; cf. Acts 17:16–34).

Four Realities About Change

As leaders within the church, it is easy for us to maintain the status quo. It requires little effort and cost. Yet we must recognize that no matter how much we may try to maintain the status quo, the reality is that we are constantly changing. Because we are inundated with options, we need to carefully think through the changes that we desire to make. This begins with understanding the importance of change.

The Small Church Must Change

Change is a biblical necessity, for without change there is no spiritual growth. This is true individually and corporately. Individually, we must change if we are to mature in Christ. The Christian life is one of constant change, as we are "transformed by the renewing of [our] mind" (Rom. 12:2). We must put off the old man and put on the new (Eph. 4:22–24). What is true of the individual is equally true of the church. To grow spiritually, the church must be continually changing; to not change is to become lethargic and to eventually die.

The church must change if the church is to maintain its relevancy. Culture is never static; society is constantly changing. Because our ministry environment is constantly changing, our methods of reaching and influencing our culture must be modified. What worked in the past no longer works today. A hundred years ago, if the church desired to evangelize the community, it would invite an evangelist for a week of services. Because the church was the social center of the community, people would attend in order to socialize with others. It was a community event, so everyone would come, especially if there was a musical group accompanying the evangelist. Today, the church is no longer a social center of the community. Consequently, people will not attend simply because it is a special event. No longer can the church reach the unchurched through a week of revival meetings. Instead, it needs new strategies.

The church also must change if it is to maintain its ministry effectiveness. New people come into the church, bringing new gifts that change the gift-mix of the congregation. As God equips the church to accomplish his desired purposes, the church needs to change and adapt its ministries to the gifts of the new people rather than force them into already established ministries. If we are to effectively accomplish God's plan for the church, we must allow the giftedness of the people (which is determined by God) to shape the program, rather than having the programs dictate what people must do.

The Small Church Can Change

Change within the church comes through the direction and empowerment of the Holy Spirit as he guides and leads the church. God is constantly working in the church to reform and transform the character and conduct of the congregation. In Philippians 1:6 we are reminded, "Being confident of this, that he who began a good work in you will carry it on to completion until the day of Christ Jesus." Change is at the very heart of sanctification. The work of sanctification is the work that God accomplishes in the heart and soul of individuals and congregations. Since it is the work that God accomplishes, and nothing is impossible with God (Luke 1:37; Phil. 4:13), no matter how difficult the church may seem, no matter how spiritually unhealthy the church is, it can be changed into a dynamic force for the kingdom of God.

The Small Church Will Change

No matter how much we may try to hold on to the past or even the present, no matter how much we may resist the changes that are occurring, the reality is that we will change. Because people are constantly changing, the congregation is continually changing. The question is not whether we will change but how we will change and what will determine the changes that are made. If we do not intentionally guide how we will change, we will slowly become secular as our society and culture infiltrate our thinking and alter our views. Like the Jews of Jesus' day, we will try to uphold the traditions of the past without realizing that we have become spiritually bankrupt in the process. While we may think we are remaining the same, in the end we become the very thing we fought so hard to avoid—individuals who are impoverished in our soul.

The Small Church Desires to Change

Contrary to the opinion of many, people want to change. Often the small church is labeled as resistant to any change, but this is not always the case. What small churches resist is being forced into a change when they cannot see its benefits. More often than not, when there is a problem with the change process, it is not a reflection of the people's attitude toward change but the way in which the leadership has introduced and handled the change. People want to change, but not at the cost of devaluing the past and alienating the people who built the church. They do not want to make changes that destroy relationships within the church. Therefore, when we make changes, it is important that we maintain the connection that people had with the past.

For example, one church had the opportunity to replace the hard, wooden pews with padded pews that were given to them. However, in the midst of the discussion, an elderly lady mentioned that her father was the one who was responsible for bringing the wooden pews into the church. For her, to replace the pews was to remove the contribution of her father and thus the visible memory of her father. Consequently, to change the pews the leadership needed to do so in a way that the memory of her father would remain in the church. It was not that she resisted the change to padded pews. She resisted the removal of her father's memory. After some discussion, they replaced the pews in the sanctuary with new pews but took the old pews and lined the fellowship hall with them. Thus they were able to have the new pews and keep "her father in the church."

❋ ❋ ❋

Pete agreed with Ken: "We do need to change our evangelistic programs. What can we do differently?"

Pastor Dave spoke up. "I have been reading on change
lately, and the author suggested a process for evaluating the
problem that might be helpful." He wrote five words on
the whiteboard: IDENTIFY, COMMUNICATE, EXPLORE,
IMPLEMENT, and EVALUATE. He then went on to explain
what each of the terms meant.

He continued, "Let's start with 'identify.' What is the key
issue that we are dealing with?"

Pete responded, "Well, it seems to me that the key issue is
how to reach new residents in our community."

"I think the issue is broader than that. To me the issue deals
with our whole approach to evangelism," countered Ken.
He continued, "It's not just the newcomers, but the youth,
the elderly, the long-time residents. When was the last time
we saw anyone new come into the church?"

"OK," Pastor Dave answered, "I agree with you. The key issue is, 'What can we do to be more effective in evangelism
and outreach?'" He wrote this on the whiteboard under the
word IDENTIFY.

✳ ✳ ✳

The Board as Agents of Change

Because the church will change, it is our responsibility as a board
to guide the process so that the changes have a positive effect upon
the health of the congregation. The danger we face in leadership is
focusing on thoughtless, superficial changes rather than in-depth
and life-altering changes. We must recognize that the greater the
change, the greater the disruption and the greater the potential to do
long-term damage to the spiritual growth of people. We must lead

the church through change toward spiritual growth and maturity, but we must do so carefully. We also must recognize that organizational changes need greater caution than spiritual changes. Changes that are required by Scripture should be made regardless of the cost. Changes that are purely organizational should be done carefully, considering the cost and evaluating the impact they will have upon the spiritual well-being of people.

As leaders, there are five occasions in particular when we need to implement change. First, we must lead the congregation in change when we are confronted with a biblical mandate. We must constantly be examining the values, beliefs, and practices of the church in the light of Scripture. As we continue to grow in Christ, we will be confronted with values and practices in the church that do not conform to the teachings of Scripture. Unless we change these values and practices, we will never be able to effectively grow in Christ. As Lyle Schaller points out, "A change in values and assumptions is essential before the behavior of either an individual or an organization can be changed substantially."[3] We are to be constantly evaluating the ministry of the church in light of the values of Scripture and the biblical mission of the church. If we are not in line with Scripture, then we need to alter our values and practices no matter how severe the change might be.

Second, we need to implement changes when new needs arise in the community that provide new opportunities for ministry. Because society is constantly changing, the needs are constantly changing. The purpose of the church is to influence the community, therefore we are to be sensitive to the changes that are occurring and seek new ways to demonstrate the reality of God's grace. For example, many communities are experiencing a rapid growth in the Hispanic population. This influx of people provides new opportunities to reach Hispanics with the gospel of Christ. Offering English classes or conducting a service in Spanish can be an effective tool for outreach.

Third, we need to make changes when old methods and programs are no longer effective in ministering to people. Many small churches struggle because they seek to maintain programs and structures that are now ineffective. The small church by nature has a past orientation. Since the small church is relationally driven, people do not want to damage present relationships by changing what is being done or what others have previously established in the church. While we always want to make sure that we maintain positive relationships in the church, we also need to recognize that we cannot afford to put our time, resources, and energy into a program that is no longer fulfilling the biblical mission of the church. This is especially critical in the small church because it has limited volunteers and resources available. As a board we must honestly and carefully evaluate the programs and ask the hard question, "Is this program accomplishing the mission of the church, which is to transform people into the image of Christ?" If the answer is no, then we must make the necessary changes, for there is too much at stake—the eternal destiny of people!

Fourth, we need to make changes when the church is slowly dying. There are a number of issues that cause a decline in a church, and many of them are outside the church's control. However, there are times when our actions do affect the growth or decline of a congregation. When we are facing a steady decline in attendance so that the viability of the church is threatened, we need to ask ourselves why. If it is something that we can or should change, then we need to address that issue. For example, while on vacation one summer, my family and I attended a small church on the east coast. We were driving several hundred miles that day but decided to stop and attend a church service. So at 10:30 AM we drove through a small town and saw a small church and decided to attend. In view of the fact that we were on vacation, we were casually dressed. Before and after the service no one in the church spoke to us, and it soon became apparent why: we were not dressed properly for the service and so we did not fit the church's cultural expectations. Because of this we were looked upon as "outsiders," and no one welcomed us. The church was dying, not because of demographics, but because of their legalism that isolated them from new people. When our actions, or lack of, hinder the work of the church, the responsibility of the board is to address these issues and make necessary changes.

Thus, key questions the board must ask are: "What are we doing to hinder the outreach of the church? What are we doing to advance the outreach of the church?"

Fifth, we need to make changes when our present structures hinder effective ministry. There are several ways structures can hinder ministry. One is when we have overly complicated structures. Often in the small church we try to duplicate the structures of a larger church. We form committees and boards to oversee the various ministries within the congregation. The result is that we become so "organized" that we spend all our time in meetings discussing ministry rather than doing ministry.

A second way our structure can hinder the work of the church is when our organization does not allow people to make any decisions without the approval of a board or committee. The result is ministry paralysis. While it is important that we have accountability and that we set the parameters by which decisions are made, we do not want to hinder people by asking them to serve but not empowering them to do the work. For example, before a Sunday school teacher can purchase any supplies, the teacher may have to have the approval of the Christian Education Committee and the Finance Committee. The result is that purchases that would improve the Sunday school class are never made because "it is not worth the hassle." Another structural hindrance might be in the way decisions are made. For example, if, instead of allowing the person in charge of the ministry to make the day-to-day decisions, all decisions must be made with the approval of the board, people will become frustrated to the point that they stop working. Structures, while important, should be simple enough to allow people to adapt their ministry to the daily needs that arise. The purpose of the structure is to empower people and support them in their ministry, not hinder or frustrate them.

Orchestrating Change in the Church

The challenge we face in effectively implementing changes within the small church is to do so in a way that strengthens the church and the relational ties within the congregation. If conducted improperly, changes can result in division and hurt that can undermine the health of the congregation. There are two extremes that will destroy the congregational health, one is to not make any changes, and the other is to make changes without properly laying a foundation for the change.

Step 1: Identify the Need

Orchestrating change begins with the assessment of the need for change. It is a grave mistake to thoughtlessly bring about a change without considering the impact it will have on the long-term vitality of the congregation. When we fail to think through why the change is needed, we will focus on the latest fads rather than on long-term health. Change must be based on our specific setting rather than on what worked somewhere else. Another mistake is attempting to initiate wholesale changes. What we must recognize is that a series of small changes will have less of a negative impact upon the health of the church than major revolutionary changes.[4]

In identifying and assessing the need for change, our responsibility as leaders is to be aware of the issues within the church and the way the church is being influenced by popular culture. When we are faced with new issues and problems challenging us with the necessity of change, we should ask a series of questions to properly appraise the need: How does the present way we are doing things reflect biblical theology? How would the proposed change reflect our theology and values? Why is the change necessary? Who will be affected by the change? How will the change affect the people involved? How will it impact their ministry? How will it affect them emotionally? How will it influence them spiritually? What resources are necessary if the change is implemented? What will be the desired result if the change is implemented? What will happen if we do not change?

Answering these questions is critical for laying the groundwork for implementing a change within the church. By carefully evaluating the issue and the impact it will have, we can lessen the risk involved. If we cannot explain why the change is necessary, then we are not ready to implement it. It is important at this point that the focus is only upon what we believe needs to be changed and why it needs to be different. Before we can determine what change to make, we must first determine why the present arrangement is not working. Then we need to get input on possible solutions. This is best done by communicating with and listening to the opinions of others, especially those most affected by the proposed change.

✳   ✳   ✳

"We have identified the issue, now we need to *communicate* the issue to people so that they understand what we are attempting to do and we can get their input in terms of what we need to do differently. How can we best communicate the issue to the congregation so that they understand why we desire to stop doing the 'tent meetings' and start doing things differently? How can we get their input and ideas on what we need to do differently?"

After discussing this for thirty minutes, they had identified five ways they were going to communicate the issue to the congregation. Dave wrote each of these on the board:

1. Pastor Dave will preach a series of messages on evangelism.
2. At the upcoming quarterly business meeting, we will tell the congregation what we want to change and why.
3. We will meet jointly with the evangelism committee to discuss the issue.
4. We will have four meetings in different people's homes to get their input and answer questions.
5. We will have a follow-up meeting at the next quarterly business meeting to share our findings with the congregation.

✳   ✳   ✳

Step 2: Communicate the Need

Only after we have carefully identified the reasons for the change are we ready to communicate the change to the congregation. If the congregation is going to endorse the proposal, they need to understand why it is needed and how the present structure or method is hindering the work of the ministry. Communication begins by informing those who will be affected or those who perceive themselves to be affected. Kirkpatrick rightly points out, "Who should be told about the change? The obvious answer is 'those who need to know.' A better answer is 'those who need to know plus those who want to know.' In other words, the change should be communicated to those who are concerned as well as those who are involved."[5]

At this point it is important that we communicate why the change is needed, even though the new method has not yet been determined. There are four areas in particular that we need to communicate about the change. First, we need to state clearly what is being changed. This needs to be clearly defined, for any ambiguity will only result in misunderstanding. Second, we need to state why there is the need for the change. Before we can proceed to exploration and implementation, people need to clearly understand the reasons why we are seeking to make changes. Third, we need to communicate what will happen if the change does not take place. If people do not understand the negative impact of the status quo, they will not be willing to alter the present. Last, we need to succinctly state what the subsequent process will be. For people to embrace a change, they need to feel that they have had a voice in the process. Consequently, they need to understand what the process will be and how and when they will be given an opportunity to voice their concerns.

When communicating about change, it is always better to over-communicate than to under-communicate. If people feel we have not openly and honestly shared all the information, then they will feel like they are being manipulated. This will result not only in resistance to any change, but also in an undermining of people's trust in our leadership. When communicating, there are three

questions we need to answer:
(1) What do people want to
know? (2) What do people need
to know? (3) What can people
be told? Our desire is to share as
much information as is morally
and ethically possible. There
may be times when we cannot
share all information due to
confidentiality. When this is
the case, we should carefully
explain why we cannot share
all the information. As we share
with people what the issues
are, we must seek to convey the
information through a number
of different avenues. The rule
of thumb is that the more significant the changes, the more
we need to publicize the issues
by various means (announcements from the pulpit, special
meetings, committee meetings,
personal and informal interac-

> **Principles for
> Effective Communication**
>
> - Communicate constructively
>   and positively. Focus upon
>   what the church needs to
>   do and why, rather than on
>   what the church has been
>   doing wrong.
> - Communicate with
>   conviction. The leadership
>   needs to be convinced of
>   the need.
> - Communicate with clarity.
> - Communicate in
>   contemporary terms. Connect
>   the issue to the present
>   experiences and reality of the
>   people.
> - Communicate continually.
> - Communicate in the context
>   of the past. How is the
>   change a reflection of the
>   past heritage and history of
>   the church?

tion, newsletters, etc.). Furthermore, we need to make sure we
are communicating about the change with the right people. This
includes the leaders, the power brokers of the church, people affected by the change, and people who have an interest in the issues.
Ultimately we need to be communicating about the process with
the whole congregation.

※ ※ ※

The meetings with the congregation went far better than
the board imagined they would. Not only were people
enthusiastic about the proposed changes, but there was

also a very high degree of interest in evangelism. Through this *exploration* phase, the board identified four areas that the church needed to address in order to better reach the community.

1. The church needed to provide training for the congregation in the area of personal evangelism.
2. The church needed to become more involved in the community.
3. The church needed to organize at least two different evangelistic events each year that would have greater appeal to the unchurched.
4. The church needed to incorporate evangelism in the various ministries of the church.

After they identified these areas, the board scheduled a meeting to talk about how to implement these changes within the church.

❈   ❈   ❈

Step 3: Explore the Options

Having identified and communicated the need for change and the reasons why those changes are necessary, the next step is to explore possible solutions. It is important at this point to gain the participation of all those interested in providing input. The more people are involved in the decision-making process and the solutions attempted, the more likely they will be to accept and support those solutions. There are a number of ways that the board can elicit the input of others: through special congregational meetings, personal contact, surveys, and small group meetings, for example. As we gain the participation of people, we want to encourage them to be creative in identifying new options for the church to consider. The one idea that a person may think is most outlandish may be the idea that works the best. We want to explore and examine all possibilities. As a result it is important that when guiding the discussion we make it clear there are no bad ideas and no one is criticized for an idea he or she comes up with.

After discussing and examining all the possibilities, the board and those involved in the decision need to develop a tentative plan for implementing the changes. This plan should be examined in light of three factors. First, we need to examine the plan based upon the resources available. However, just because we do not have all the resources available to implement a plan does not necessarily mean that we should rule the plan out. There are times when we must step out in faith, believing that God will provide. Nevertheless, we are to use wisdom in making our decisions, and part of that is being good stewards with the finances God has provided. Second, we need to examine the plan based upon the time availability of those who will be responsible to implement the change. Often those who will be most involved are already overcommitted in ministry. If we are adding more to their responsibilities, we are placing them on the road to burnout. Part of the responsibility of the board is not only to get everyone involved in ministry but also to protect people from getting overly involved. Third, we need to examine the plan based upon people's giftedness and abilities. If we implement the plan, are there people who are gifted in the area and have abilities to perform the task? We must realize by faith that God never calls us to accomplish anything he has not already given us the ability, resources, and time to accomplish. If any of these is lacking, then the solution may not be the correct one.

✳   ✳   ✳

As was now the custom, the board spent the first part of the meeting in prayer, specifically praying for the lost and for wisdom to develop a more evangelistic focus in the church.

Ken opened the discussion. "I don't know what the rest of you think, but I was really pleased with the ideas the church came up with for changing our evangelistic program. I really believe that God has given us a clear mandate. But now where do we go from here?"

"Good question. The next step is for us to *implement* these changes within the church," said Pastor Dave. "The first change we have already implemented. Ken has begun a class on personal evangelism for the adult Sunday school class, using the book *The Way of the Master* by Ray Comfort.[6] So far it is going well, and the people have responded with enthusiasm. The evangelism committee is already working on planning the two evangelistic events for next year. The one area that I think we need to spend some time working on is the area of community involvement. Any ideas?"

It was quiet for a time as the men thought about the issues. John was the first to speak up. "I have been thinking about the new people in the community. The other day I was talking with a new person in the community, and he was expressing to me how difficult it was for his family to be in a new community without any friends and how difficult it has been for them to meet new people. I think that one of the ways we can get more involved is by having social events for people to get to know one another."

"But what does that have to do with evangelism?" asked Steve.

"I don't know, I was just thinking about how difficult it is for new people to develop friends," responded John.

"That is exactly right," Pete interjected. "It was difficult for our family when we moved here. We were outsiders, and so people were reluctant to get to know us. We were thankful we had a church that accepted us and made us feel at home."

"I think there is something that we can do," replied Pastor Dave. "I know of a church that had what they called

'Supper for Six.' Each month a couple would invite one unsaved couple from their neighborhood and one other church couple over for supper. It was a great way to build relationships. How would it be if we did that in our church with a focus upon new people? When a new person moves into the neighborhood, someone from the church could invite the couple and someone else from the church over for dinner."

"That's a great idea!" Pete excitedly exclaimed. "I will go ahead and get it organized, and then we will get a sign-up sheet of people who want to be involved."

※   ※   ※

Step 4: Implement the Change

Once a plan is determined, then the next course of action is to develop a strategy to implement the change. This involves three critical elements. First, it is critical that we gain support from the congregation and especially the key leadership within the congregation. We must recognize that change can never be forced; rather, people must accept the change if it is to have a lasting impact. This begins with the leadership of the church. It is important that the board be in agreement; otherwise it will only cause division both within the board and the congregation. This does not mean that we all have to think it is the best option. Rather, it means that we will all be committed to support the implementation of the change. Second, we must determine the timetable by which the change will take place. This involves not only the time frame for the implementation of the change but also the length of time before we will evaluate the change. Third, we must identify who is responsible to implement the change. Here again, it is crucial that these individuals demonstrate their full support for the change. If the person who is responsible to implement the change is not in full agreement, then the changes will never occur, for the individual will not put forth the energy to implement the strategies.

✳ ✳ ✳

It had now been a year since they had made changes in the evangelistic programs in the church. Pastor Dave called up Ken to discuss the agenda for the upcoming board meeting.

"Ken, I would like for us to set aside the next board meeting to focus on what we have been doing in our evangelistic programs. We need to *evaluate* how things are going."

Ken agreed, "I've been thinking about that since you talked about the importance of evaluation. The Supper for Six worked well, and we have seen two new families coming as a result. But we had mixed results on the two evangelistic events. The committee did a great job organizing them, but we still did not get any unchurched people to attend."

"I would agree. Perhaps we should invite the committee to attend the meeting as well so that we can get their input. I think they did a good job and worked hard, so I don't think it was their fault. But I do think we need to evaluate it further," Dave responded.

When they met with the evangelism committee the following week, they all agreed that the events went well but missed the target. After much discussion it was decided that the events were well planned, but the problem was in the area of publicity. While the church had advertised in the local paper, the congregation had not been properly trained to invite people and utilize the relationships they had developed through the lifestyle evangelism they had been taught. For this coming year, it was decided that two months before the next event, the church would again have a refresher course on lifestyle evangelism and spend time teaching people how to personally invite people to the event.

✳ ✳ ✳

Step 5: Evaluate the Change

When implementing change, it is important that we do not become so rigid that we are not willing to alter the plan if it is not working. The purpose of the evaluation is to determine if the results achieved by the change meet the purpose set forth by the board and congregation. Even before the implementation is started, the timetable for implementing the change should be clearly communicated, as well as when and how we will then evaluate the change. Often people are much more willing to implement a change if they know that sometime down the road they will have the opportunity to evaluate and reject the change if it is not working. Furthermore, while there will be a specific time when the change will be examined completely, evaluation should be an ongoing process in the whole procedure. This way corrective action can be taken when it becomes apparent that the strategy must be adjusted.

Change is an important part of the continued health of the congregation. If the church does not change, then it will eventually die as it finds itself no longer relevant to the needs and issues confronting the community in which it lives. While we never change the message of the gospel, the methods and manner in which we fulfill the Great Commission will change as society changes. As leaders of the church, we must be change agents. We must be leaders in guiding the church through the process of change so that we are making changes that have a positive effect upon the ministry of the church. If we are not intentional in the changes we make, the church will change, but it will slowly decay into a dead organization that no longer has any spiritual or organizational vitality.

ELEVEN

The Responsibility of Administration

When we gather together to discuss the business of the church, we wrestle with the challenge of leading the church in the right direction and overseeing the various ministries of the church. While the daily operation of the different programs falls upon the shoulders of those responsible for the ministries, the board is to provide the general oversight by establishing the goals and direction of the church. If the church does not have a clear focus, it can splinter into a number of different ministries, each pursuing its own self-interest. The result is the church becomes fractured as people compete over the various resources within the church. If we had unlimited resources, this would not be as big a problem. However, in the small church we struggle for adequate finances to fund even essential programs, and we face a continual shortage of volunteers, even though people are actively involved in the church. We deal with limited space and facilities to house the ministries we have.

Not only do we have a practical reason to have adequate organization, but we also are mandated by God to maintain an orderly and cohesive ministry. One of the gifts that God gives the church is the gift of leadership (Rom. 12:8). The term the Bible uses refers to those who are given charge of the administration of the various charitable ministries of the church.[1] Ministry is not to be conducted haphazardly and inefficiently; rather, we are to recognize the seriousness of the ministry and organize the ministry so that it is effective. This does not mean that we must manage the church like a large corporation. The small church can be effective without being completely efficient. As David Ray points out, "[Small churches] may not be punctual, business-like, or efficient, but they work. And the lack of orderliness is part of their genius. The small church can function and thrive without being efficient because of its size."[2] Because the small church is small, it can operate more informally than the larger church. Discussion and decisions can be made over a cup of coffee rather than a "formal meeting." However, this is not an excuse for becoming sloppy in our business. Our task as leaders is to assure that the church is working together to accomplish its biblical mission.

Overseeing the Planning

Providing oversight begins with the overall planning and strategy of the congregation. This starts with the conviction that every small church has the potential to accomplish great things for God simply because it can be used by God and is called by God to accomplish his will. We must always keep in mind that in God's economy there is no small church and no small task. If we are a part of God's plan and purpose, there is nothing that is insignificant. Consequently, the greatness of the ministry of the small church is not determined by the world's standard of achievement but by the accomplishment of God's will and purpose. The goal of planning is not efficiency, so that everything runs smoothly. *The goal of planning is to discern the will of God so that we can channel our activities, resources, and energies in that direction.*

❋ ❋ ❋

As they were preparing for the annual meeting, Pastor Dave shared with the board some of the goals he would like to have for the coming year. As he was sharing, Steve objected, saying, "Pastor, I appreciate all that you have been teaching us about leadership and what it means to be a spiritual leader, but I don't think we need to worry about setting goals for this coming year. After all, you have repeatedly said that we need to focus on the spiritual not the organizational.

Furthermore, aren't goals for the big churches? We are just a small church. I don't see where we need to worry about goals. If it ain't broke, then why fix it?"

Pastor Dave appreciated Steve's objection. "Steve, you raise an important issue that we need to discuss regarding leadership. Often we think that goals are not important, especially in a small church. But wouldn't you all agree that as a church we are to seek to understand and accomplish God's will for the church?"

All the board members, including Steve, nodded their approval.

Dave continued, "Well, goals are merely the means by which we make sure that we are effectively accomplishing the will of God. We can identify and talk about God's will all we want, but if we are not taking any steps to achieve that will, then what good is it?"

Again, all gave their approval.

"Goals, objectives, and plans answer the question, 'What specific steps do we need to take to accomplish the will of God?' Without these, we just talk about the will of God but we never make any progress in achieving it."

Because of his business background, Pete understood what Dave was trying to say. "I agree. Without goals, all we do is maintain the status quo. As we have already seen, if we are to lead the church in transformation, then we must lead the church in change. Furthermore, goals make sure that the changes we make are the right ones, moving us in the right direction."

Steve was still not convinced. "I agree we need to be leading the church in change, but I have seen many churches become so focused on goals and objectives that they no longer are focused on people. They become controlled by the goals rather than the leading of the Holy Spirit."

"Again, Steve, you are making an important point," agreed Dave. "I agree wholeheartedly that we must be adaptable to the leading of the Spirit and we must always be willing to change our goals as the Holy Spirit directs us and as the circumstances change. I also wholeheartedly agree that we need to be people focused rather than goal driven. But the one does not preclude the other. In fact, I think we see in the life of Paul a balance between the two. Paul had specific plans and goals that he sought to achieve. We see examples of those in Acts 15:36 and in 2 Corinthians 1:15–16. But we also see flexibility in those goals in Acts 16:7–11."

While Steve was not fully convinced, he was beginning to see their point. For the rest of the board meeting, they discussed what the goals for the coming year should be.

❋   ❋   ❋

The Importance of Planning

It takes careful planning to accomplish the will of God. Without planning we may be extremely busy, but we will accomplish little. The sage in Proverbs 24:27 writes, "Finish your outdoor work and get your fields ready; after that, build your house." This proverb points to the importance of carefully planning and developing clear priorities that govern the allocation of our resources. Contrary to the popular notion, the more limited the resources we have, the more critical it is that we carefully plan how we use those resources. Otherwise, we will misuse what has been given us and thus further undermine the health and viability of the church. Again, the writer of Proverbs warns, "The plans of the diligent lead to profit as surely as haste leads to poverty" (Prov. 21:5).

In the small church, we often view planning as something secular and unspiritual. However, for the writer of Proverbs it was conducted in the context of one's spiritual dependency upon God. Proverbs 19:21 reminds us, "Many are the plans in a man's heart, but it is the LORD's purpose that prevails." When we make plans for the church, we are seeking the purpose and will of God. We are prayerfully seeking God's direction for the congregation and for the ministry of the church (Rom. 12:1–2). When we do so, then our ministry will be effective, for when we seek to follow his agenda, our plans become effective: "Commit to the LORD whatever you do, and your plans will succeed" (Prov. 16:3).

The task of the board is not just to oversee who uses the building and when; it is to develop a cohesive plan for the ministry of the church that provides direction for all aspects of the church. This involves establishing clear goals and objectives and then developing ministries that accomplish those goals.

Establishing the Goals and Direction of the Church

Within the small church, people are often reluctant to discuss and set goals for the church because they view them as divisive. When we talk about setting goals, we often believe they will force a congregation to make choices between possible alternatives, which will then divide the church and undermine the close relationships that undergird the church's ministry. Furthermore, we are reluctant to set goals because we often have an aversion to organizational bureaucracy. What attracts us to the small church is the simplicity of its ministry. We like the small church because there is freedom to conduct ministry without the constraints of "management" trying to control our actions. Furthermore, especially in rural areas, churches are reluctant to set goals because it is outside the realm of their daily experience. By nature farmers and ranchers are not goal setters. Their only goal is to make enough money to continue farming and ranching. In reality, however, we all set goals; it is just that we do so without consciously thinking about them as goals. Instead, we merely identify what needs to be done and then set about doing it. For example, at the beginning of spring planting, a farmer never sits down and states that his goal is to get the planting done by the June 1. Instead, he sets about getting his crops in as soon as possible, because if the crops are planted later, the plants will not get firmly established before the dry period in July. Yet, in reality, this is setting goals (the goal is to plant the crops as soon as possible in the spring). Because of this goal, when the weather is fair and the farmer is able to work in the field, he does not take the time to overhaul the lawn mower.

While the church can (and often does) function without clearly stating its goals, there are four key times when it is necessary for the board to work with the ministry leaders to establish clear goals and objectives. First, the church needs to clarify its goals when it is faced with a crisis that threatens the existence of the church. Clarifying goals enables the church to establish a strategy for moving out of the crisis and strengthening the morale of the congregation. Developing goals, even small goals, enables the church to gain a sense of progress.

Second, goals should be established when the church is faced with a new ministry opportunity. When God opens the church to new opportunities for ministry, it is important to realize that we can no longer continue doing things the way they have always been done. New ministries require new strategies to meet new opportunities. Setting goals enables the congregation to evaluate whether or not it is being effective in accomplishing God's purpose.

Third, goals are needed when the church is faced with the need for change. While the small church operates in the present and focuses upon maintaining existing programs, there are times when maintaining the status quo is no longer valid and can become a hindrance to the biblical purpose of the church. For example, when the church is no longer reaching the community with the gospel, then it is no longer fulfilling the biblical mission of evangelism. Consequently, the church needs to change the way it is conducting its ministry. Developing new goals enables the church to identify what needs to be changed, why it needs to be changed, how it will change, and if the changes are effective.

Finally, the church needs to establish new goals when it is no longer reaching its potential. Instead of seeking to identify and accomplish God's will and purpose in the church, a church can become bogged down by past methods and traditions. Without occasionally reevaluating our ministry, we can focus on doing what we have done in the past but fail to realize that it is no longer valid in the present ministry environment.

Developing clear goals involves a five-step process. The first step, and perhaps the most important, is to clarify the purpose and mission of the church (see chapter 8). Paul establishes the purpose of the church in Colossians 1:28–29, when he states, "We proclaim him, admonishing and teaching everyone with all wisdom, so that we may present everyone perfect in Christ. To this end I labor, struggling with all his energy, which so powerfully works in me." The purpose of the church is to lead people into spiritual transformation. As outlined in Matthew 22:37–40, this purpose involves developing an intense relationship with God and in-depth love for one another. This purpose is to govern the identification and implementation of every goal and objective established by the church.

The second step is to clarify the purpose of each ministry. Lyle Schaller identifies two types of ministries the church conducts.[3] The first is "basic ministries." These are the ongoing core ministries that are essential to the overall health of the church. These ministries, which are conducted on an ongoing basis, are critical to the survival of the church and are the foundation of the ministry. These would include the Sunday worship service, pastoral visits to the sick, children's ministries, and so on. The second type of ministries is the "advancing ministries." These serve to expand the ministries and influence of the church. These would include new ministries that are started to meet new needs in the community, significant advancement of a current ministry, or

---

Principles for Setting Goals

- Avoid making goals that only focus upon numbers.
- Goals should be consistent with the purpose and mission of the church.
- Goals should be consistent with the resources.
- Goals should be clear and understood.
- Goals should challenge.
- Goals should be achievable.
- Goals should be unifying.
- Set few goals but make them critical goals.

strengthening areas that need special attention. Advancing ministries would include a new outreach program or a significant increase in the budget for the youth ministry. While the church will devote most of its focus to basic ministries, it should always have at least one expansion ministry goal so that the church is moving beyond the maintenance mind-set that can easily plague the small church.

The third step is to identify and clarify the goals for each ministry. Goals are the specific accomplishments we wish to achieve for the ministry, and they encompass both short-term (6–12 months) and long-term (1–2 years) goals. If a ministry or church is struggling or discouraged, it is important that we set attainable goals in order to gain a sense of accomplishment for the church. The purpose and mission of the church answer the question, "Why is this ministry important?" Goals answer the question, "What do we want to accomplish in the next six months, next year, next two years in this ministry?" As the board oversees the ministries, they should work with the ministry leaders to establish goals and objectives for the specific ministries. The task of the board is not to set the goals for each ministry but to set the goals for the whole church and then work with the ministry leaders to ensure that each ministry goal works in conjunction with, and not in opposition to, the overall church ministries.

The fourth step is to clarify the objectives. Objectives are the specific activities to be accomplished in order to achieve the goals. Objectives answer the question, "What must we specifically do to accomplish the goals we have established?" For example, if the goal is to reach the unchurched parents of the children involved in the children's program, two objectives might be to send home literature for the parents to read and to establish a parent's night to acquaint them with the ministry. As we establish goals for the church, we should establish two or three objectives for each goal.

As the fifth and final step, we need to evaluate the outcome. Did we accomplish what we desired to achieve? Evaluation should take place during the process as well as at the end. By continually evaluating the goals and objectives during the process, we can make necessary changes if we discover that the goal was misguided and changes are needed. Furthermore, by evaluating the process at the end, we can identify what God has accomplished. It may be that the outcome did not accomplish what we desired, but it still changed people's lives. In this case we can still rejoice that God used the program to achieve what he desired rather than what we expected.

Overseeing the Budget

Setting goals and establishing ministries will have little value if we do not have the finances to fund the programs. In the small church we constantly face the struggle of dealing with limited financial resources. This raises a number of different questions that we have to wrestle with as a board. Where will the money come from? How will the church handle the income and expenditures of the programs? How will we keep track of the expenses? Should the programs be under the general budget? Often in the small church we never itemize our expenses. When someone requests money to purchase something for the church, as long as there is money in the checking account, we authorize it. However, because we have limited finances, how we handle the finances is all the more critical.

❋   ❋   ❋

After spending the evening discussing the goals of the church, the board came up with three they felt were critical for the church in the coming year. These Pastor Dave wrote on the whiteboard:

1. To have three outreach events that reach the community.
2. To develop a greater prayer focus within the church.
3. To provide training for Sunday school teachers so that they will be more effective in training the kids.

After writing these, Dave turned to the board members. "Does everyone agree that these are critical for the church to be effective?" Everyone agreed. "There is one problem, then; how will this be reflected in the budget?" Pete groaned. Everyone laughed because they knew how much Pete hated budgets. Dave continued, "I know that we often do not look at the budget, but if these goals are important, then we need to make sure that they are properly funded. Too often we make our budget based upon what we spent last year, rather than on what we are seeking to accomplish this coming year."

Pete raised a familiar question: "Pastor, why do we need a budget? If we have a need, you know the money is always somehow there. If it is in the checkbook, we can make the purchase; if not, then we have to wait."

Dave responded, "The problem is that if we always operate without a clear budget, we can end up spending our money on projects that are not essential to our mission and goals. We have to recognize that there are two things that we are limited in: time and money. In the small church we often don't worry about budgets. We think of that as a big church concern. In reality, the opposite is true. The more limited our resources, the more careful we need to be in how we use them."

Steve again agreed with Dave. "I agree, Pete, that we should be focused on ministering to the needs of people and that we should not lose sight of that, but I think Dave has a point. We need to be good stewards with what God has provided. A budget is not written in concrete, but it should serve to guide us to make sure that we are using our resources in the right way."

John spoke up, "Let's get back to the issue. I agree that we need to have a budget so that we use our financial resources wisely. But how will we budget for the goals that we established?"

For the next hour they talked about the budget and how much money would be needed for each of the goals. In the end they budgeted $1,000 for the goals they established. While it was not much, they felt it would provide for the necessary requirements. By faith they trusted that God would provide for this, even though it led to an increase from last year's budget.

❋   ❋   ❋

Building a Budget upon a Biblical Foundation

Proper financial principles are not just an organizational necessity but a biblical responsibility that the church needs to uphold. Developing a budget for the church begins with a biblical perspective of giving and stewardship.

The basis for a budget is faith. Faith is not necessarily trusting that God will provide more; rather, it is the firm conviction that God will provide all that is needed to accomplish what he is calling the church to perform (2 Cor. 9:8; Phil. 4:19). If the church follows the leadership of God, it will have all the needed finances, no matter how small the budget may be.

The budget should reflect the priorities. In evaluating a church budget, it is important that the church does so in light of its priorities and values (Matt. 6:21). Without a clear assessment of the priorities, the budget, rather than the purpose, mission, and vision, can drive the church.

The budget reflects the spiritual maturity of the congregation. How people give, what they give to, and how much they give is an indication of the priorities and spirituality of the people (2 Cor. 8:7). Preaching and teaching on the importance of giving is part of developing the maturity of the congregation. Abe Funk rightly points out, "A budget is a church's statement of values. It tells you what is important to your church. In that sense, it is the most important item on your annual meeting agenda."[4]

The budget should challenge. The church should continually be encouraging people to give generously and sacrificially (2 Cor. 9:6–7).

This is not just because of the financial needs of the church but also because of the importance of the discipline of giving (Phil. 4:17). We must always remember that giving is an expression of our worship to God. The church should not challenge people to give in order to meet the budget. Rather our giving is to be a reflection of our recognition that everything we have is a gift from God, belongs to him, and is to be used for his glory.

The foundation of giving is obedience. More important than the amount people give is their attitude toward God and toward the Scriptures (2 Cor. 8:5). The ultimate strength of the church is not found in its budget but in its obedience to God's Word. The church's spirituality determines the viability and stability of the church, not its bank account. When people are taught correctly about giving, so that they are first obedient to Scripture, the finances will be sufficient for the needs God has called us to meet. Ultimately, giving is not a budgetary issue but an obedience issue.

The church must manifest integrity in its financial practices. The church is to be the model of financial responsibility. Therefore, care should be given concerning how it handles its finances (Prov. 13:11). Designated money should be used only for the designated project. Quick fund-raisers that compromise the church's integrity will ultimately be destructive (Prov. 10:16). The resources also should be used to benefit people outside the church and not just for the church's own organizational benefit (Prov. 28:8).

Four Budgeting Errors to Avoid

Avoid developing a budget based solely upon past performance. Typically a budget is developed by examining last year's income and expenditures. While it is important to examine the past, it should not dictate what the future will be. If the formation of the budget is based only on the past, then there will be no room for growth, little challenge to the people, no avenue for faith, and no need for dependency upon God.

Avoid developing a budget that does not require faith. The focus of developing a budget should be upon God's provision rather than upon the bank account. Too often the church determines its fiscal plans based upon past receipts, instead of prayerfully seeking God's direction.

Avoid developing a budget without prayer. The church is not merely an organization but a spiritual organism that is to be organized around spiritual principles. The financial needs of the church are ultimately a question of God's sovereign supply rather than people's giving. Therefore, prayer should be made not only for wisdom in forming a budget, but also for the realization of the budget, and the attitude of people in giving.

Avoid developing a budget that is unrealistic. Asking a church of fifty to support a $600,000 building not only may be unrealistic but also may put the future of the church at risk. Overspending the amount people can realistically give can cause a church to become financially strapped so that it will be unable to support its core ministries. This is not to say that the church should never take any financial risks, but it should do so very carefully, thoughtfully, and prayerfully. Developing a budget involves the interplay between wisdom and faith. Without wisdom it becomes a burden. Without faith it remains shortsighted.

Principles for Developing a Sound Budget

How the church goes about forming its budget will influence its effectiveness in meeting that budget, and it will also affect the way people give. A budget-driven church is one in which the financial plan is formed by transferring the previous year's expenditures (with any increases in utilities, etc.) to the new budget with its projected funds for the coming year. The ministries then must operate for the coming year within the confines of this plan. As a result, the budget dictates the programs. When this occurs people will be reluctant to give because they have little desire to contribute to a perceived organization. A ministry-driven church forms its budget based upon the needs of the ministries and programs that serve people. Then the congregation is challenged to meet the needs of people rather than the organizational requirements. When ministries, programs, and needs of others dictate the finances, people readily give because they see the importance of their contribution. To have a ministry-driven budget, the following steps should be taken.

Step One: Develop goals for each area of ministry. Each area of ministry should determine the goals for the following year. These should be developed through a prayerful consideration of what God desires the church to accomplish within the particular program. While the goals should take into account the previous financial giving of the church, they should not necessarily be dictated by it.

Step Two: Each ministry should formulate a budget for their ministry goals. Once a ministry team has identified the goals for their programs, they should then determine the specific costs that will be involved in accomplishing them. These costs are not organizational expenditures but money invested in the lives of people through the particular ministry.

Step Three: The board should review the goals and needs of each ministry. The purpose of this review is to assure that the goals of each ministry correspond to the vision and direction of the church. Ministry goals should be examined to assure that they are realistic, achievable, and beneficial to the overall health of the congregation.

Step Four: The board must review each proposed budget for each program. The board has a twofold responsibility. First, they make sure that the budget of each program is realistic and cost effective. Second, they evaluate each individual budget in view of the overall church financial status to assure that the expenses of each program correspond to the overall strategy of the church. If the board determines that cost reduction is needed, it communicates to the ministry teams the reasons for the reduction and works with them to formulate a revised budget proposal.

Step Five: The board should develop a church budget to propose to the congregation. Once each ministry budget has been reviewed, the information is condensed into a proposed church budget. This proposal does not just communicate the amount of giving that will be required for the coming year, but also includes an explanation showing how each item relates to the goals and ministries of the church. When it is presented to the congregation, people should understand why this money is needed. The report is not a financial statement but a statement of ministry objectives.

Step Six: Challenge people to commit to the ministry rather than just the budget. When people are asked to vote on the budget, they are not voting on a financial report but on a ministry plan for the coming year. People are more willing to give to the needs of people than to a perceived administrative institution. When the budget is presented, it must be clearly communicated that the fiscal plan is not just an assessment of monetary needs to keep the church fiscally solvent but a projection of the needed resources to minister effectively and accomplish God's will for the church.

Step Seven: Pray and trust God for provision. Once the ministry goals and budget have been accepted, the church should commit to pray regularly for the ministry and for the financial provisions. When there is a shortfall in the giving, the prayers focus not just upon the church finances but upon the ministries of the church and the people affected by the lack of resources.

Step Eight: Maintain flexibility within the budget. The budget guides the church budget, rather than dictating it. Inevitably needs will arise that were not foreseen. Since the ministry environment is always changing, the budget needs to be adaptable and flexible. The church should develop policies and procedures for adjusting to these ongoing changes so that the ministry is not hampered by an outdated budget.

Providing for the Pastor

Within the small church, one of the greatest struggles is not only how much to pay the pastor, but also how the church can afford to pay the pastor. Scripture makes it clear that it is the responsibility of the church to provide for the financial needs of the pastor (Gal. 6:6; 1 Tim. 5:17–20). Formulating a budget for the pastor is often one of the most difficult tasks the board faces. Tragically, one of the reasons small churches struggle to recruit and keep qualified pastors is because of the salary package the church offers. How much should we pay the pastor, and how much of the budget should go to the pastor? While there is no rule that can govern every situation, there are several guidelines that can provide helpful direction.

First, the church needs to recognize that it is responsible to provide adequately for the pastor and his family. It is a poor testimony in the community when the pastor is living in poverty. If the church cannot afford to pay the pastor a full-time salary, then the church needs to allow the pastor to have employment outside the church and recognize that the amount of hours the pastor devotes to the church should be adjusted accordingly.

Second, there are two measurements that can help the church assess what is an adequate salary for the pastor. One way to measure how much to pay the pastor is to take the average of all the incomes of the working families within the church. Another way to determine a base salary is to use the salary of a tenured schoolteacher in the area. These standards, while not absolute, can provide a starting point in the discussion of what is appropriate for the salary of the pastor. The ultimate goal is to pay the pastor a salary that provides for his family so that he will not be under financial stress.

Third, the church can be creative in providing for the needs of the pastor. In many rural communities, people can provide support other than just financial. Giving the pastor an occasional side of beef or providing free mechanical work on his car can decrease the pastor's cost of living.

Fourth, the church needs to recognize that there are many expenses pastors face that are often undetected in the budget. Even though the church may provide a parsonage, the pastor will have to pay social security tax on the fair rental value of the home. For example if a home of equal size as the parsonage rents for $1,000 a month, the pastor will have to pay $150 a month in social security tax for the parsonage. This should then be taken into consideration when developing the salary package for the pastor. Furthermore, there are many ministry expenses that the pastor has (for example, gas for the car when visiting people) that the church needs to recognize. Every church should have in the budget funds for "professional reimbursements," which cover the expenses the pastor has for ministry.

Fifth, the church needs to make sure that the pastor is provided comprehensive insurance to cover the medical needs of his family. In order to save money, the church often provides minimal medical coverage. This is especially true in rural areas, where many farmers have a high deductible for their own insurance. Consequently, they reason, "We just have major medical, so that is all the pastor needs." However, the problem is that farmers often have enough cash flow to cover any minor medical bills that arise. This is often not the case with the pastor. The pastor in a small church often does not have much discretionary income. As a result, a $1,000 medical expense creates a major financial strain for the family. An important part of providing for the pastor is providing for his family's medical and dental expenses.

Last, the church needs to recognize that in most cases denominations and associations do not have a retirement program for pastors. Many pastors in rural communities retire with no funds other than social security. This can be especially difficult for pastors who have never purchased a home. Consequently the church should establish its own retirement for the pastor.

Overseeing the Policies

In a world where litigation affects the church, it is becoming more and more important to develop policies and procedures that govern the activities and actions within the church. Policies are implemented in order to protect both the church and individuals within the church from accusations of inappropriate action. This is especially critical since sexual predators often target the church as a means of gaining access to children for the purpose of fulfilling their perverted gratification.

The purpose of policies is to indicate the position and values of the church on specific issues. They contain the guidelines and inform people in terms of what they are to do in specific situations. Policies are the broad guidelines that establish the course of action needed to determine a decision. Procedures, on the other hand, are a set of instructions that describe the approved and recommended steps for a particular act or sequence of acts. Procedures inform people how they are to perform their ministry in a way that is in line with the values, beliefs, and doctrines of the church. For example, when writing a policy-and-procedure statement for sexual misconduct, the policy states that any hint of sexual misconduct will be reported to the proper authorities. The procedure for reporting would include filing a report with the sheriff's office and social services, as well as immediately informing the pastor and the chairperson of the board. The report to the pastor and chairperson should be in a written form, describing the date and time of incident, the detailed description of what happened and the detailed description of the action that was taken.

❋　❋　❋

The budget had been approved by the congregation, but several months later a question arose about the application of the budget. When Alice, the Sunday school superintendent, wanted to buy some new storage cabinets, her request was outside the budget. In the past, when someone made a request, Pete would just look at the checking account of the church. If there were enough money to pay the monthly bills, he would simply write a check for the purchase. But with the new budget in place, he was uncertain what to do. So he called Pastor Dave.

"Dave, I have a problem. In the past we always made the purchases if there was enough money in the account, but with the new budget I am not sure what we should do."

Dave thought for a moment, "Pete, it is not fair for you to be put in a position to make these decisions on your own since it will affect others." Pete agreed. Dave continued, "What we need to do is to develop a policy regarding expenditures so that you have clear guidelines about what should be done. Tell Alice that we will discuss it next week at our board meeting and get back to her."

The next week, Dave brought up the issue to the board.

Pete started the conversation. "I talked with Alice this week about this issue. At first she was a little upset that we would question the legitimacy of her request. She felt that we did not trust her and her decisions. I explained to her what we were trying to do. I assured her that we trusted her completely but we needed to make sure we were not circumventing the budget and thus violating the decision made by the congregation. After a little more explaining, I think she understood. I told her that we would be writing up a policy regarding it."

Steve voiced his concerns, "I kind of agree with Alice on this. It seems to me that policies are built upon a lack of trust for people. We are a small church, and we know everyone. I trust Alice. If she thinks it is important and we have the money, then let's make the purchase. We don't need a policy to decide that."

Pete disagreed, "Steve, I appreciate what you are saying. However, in the last church I was in, this very issue was raised. But in that case the person went ahead and made the purchase before asking for permission. When someone else found out, she was upset because then there was not enough money for her to make the purchase she wanted. While no one really said much, there were some hard feelings over it. If the church had a clear policy, then it would have prevented this whole thing. If we have policies in place, people are not as apt to be hurt. I think they are a good idea, not just because of the need to be careful with our money, but also to protect the people who are in leadership."

Dave interjected his perspective. "I agree with Pete. The purpose of a policy is not to control people or express a lack of trust in them, but to protect people and protect relationships. If we do not clearly outline what is expected of people, then people can get their feelings hurt. That is why we need policies not only on expenditures, but also on all our workers. However, this will require a lot of work on our part as we research and write clear policies. I would like to suggest that we approve Alice's request and that we set aside a meeting next month to develop policies for the church. Then at our church meeting next month, we can communicate them to the congregation." Everyone agreed, and so the issue was put on the agenda for the next meeting.

✳ ✳ ✳

The Necessity of Policies and Procedures

The purpose of policies and procedures is to make sure there is proper accountability within the church so that people working within the various ministries are upholding biblical values and the desires and values of the congregation. By establishing the rules and regulations of a ministry, they further protect people and the church from the harmful actions of others and the false accusations that people may bring against those within the church. Policies assist people in making decisions within the ministry so that there are no misunderstandings and/or inappropriate actions taken that might cause the hurt of others.

Writing Effective Policies

Policies should be clear and concise. They should clearly state the problem being addressed and how the policy deals with the issue. Because the purpose of policies is to give people a clear understanding of what they should do, there should be only one policy for each issue. When questions arise about the policy, the wording should be evaluated in order to clarify the question. The policy statement may not address every conceivable event, but it should set clearly

Policy Questions That Statements Should Answer
• Why is the policy being implemented?
• What does the policy cover, and what actions or decisions does the policy apply to?
• What is the policy?
• What is the procedure to be followed in implementing the policy?

defined parameters that would serve to give people guidelines. Policies should be easy to use. They should not be complicated or difficult; otherwise, they will not be implemented.

Policies should be consistent. One policy should not be in conflict with any other policy or the values of the church. The purpose is to make sure that the values are being upheld, not undermined.

Policies should address legal concerns. Especially in dealing with finances and with sexual misconduct, the church needs to make sure that the policies are in line with current laws. When dealing with issues that may have legal ramifications, it is always advisable to have a lawyer examine the policy before it is implemented.

Policies should be specifically followed. A policy is only as good as its enforcement. Furthermore, if the church fails to follow the policy, it can face legal action that can result in a major financial loss for the church.

Each policy should specify the consequences if it is not followed. This will range from a verbal reprimand to dismissal from the ministry. This is especially critical in dealing with children, where the potential exists for inappropriate activity that can devastate the lives of children and families and destroy the reputation of the church and the people involved in ministry.

Each policy should be clearly communicated to all the involved parties and should be reviewed on a regular basis. It is important for people to have a clear understanding of what the policy is, why it was written, and what will happen should the person not follow the policy. When there is a question, then the policy should be examined to make sure it is clear.

Although we are primarily spiritual leaders, we do have a responsibility to provide organizational oversight and direction as well. Central to this role is developing a strate-

---

Critical Areas the Church Policy Manual Should Address

- Sexual misconduct.
- Child protection and child workers.
- Financial expenditures (who is authorized to purchase what).
- Use of facilities (when and by whom).
- Marriage policy.

gic plan for the church. When the small church neglects administration, ministry becomes haphazard at best. However, if the church is to be effective, there must be careful planning. We are continually to be asking, "Where are we at as a church, and where do we need to be going as a church?" As someone once stated, "If you don't know where you are going, you will probably end up somewhere else." In other words, without clear direction, we end up going off track from what we want to accomplish. Clear direction comes through setting clear goals and developing sound budgeting in order to effectively utilize our resources to accomplish those goals.

TWELVE

Maintaining the Structure

Developing and Rewriting an Effective Constitution

*N*othing can galvanize more hostility and frustration than the process of developing or revising a church constitution. For some, the church constitution is a sacred document; it is never to be changed and must be followed meticulously. They use the constitution like a club, browbeating people into conformity to it. For these people, the constitution is to be followed regardless of the damaging effect it might have upon individuals. They think deviating from it will only cause further problems and hurts, opening a Pandora's box that will result in the downfall of the church.

For others, the constitution is simply a product of man and is to be regarded as just another attempt by man to run the church of which Christ is to be the Head. They ignore the constitution altogether, placing it upon the shelf and seeing it only as a hindrance to the real task of the church, which is to minister to the needs of people, even if it means violating and defying the rules of organizational structure outlined within the constitution. The result is equally disastrous as confusion leads to conflict because of a lack of clearly defined roles and responsibilities.

Into this minefield the leadership walks, seeking to develop a constitution that serves to set the guidelines of the church while allowing for flexibility in order to permit the church to minister to individuals with unique issues in an ever-changing world.

❋ ❋ ❋

Alice called Pastor Dave, venting her frustration about the last business meeting. She had proposed that the church form a new ministry team to reach the Hispanics in the community. However, the constitution stated that there were to be only four ministry teams that organized the various ministries of the church. The people who were on these teams were not excited about another job being assigned to them since they already had too much to do. Consequently, the proposal was voted down.

"Pastor, you are always saying that we need to be driven by our mission. Here is an opportunity for us to minister to people in our community, but we can't do it because of our constitution. I expect that kind of bureaucracy at work, but not in the church. Who are we serving here, God or some human structure?"

Dave remained calm. "Alice, I fully understand your frustration. I was frustrated as well. But I have learned that when we violate the constitution it usually comes back to cause us problems in the future. I think your idea for the formation of a new team is a great idea. I am all for it. But we can't go against the constitution. At the next board meeting, I am going to propose to the board that we revise our constitution so that we can have more flexibility in ministry."

Alice was still not happy, but she seemed to be satisfied for now.

❋ ❋ ❋

The Role of the Constitution

To understand the importance of the constitution, we must understand the role it plays within the life and organization of the church. It is neither an inspired text that cannot be changed nor a useless, man-made institution that should be ignored.

The Biblical Basis

Within the pages of Scripture we find that the people of God were not to approach the development of the community haphazardly and without structure. Instead, we find that organization and structure were integral parts of the health and movement of God's people. When God established the nation of Israel, he did not tell them just to take possession of the land and then live without guidelines and rules. Rather, in establishing the nation, God set down many specific rules and regulations governing their spiritual life and many other aspects of their existence as well. These rules dealt with such things as spiritual worship; the use, acquisition, and selling of land (Lev. 25); when and where the people were to gather together for the feasts (Exod. 23:14–19); and the manner in which a king was to be chosen and how he was to govern (Deut. 17:14–20). The purpose of these rules was not just governmental but ultimately social in that the establishment of procedures and structures were designed to protect individuals and assure the unity and health of the whole community.

Even though it is not so specifically outlined in the New Testament, we do find hints that there were organizational structures that served to govern the early church. In Acts 6 we find that certain individuals were being overlooked, thus creating the need to establish better organizational structures. There we also find the priorities and responsibilities of those in leadership articulated. While the deacons were to oversee the assistance programs, the elders were to focus upon the spiritual health of the community. We also find that part of the establishment of the church involved the creation of leadership structures (Acts 14:23; Titus 1:5). While there is certainly freedom and latitude in terms of how the church is organized, this should never be construed to mean that the church does not require organization.

In 1 Corinthians 14:40 Paul writes that "everything should be done in a fitting and orderly way." This statement comes after

Paul's extended discussion regarding propriety in worship. The phrase refers to the fact that things are to be done in a way that is conducive to orderliness and proper arrangement. While the focus is primarily on worship, the principle applies to all the functions of the church.

Developing a constitution that outlines the order in which things are to be done is not a violation of Scripture but an application of it. An effective church does not run haphazardly but with order and clarity (1 Cor. 9:26). The purpose of the constitution is to provide such order and assure that the church is run in a way that properly reflects God's character.

The Purpose of the Constitution

The constitution of the church has a twofold purpose. The first is to protect the congregation from conflict. When the church does not operate in an orderly manner, conflicts begin to arise as people struggle over authority structures. The constitution should bring clarity to the roles people have within the church and the responsibility each person shares within the congregation. When the structure of the church is clearly delineated, then people are less likely to misunderstand or be hurt by the actions of others.

The constitution further serves to protect the church from false accusations from those outside the church. As the church becomes more visible, it comes under greater scrutiny from the secular community. This scrutiny has been further sharpened as people have seen financial and moral failures in the leadership of the church. Harold Longnecker rightly points out, "Careful handling of funds, proper records, sound management, all tend to command the respect of those within the church, and what is more important, those outside whom we are trying to reach. It seems senseless to be so concerned that our secular businesses are carefully administered while the Lord's work, which is many times more important, is carried on in a slipshod fashion."[1]

Having a clear organizational structure and doctrinal statement that people must agree to in order to become members also protects the church from error. Paul warns us that there will arise those who seek to destroy the church (Acts 20:30). While a clearly established doctrinal statement will not eliminate all possibility of someone negatively influencing the church, it does serve as an essential safe-guard in preventing individuals who do not agree to the doctrine of the church from gaining positions of leadership. Furthermore, should such individuals arise, the doctrinal statement provides a basis for dealing with the individuals and removing them from any position of authority. It also serves as a foundation for requir-ing people to teach in accordance with the doctrine of the church so that people are not teaching what is contrary to the position of the congregation.

Additionally, the constitution protects the congregation from unclear priorities and direction. It is easy for the church to become divided not only over doctrinal issues, but also over the direction and priorities of the church and of the roles of those in leadership in the church. The constitution brings clarity both to the purpose and mission of the church and to the role each person in leader-ship has in relationship to that purpose. It also serves to assist the congregation in making wise decisions by outlining the process by which decisions are made.

The second purpose of the constitution is to provide direction for the congregation. This is done by clearly outlining the mission of the church. If it is correctly done, the constitution continually calls the church back to its biblical mission by challenging the church to examine what it is doing and why it is doing it. It is this mission that defines what the church is to do and how it is to go about do-ing it. The constitution provides direction for the congregation by outlining the overall structure of the church. While the constitution will not give (nor should it) every detail in terms of the structure of the church and how decisions are made, it should serve to set the parameters for the structure. These parameters should give latitude to the church to make changes within the structure as needs arise and the ministry environment changes, while at the same time it sets forth governing principles that provide direction for how the decisions are made and how the programs and ministries will oper-ate within the church.

When to Revise the Constitution

Choosing when to revise the constitution is just as important as determining the areas needing to be revised. Since doing a revision can place a congregation under a certain amount of stress, it is important that the leadership carefully determine when it is needed. Three important questions should be asked before the topic of revision is presented to the congregation: Why do we want to revise the constitution? What areas of the constitution need to be changed? What would happen if we did not make the changes? Asking these questions provides the basis for deciding when it is necessary to make the revisions. There are three issues that would give rise to the need for revision.

First, it is necessary to change the constitution when it does not reflect biblical teaching. Since the church is first and foremost a spiritual organization in vital relationship with God and striving to live in obedience to Scripture, then it is necessary that the church's constitution reflect this. Often the discrepancy will be reflected in the doctrinal statement, where the doctrine expressed in the constitution is either inadequate or does not properly convey the distinctives of the church that define its theological perspective. The discrepancy also may be reflected in the function and purpose of the board, where the focus is upon the organizational function rather than the spiritual responsibilities. Or, the discrepancy may be reflected in the purpose and mission of the church. The purpose and mission of the church should be derived from Scripture and reflect the mandate that God has given the church. Here again, the constitution may reflect an incomplete view of the mission of the church. For example, a mission statement might read, "The mission of our church is to provide a place of fellowship for all believers." While this is part of the biblical mission, it is also inadequate, for it leaves out the mission of evangelism and discipleship. While fellowship is an integral part of the mission, it is not all the church is to be doing. Consequently, it is necessary to develop a more in-depth statement that more adequately expresses the biblical mandate of the church.

Second, it is necessary to revise the constitution when it hinders the present ministry of the church. Because the community and ministry opportunities change over time, the constitution may reflect a structure that was effective in the past but not in the present. This often occurs when the organizational structure of the church was written in the past when the programs and ministries were different. An example of this might be a church constitution that was written in the 1950s, when revival meetings were effective. Consequently, the constitution may have the requirement of a "Revival Committee" whose responsibility is to plan for and conduct yearly revival meetings. However, in today's culture such meetings no longer are effective in reaching the lost. Nevertheless, the church faithfully selects a committee each year to perform a job that is no longer required. Another instance is when the constitution reflects organizational structures of a church that was much larger. If the constitution was written years previously when the congregation was larger, it may reflect past structures that overly tax the available volunteers presently in the church today. In this case the church may need to simplify its structures. If, on the other hand, the church has grown significantly over the years, it may need to revamp the structures in order to provide for the expanded organizational needs of the church. For example, three board members were all that was needed when the church had fifty people attending, but with four hundred now attending it needs many more individuals on the board to oversee the spiritual needs of the congregation.

Third, revising the constitution is needed when conflicts arise because of a lack of clarity within the structures of the church. The constitution may not adequately define the lines of authority and accountability within the church. For example, someone may become upset because he or she was placed on the inactive member list because it was not properly conveyed in the constitution when a person is classified as inactive. A conflict may arise over the board's action in an instance of church discipline because some people believe the board overstepped their authority in their actions. In these cases, the church may need to revisit the constitution in order to bring greater clarity. However, it may be possible to address the problem through a policy statement rather than a constitutional change. The advantage is that policy statements are easier to alter and change than the church constitution. The policy statement should not conflict with the constitution, but it may address areas not covered by the constitution. For instance, rather than putting into the constitution how much each ministry can spend that is not expressly stated in the church budget, it would better to draft a policy statement to address the issue.

✳ ✳ ✳

At the next board meeting, Pastor Dave shared the frustration that Alice had expressed.

Ken, who was the most vocal about following the constitution, said, "Pastor, I know that Alice was frustrated, but we can't disregard the constitution. If we do, then we are setting a precedent that will only cause problems."

John spoke up. "Ken, you're right, but we also need to be driven by our mission, not by our organization. Not only that, but there are a couple of other areas where we are not following the constitution. The constitution states that we are to have six board members, but we only have five, so we are already violating it. I think we need to change the constitution. We haven't revised the constitution for years, and there are a number of areas that need to be addressed."

Steve concurred. "I move that we formulate a constitution revision committee that will consist of the pastor, two members of the church, and one board member."

After further discussion, it was agreed that they would take the proposal to the congregation.

✳ ✳ ✳

Developing or Rewriting an Effective Constitution

Understanding the principles for writing an effective constitution is critical to developing and implementing the process within the congregation. A constitution that is well written will not only serve as a guideline for the church and prevent many misunderstandings and organizational errors, but it will also serve to promote the effectiveness of the ministry.

Principles for Writing the Constitution

Too often little thought is given to the principles of writing an effective constitution. Instead, it is developed based upon previously established organizational structures. The following principles should serve as the guidelines for how the constitution should be written.

The Constitution Should Reflect Biblical Theology

Because the church is to be a spiritual organization that is biblically driven, the first consideration when writing an effective constitution is its relationship to biblical theology. The constitution should convey our responsibility before God and his will and purpose for the church. God calls the church not only to be a visible presence in the community but also to live and conduct itself in a manner that is consistent with his character. Therefore, the values and beliefs reflected in the constitution should be derived from our understanding of the biblical responsibility God has given the congregation.

The Constitution Should Reflect Biblical Structures

While there is debate concerning the correct polity and structure that are outlined in Scripture, the constitution should reflect the congregation's belief concerning the role and nature of authority within the church. The constitution should reflect the role and responsibility of the pastor, elders, and deacons within the life of the church. It should outline the spiritual authority the Bible gives to these leadership positions. The constitution conveys the qualifications for these positions, the responsibilities assigned to them, and the extent of authority that the Bible gives to each one. The constitution should further define the biblical role and responsibility of the congregation within the church. It should outline the church's beliefs concerning the biblical authority that is given to the congregation in terms of decisions, church discipline, and authority.

The Constitution Should Reflect Cultural Values and Structures

While elements of structure are outlined in Scripture, a great deal of latitude is given in Scripture concerning the organization of the church. This latitude is reflected in the cultural and social setting of the individual church. Consequently, the constitution will reflect the history of the church and the views it has historically maintained regarding church polity. The constitution will be unique, reflecting the uniqueness and individuality of the specific congregation. While it is always helpful and advisable to examine other church constitutions for guidelines, it is important to recognize that each constitution is to reflect the individual church. The constitution will reflect specific doctrinal issues that are unique to the specific church and/or denomination (e.g., mode of baptism, eschatology, spiritual gifts). It will also reflect unique practices (e.g., selection of the pastor, types of membership, officers, committees, ordination).

The Constitution Should Be Followed

The constitution is effective only when the church follows it. When the congregation no longer follows the constitution, it not only renders the constitution ineffective and irrelevant, but it also invites misunderstandings and conflict within the church. When the constitution is not followed, decisions are made haphazardly. When authority is not clearly delineated, conflicts arise as people question who has authority over what areas of ministry.

The Constitution Should Be Simple

The purpose of the constitution is to set the parameters for how the church is to operate rather than give a detailed outline that covers every specific aspect of the ministry. The details of the church structure should be established in policy statements that serve to govern the daily affairs, while the constitution serves to discuss how things are to be done rather than what things are to be done. For example, the constitution would cover how committees or ministry teams are formulated and what roles committees have within the ministry of the church. The policy and procedure manual would deal with what specific committees there will be and what their responsibilities within the church will be. The constitution gives the general framework of structures (the pastor, the board, the legal structures), while the policies provide the specific details (the ministry teams, the committees, the positions of the volunteer staff). The constitution sets the direction; policies govern the day-to-day implementation of the decisions and actions the church takes to accomplish its mission and purpose. The more complex the organizational structure is, the more likely it will hinder growth and effectiveness. This means that the constitution should outline the minimum number of official positions needed to effectively oversee the ministry of the church. These positions then form the basis for accountability and authority within the church. Other positions may be added, but they are subservient to the authority of these positions.

The Constitution Should Be Flexible

The constitution should be flexible enough in the organizational structures to allow the church to change and adapt its structures and ministries as needs arise. When developing the structure, the constitution should outline the procedure for developing new ministry teams rather than outline what the ministry teams are to be. For instance, the constitution should be flexible enough that if the need arises for the development of an ethnic ministry team it should not require a change in the constitution to do so. If the church determines that it wants to discontinue or change a particular ministry (such as changing the children's program), it should not necessitate a change in the constitution.

The Constitution Should Be Ministry Driven and Empowering

Since the goal of the constitution is to provide the necessary guidelines for effectiveness in ministry, it should assist, not hinder, the ministry of the church. It should help to keep the ministry running smoothly and to avoid unnecessary misunderstanding. While the constitution should outline the accountability structure within the church, it also should empower people to make decisions and take actions within the specified parameters. Having multiple decision-making bodies will only slow down the ministry of the church.

✳ ✳ ✳

At the church meeting it was agreed to form a revision com-
mittee. Alice was the first to be nominated, along with Fred.
Ken was the one selected from the board. The following
Tuesday they met.

Pastor Dave began the discussion. "I want to thank each of
you who are willing to serve on this committee. We have a
lot of work ahead of us. Let me outline the way I have approached this in the past and see if that is agreeable with
everyone. What we followed in our previous church was a
three-step process: research, revise, and recommend. First we
research what is a good constitution. I would recommend
that we obtain five or six constitutions from other churches
in our association to get an idea of some things that we want
to put in the constitution. Second, we revise a section at a
time rather than try to do the whole thing at once. Third, as
we revise each section, we recommend the revision to the
congregation for their approval."

Everyone agreed that this approach seemed to be the best.

✳ ✳ ✳

Characteristics of an Effective Constitution

A well-written constitution should answer these questions: Why
do we exist? What do we believe? Who makes what decisions? What
are our legal responsibilities? If these questions are not answered,
then the constitution will be ineffective as a guideline for the church.

Why Do We Exist? Answering the Question of Purpose and Mission

The purpose and mission of the church are biblically derived and
involve a focus upon the nature of the church and the God-given
task of the church. The purpose of the church gives the distinct
reason why the church exists within the world and its relationship

to God. The mission of the church describes what the church is to do from a biblical perspective. The constitution should reflect the biblical mission of the church. While the vision of the church will always be distinct to the individual church, it should be derived from the Great Commission. If the vision and structures of the church are not determined by the biblical mission, then the church will not be effective; and instead of the constitution strengthening and assisting the church in accomplishing its purpose, it will become a hindrance.

What Do We Believe? Answering the Question of Doctrinal Clarity

Perhaps the biggest mistake churches make in drafting the constitution is spending a great deal of time outlining how the structure operates within the church but very little time defining what the church believes. Yet, in terms of the health and growth of the church, the doctrine of the church is far more important. When developing the statement of faith, two elements need to be addressed.

First, the doctrinal statement should focus on the foundations of the Christian faith. It should clearly articulate those aspects of doctrine that are central to the Christian church. This would include an outline of what the church believes about the nature and authority of Scripture; the person and work of God the Father, the Son, and the Holy Spirit; and the church's position regarding salvation and the sinfulness of man.

Second, the statement of faith should include the distinctive theology of the specific church. While it should not seek to go into all details, it should reflect the theological perspective of the church. For example, this might include a statement regarding the mode of baptism. Other issues that might be addressed are the church's position on the nature of spiritual gifts and Spirit baptism, on ecclesiology, or on church polity (for example: congregational or elder rule).

There are, however, two errors a church should avoid in drafting the doctrinal statement. The first error is writing a statement that is so general it does not adequately convey the theological positions and distinctives of the church. The second error is being so specific in the statement that it expresses a very narrow theological stance that hinders people's involvement. How the church positions itself between these two extremes will depend greatly upon the individual congregation and the history of the church. What is important is that the doctrinal statement properly conveys the theological position of the church while at the same time adequately allowing for the theological latitude that is acceptable to the congregation.

Who Makes the Decisions? Answering Questions of Organizational Responsibility

As has already been pointed out, the constitution should outline the general guidelines of structure and responsibility. The specifics may be further outlined in a policy manual. By focusing upon the general guidelines rather than specifics, the church will have more flexibility to change structure as ministry needs fluctuate in the church and community. The constitution should give the basis for the overall governing board (i.e., the church board and pastor) and any other committees whose ongoing existence is necessary to oversee the structure of the church (i.e., nominating committee, search committee, etc.).

What Are Our Legal Responsibilities? Answering the Legal Requirements of the Church

The last component of an effective constitution addresses the legal decisions of the church. This would include the process of church discipline. It would also deal with the process for hiring and firing of staff and how each of these is accomplished. It should outline who has the authority to make legally binding decisions (such as the purchase of property, entering contracts, etc.). The constitution also should address the issue of licensing and ordination.

✳   ✳   ✳

Pastor Dave acquired several different constitutions from churches of various sizes in the denomination. He also called several churches outside the denomination that had just rewritten their constitution to get ideas from them.

Before the next meeting, he passed the examples to each of the committee members. He asked that the members each read the examples provided and mark any areas that they felt needed to be added to their constitution.

At the meeting, Ken was the first to speak up. "As I compared our constitution with the other ones, I thought that in most areas we have a pretty good constitution." Everyone agreed. Ken continued, "However, as you know, the last couple of years our board has spent a great deal of time evaluating our role and responsibility. I think there are some areas that we need to change to reflect this new focus on the board."

Alice was next, not surprisingly she brought up the ministry teams. "There were a couple of churches that I thought had a well-written organizational structure that provided both accountability and flexibility for how we organize the ministries of the church."

"Anyone else have anything to add?" asked Dave.

Fred spoke up, "After looking at the doctrinal statements of the churches, I think ours is pretty weak."

After more discussion it was decided they would first focus on revising the section about ministry teams since this would be the least controversial of the changes.

Contents of the Constitution

The contents of the constitution should include a biblical basis for the church, the organizational parameters of the church, and coverage of legal issues. In formulating a constitution, keep in mind that while the constitution will cover a number of different areas, it should remain brief. A well-written constitution should not exceed ten to fifteen single-spaced pages. Anything that exceeds this is probably much too specific and needs to be abbreviated.

The Legal Name and Location of the Church

The legal name and location serve to establish the basis upon which all legal documents and governmental records are recorded.

The Purpose of the Church

The purpose provides a general statement that defines who we are and why we exist. This purpose statement should address two areas. First, it should provide a statement regarding the biblical purpose of the church. This statement answers the question of "why the church exists" from a biblical perspective. Second, it should include an organizational purpose. The organizational purpose should include a statement that the purpose of the church is exclusively charitable and that it is a non-profit organization.

The Mission of the Church

The mission of the church serves to provide a general outline of what the church is to do. Like the purpose statement, this is derived from the pages of Scripture and should reflect biblical theology. Because it is derived biblically rather than sociologically, the mission should be applicable to any given church in any location and should serve to guide the church in the formation and development of its programs and ministries.

The Doctrine of the Church

Perhaps the most important element of the constitution (at least from its spiritual function) is the doctrinal statement of the congregation. It should give new people a clear idea of what the church believes so that they might make an informed decision as to whether they will be comfortable with the church. It should also be the basis for what the church teaches and what it requires people in teaching positions to uphold. Anyone who cannot teach in conformity with the doctrinal statement of the church should not be asked to teach. Furthermore, for those issues that are not specifically stated in the doctrinal statement, latitude should be given to teachers to present their own specific views as long as they do not disrespect others who have a different position. Consequently, when formulating the doctrinal statement, the congregation should clearly identify which doctrines are nonnegotiable for the church and which ones the church can have latitude in regarding its teaching and beliefs.

The Membership of the Church

While some churches do not have formal membership, most churches do. The constitution should outline the process and the expectations of those who are members. The membership portion of the constitution should include five components.

First, it should include a brief statement regarding the biblical basis for membership. While this should not involve an extended discussion, a short statement enables the congregation to see that this is not just a human institution but a God-ordained responsibility.

Second, the constitution should outline both the requirements for membership and the process for becoming a member. The requirements for membership might include the submission of a membership request form that would involve a brief, written testimony of the individual's acceptance of Christ. It might include a requirement for an interview from the pastor and/or board. While the requirements may differ from one congregation to another, they should always include the requirement of a confession of personal faith in Christ.

Third, the membership portion also should involve an outline of the expectations of membership. However, here a word of caution must be given. Two errors need to be avoided in terms of the expectations that are outlined. It should not reflect levels of maturity. Inclusion in the body of Christ is grounded in salvation rather than sanctification. While the expectations are such that the individual should desire to grow, the church must be accepting of new Christians who still might be struggling in particular areas within their lives (for example the use of tobacco or alcohol). The second error is to become focused upon cultural expectations (dress, behavior) rather than godly character. The focus must be upon character development rather than outward performance. In developing these expectations, we should focus upon the major character qualities (Christlikeness, love for God, support of the church, etc.) rather than specific actions (avoidance of certain activities, clothing, etc.).

Fourth, the constitution should outline what happens when people become inactive within the church. This will include a definition of an inactive member, as well as the process for being placed on the inactive list. Also included in the statement would be the process for removal from the inactive list. The purpose for the inactive list is not to exclude individuals but to make sure the church rolls are kept current and that inactive individuals are not counted with respect to a quorum of voting members. Consequently, the process for removal from the inactive list would normally be a renewed participation and attendance in the church. Before a person is placed on the inactive list, attempts should be made by the board and the pastor to meet with the individual in order to encourage the person's renewed involvement in the church.

Fifth, the constitution should outline the process for disciplining a member. This process should reflect the biblical process of discipline (see Matt. 18:15–20) and give the specific steps the church will use to implement the discipline. It is important that when issues of discipline arise, the church carefully follows the outline provided in the constitution in order to avoid the possibility of legal litigation.

The Government of the Church

The constitution will outline the organizational structure of the congregation. First, this will include a statement outlining who the legal officers of the church are, thus defining who has the authority to make legal decisions for the congregation. In most cases this will include the pastor, board chairperson, church clerk, and treasurer.

Second, this section will provide the structure for the church board. This outlines the role and responsibility of the board, the requirements for being a board member, the process for selecting the board, and the process for filling a vacancy on the church board.

Third, the government portion outlines the role and responsibility of the church clerk. The responsibility of this position is to keep accurate records of the business minutes and membership roles within the congregation. In some cases this role may be assigned to the board.

Fourth, the position and duties of the treasurer are given. The role of the treasurer should be communicated, as well as the limitations the treasurer has in regard to the expenditure of funds.

Fifth, the constitution may outline the process for formulating ministry teams or committees. While it is recommended that the constitution not be too specific, it should give the general guidelines in order to assure clarity in responsibility and accountability, while at the same time providing for flexibility and changes within the ministry programs of the congregation.

Last, depending on the polity of the church, the congregation will outline who is responsible to appoint and select positions of leadership within the church. This role may be given to the church board, to a specially formulated nominating committee, or to the whole congregation.

The Role and Responsibility of the Senior Pastor

The role and responsibility of the pastor should be outlined in order to guide the pastor in the performance of the duties assigned. This section should include the process for appointing a pastor when a vacancy occurs. For independent, congregational churches, this may include the formation of a search committee. In this case the roles and responsibilities of the search committee and the process they are to use in bringing individuals to the church for consideration should be outlined. For churches that are part of an association or denomination where the pastor is appointed, this process also should be given, outlining the relationship with the denomination and the nature of that relationship. Included within this is a statement concerning the nature of the appointment. In most cases this would involve the pastor being called to serve for an indefinite period. Finally, the process for the dismissal of the pastor should be given. This serves to protect the pastor from frivolous attempts to remove him and also to protect the church should the removal of the pastor be required.

Legal Issues in the Church

Within the constitution there are a number of legal issues that will need to be addressed in order to satisfy the requirements of the state. While this may fluctuate depending on the state, there are certain areas that will need to be addressed. First, a statement should be included concerning the incorporated status of the church. This will often be included at the beginning of the constitution, under the heading of the church's name and address.

Second, the manner in which business meetings are conducted and called should be given. This will address such issues as: When is the annual meeting, and what is the fiscal year of the church? Who can call a special meeting, and what is the process for calling a special meeting? What notification is required to have a business meeting? What constitutes a quorum for the purpose of making decisions?

Third, a statement should be given concerning the real property and contracts of the church. This statement should answer these questions: Whom does the real property belong to? What happens to the property if the corporation is dissolved? Who is authorized to enter into legal contracts on behalf of the church?

Fourth, the constitution should outline the process for licensing and ordaining of individuals to serve. This would involve both the purpose of the licensing in terms of the performance of marriages and the purpose and process for ordaining an individual within the church.

Last, the constitution should include a statement providing for the process and requirements needed to amend the constitution.

✳   ✳   ✳

After rewriting the section on the ministry teams, the committee was ready to bring the recommendation to the church. Two weeks before the scheduled church meeting they passed out the revision to everyone in the congregation as well as sent it out to anyone who was absent that Sunday. They then asked for anyone who had any questions to call one of the members of the committee.

Thursday night before the congregational meeting, the committee met to discuss any issues that people had raised with regard to the proposed changes. Surprisingly people had very few questions. Instead, everyone seemed excited about the new direction the church was taking.

The following Sunday, the church quickly ratified the changes. The committee was pleased. While they knew they still had a great deal of work ahead, the first step had gone smoothly. They knew that the changes to the doctrinal statement would generate more discussion, but everyone seemed to be satisfied with how things were going.

※   ※   ※

It is important that we follow the constitution that has been established. When we fail to do so, we become vulnerable to accusations of manipulation and deceit. When the constitution hinders ministry or we find that we cannot follow it because it is outdated or unbiblical, then we need to take the necessary steps to change the constitution. A well-written constitution can protect the church and enhance the ministry of the church. It should provide the direction we go as a church, as well as set the parameters by which we conduct our business.

Developing Leaders for the Small Church Study Guide

INTRODUCTION

The call to leadership in the church is a call to be *spiritual* leaders of the church. While this involves organizational oversight of the programs, ministries, and structures of the church, the focus in Scripture is upon the spiritual responsibilities. This call is one of the greatest privileges and yet one of the most challenging responsibilities we find in the pages of Scripture. While we should not shrink back from the task in fear, we should dive into the Scriptures for clarification and be driven to the Holy Spirit for supernatural empowerment.

Dispelling the Myths of Leadership

The Myth of Inadequacy

Read 1 Corinthians 2:1–5.

1. According to verse 1, what natural abilities could Paul have easily relied upon for his ministry?
2. Instead of being confident in his abilities, what were Paul's feelings about himself and his ministry (v. 3)?
3. Why did Paul see his inabilities and inadequacies as strengths for his ministry rather than weaknesses (vv. 4–5)?
4. What are some of the doubts that we have about our own abilities that cause us to be reluctant to serve on the board?

The Myth of Being Too Small

Read Matthew 14:13–21.

1. When confronted with the needs of the people, what was the response of the disciples (v. 15)?
2. How was Christ's perspective different from that of the disciples (vv. 16–17)?
3. What was the lesson that Jesus was teaching the disciples when they gathered up the leftover food (v. 20)?
4. How does our size affect our perception of what God can do through us?

The Myth of Numbers

Read Judges 6:15 and 7:1–25.

1. Why did Gideon initially object to his being called by God to deliver Israel?
2. Why did God have Gideon select only three hundred men to go against the massive army of the Midianites?
3. What does this teach us about the numbers needed by God to accomplish his purpose?

The Myth of Visionary Leadership

Read Nehemiah 1:1–11.

1. What were the problems confronting the Jews during the time of Nehemiah?
2. How did the Scriptures provide the answer for Nehemiah in determining God's will (vv. 8–9)?
3. How does Scripture provide us clear direction for determining God's will for the church today?

The Myth of Talents and Gifts

Read Ephesians 4:11–16 and 1 Timothy 3:1–7.

1. How does the gift of being a pastor differ from the role of the elders?

2. What is the basis by which a person is qualified to be a pastor? (See also 1 Cor. 12:11, 18.)
3. What is the basis by which a person is qualified to be an elder?

The Myth of the "Hired Gun"

Read James 5:14 and 1 Timothy 5:17–18.

1. What is the board to do when people are ill?
2. What is the responsibility of the board in relationship to the congregation?
3. Why are we reluctant to be spiritual leaders? How does this relate to what the Scriptures teach us about our role?

The Myth of Time

Read Ecclesiastes 3:1–11 and Philippians 4:19.

1. How does the use of our time reflect our priorities in life?
2. What does Ecclesiastes 3:1–11 teach us about time?
3. How does Philippians 4:19 challenge our perspective that we do not have enough time?

Understanding Biblical Leadership

In response to the misconceptions we have (or the church has) about leadership, it is important that we develop a biblical perspective. Instead of viewing our responsibility as leaders through the eyes of our society, we must develop a biblical perspective, one that is derived from and governed by the biblical teachings regarding the role and responsibility we have as board members within the church.

Leadership Is Spiritual Rather Than Organizational

Read Hebrews 13:17.

1. The expression "keep watch" portrays the imagery of a shepherd who is vigilantly keeping guard over the flock under his care, lest some danger threaten the sheep. How does this portray the responsibility of the board?

2. Who will be held accountable for the spiritual well-being of the congregation?
3. In what ways does spiritual oversight differ from organizational oversight?

Leadership Is Based on Empowerment Rather Than Abilities

Read Exodus 4:1–17.

1. What was Moses' first objection to God's calling him to ministry (vv. 1–9)?
2. Why did God give miraculous signs to Moses?
3. What was Moses' second objection (v. 10)?
4. What did God say in response?
5. Why did God become angry with Moses? Was Moses' problem a lack of understanding of his own abilities or a lack of understanding of God's ability? How does this give us a different perspective on ourselves and our call to ministry?

Leadership Is Service Rather Than Power and Authority

Read Matthew 20:25–34.

1. How did the perception of the disciples and the perspective of Christ differ with regard to leadership?
2. How did the actions of Christ in healing the two blind men provide an illustration of biblical leadership?

Application

1. What are the struggles that you face in your understanding of your role as a board member?
2. What are some of the ways that the board can become stronger spiritual leaders in the church?
3. What are some ways that you can become a servant to people within the church?

LESSON 1
THE BIBLICAL OFFICES OF LEADERSHIP

Help: I've Been Put on the Board!

When asked to serve on the board, we often become fearful. There always remains something mysterious about the church board that places it upon a different plane from any other committee or team within the church. However, the bulk of our confusion and fear about being a board member comes not from the significance of the responsibility but from our failure to understand the nature, purpose, and calling of the board.

The Biblical Role of the Board: Understanding the Terms

Elder

Read Acts 14:23 and Titus 1:5.

1. What did Paul and Barnabas do in each of the churches they established?
2. What is significant about the appointment of a plurality of elders? Why do you think Paul, Barnabas, and Titus practiced this? What are the benefits of a plurality over a single person?

Read Hebrews 13:17

1. What is the responsibility of the church leaders?
2. To whom is the church board accountable?

Overseer

Overseer is the translation of a Greek term from which we obtain the English word *episcopal*. The term refers to one who is a protector and who gives oversight of the church.

Read 1 Timothy 3:1.

1. How does the term *overseer* differ from the term *elder*?
2. What is to be our attitude about being an overseer?

Pastor

The term *pastor* refers both to those who have a special gift of teaching and to the function and purpose of the leadership in the church.

Read Ephesians 4:11, 1 Corinthians 12:28–29, and 1 Timothy 5:17.

1. How were certain individuals gifted by God to provide care for the spiritual needs of the church?
2. How does this relate to the modern position of the pastor in the church?

Read 1 Peter 5:1–2.

1. What is the responsibility of the leadership of the church?
2. How does the role of the board and the role of the pastor overlap in relationship to the ministry of the church?

"The term elder emphasizes who the man is. Bishop speaks of what he does. And pastor ('shepherd') deals with how he ministers."[1]

Deacon

The term *deacon* refers to individuals who are responsible for the material needs and ministries of the church.

Read Acts 6:1–7.

1. Why were deacons first appointed?
2. How did their responsibilities differ from the elders in the church?

The Office of the Board and the Gift of Pastor

Pastors, or paid "ministers," possess specific *gifts*, while the board members hold the *offices* of leadership.

Read 1 Corinthians 12:11, Acts 6:5, and 1 Peter 4:10.

1. How does the appointment of the person with the gift of teaching and the appointment of individuals selected for leadership differ? How do they differ in terms of their qualifications?

2. What are the implications in terms of our view of the board and its responsibilities?

Read the following verses. What do they each tell us about how the board is selected, the necessary requirements for the appointment of the board within the church, and what our attitude should be as leaders in the church?

- Acts 6:3
- Acts 20:28
- Ephesians 5:23
- 1 Timothy 3:1
- 1 Peter 5:2–3

Plurality of Leadership

Elders are always referred to in the plural form in the New Testament (see Acts 20:17; Phil. 1:1; Heb. 13:17). What are the implications of this for the church today?

Read Acts 14:23 and Titus 1:5.

1. What was the normal practice of Paul when appointing leaders in a newly established church?
2. What are the implications for us today?

Read 1 Timothy 5:17 again.

While having the same position, how do individuals have different functions within the church?

Application

1. What are some ways the church can improve its selection process for the board?
2. How do the responsibilities of the board and pastor differ? How do they overlap?

LESSON 2
CHARACTER

Finding the Right Person in All the Right Places

What do we look for when we look for someone to be on the board? Because we often feel compelled to fill the position regardless of the qualifications of the individual, we look only for someone who is willing to serve on the board. However, Scripture outlines strict guidelines for those who will serve on the board. In this lesson we desire to take a careful look at the type of qualifications that Scripture demands of those who would serve as leaders within the church.

Leaders Serve as Living Models

Read 1 Timothy 4:12 and Titus 2:7.

1. What does it mean to be an example for others?
2. Why does Paul make this central to leadership?

Read 1 Corinthians 11:1.

1. How does Paul describe the process by which we become examples for others?
2. How does this define what type of example we are to be?

Demonstrating a Right Relationship with God

Read 1 Timothy 3:1–13 and Titus 1:5–9.

1. What does Paul mean when he states that we are to "hold firmly to the trustworthy message as it has been taught" (Titus 1:9)?
2. In what way is doctrine crucial to the health of the church (see 2 Tim. 1:13; Titus 1:9)?
3. What does it mean that we must "be able to teach" (1 Tim. 3:2)?
4. What does it mean to be "upright" and "holy" (Titus 1:8)?
5. To be blameless (Titus 1:6–7) means that we are not called into question. Thus, we are responsible for our actions. How are we accountable to people? To God?
6. What does it mean to be a recent convert (1 Tim. 3:6)? What are some ways that we demonstrate maturity?

7. We are called upon to love what is good. What are some practical ways we demonstrate that?

Demonstrating a Right Relationship with Others

One of the hallmarks of a transformed life is an intense and unconditional love for others (John 13:35). The love we are to have is to be radically different from the attitudes of the world. To be qualified for the position of a leader requires that we maintain this higher standard in our personal relationships.

1. To be respectable (1 Tim. 3:2) means that we live in such a way that people cannot speak negatively about us. What are some ways that we gain the respect as a church (see 1 Cor. 14:40)?
2. How can we demonstrate hospitality toward people, especially new people in the church?
3. Why is a quarrelsome person to be avoided in leadership (1 Tim. 3:3)? What are a quarrelsome person's characteristics?
4. Why is it important that we have a good reputation with the unsaved (1 Tim. 3:7)?
5. How is "overbearing" (Titus 1:7) the opposite of being humble?
6. What is the right attitude to have toward money (1 Tim. 3:3; 1 Peter 5:2)?

Demonstrating Godly Character in Relationship to Family

No one should be a leader who is not first a spiritual leader in the home. Those who aspire to serve on the board must first be servant-leaders within the home, modeling godly servanthood with their family and spouse.

1. What does it mean to be a leader at home (1 Tim. 3:4; Titus 1:6)?
2. What does it mean to be the "husband of but one wife" (1 Tim. 3:2)? How can we "commit adultery" apart from sexual relationships?
3. Why does Paul expand upon the importance of having a right relationship with our children? What are ways that you can improve your relationships with your children?

4. How does the scriptural emphasis on a leader's relationship with the family differ from the world's perspective?

Demonstrating Godly Character in Relationship to Ourselves

When we desire to serve within the church, we need to recognize our responsibility to control our own natural desires and feelings so that we are governed by the truth of Scripture rather than the cultural norms and expectations of others.

1. What are ways in which a lack of discipline (Titus 1:8; see also 1 Cor. 9:27) can disqualify us from ministry?
2. What things can hinder the Holy Spirit's work in our life by controlling our actions? How can tradition and culture "control" the life of the church?
3. Why is it important that the leader be one who is self-controlled (which means to be of sound mind, rational and prudent)? What attitudes and actions can hinder us from thinking clearly about issues?
4. Why is it important that we be patient with people?
5. What should motivate us in ministry?

Application

1. In light of this study, what are some areas in your life that you need to improve upon?
2. How can our board become a better model for the church?
3. If everyone in the church were demonstrating their faith in Christ and commitment to him to the same degree that you are, what impact would it have on the church?

LESSON 3
THE PRIORITY OF LEADERSHIP

Within the small church there is often only one governing board. The result is that the board sometimes becomes focused primarily on the physical maintenance and organization of the church. However, in Scripture we find that the focus is on the spiritual responsibilities we have. To be a board member is to be called by God to guide the church toward spiritual growth and the fulfillment of its biblical mission. To be effective we must clearly maintain our biblical priorities as leaders.

Leaders Are to Evaluate Their Relationship with Christ

Read Acts 20:28–38.

1. Why was Paul addressing the leaders of the church at Ephesus? Why was this an important and emotional time for them?
2. Why did Paul challenge them to "keep watch over [themselves]" (v. 28)?

Read Psalm 119:9–16.

1. How do we protect ourselves from the dangers of sin?
2. How is obedience the test of the authenticity of our relationship with God?

Read Isaiah 30:1.

1. What is the danger that we face both within our own lives and in our decision making within the church?
2. How can the pursuit of our own agenda become a hindrance to our spiritual growth?

Read John 13:35 and Matthew 5:23–24.

1. In what ways is our relationship with others an indication of our relationship with Christ?
2. What are we to do when we have a strained relationship with someone?

Leaders Are to Care for the Congregation

Read Acts 20:28.

1. How does this verse move our priority from the organizational to the spiritual?
2. How does this influence our agenda at the board meetings?
3. How do we provide oversight of each person within the church?

4. What are the dangers that the church faces today? How can we protect the church from these dangers?

Leaders Are to Live in Dependency upon God

Read Acts 20:32.

1. Why was it necessary for Paul to commit the leaders to God? What does that mean?
2. What are some of the struggles and limitations we face as leaders in the church?

Read Philippians 4:13.

1. How does this verse provide the answers to the limitations we have in ministry?
2. Look up the following verses, and write down the limitations we face and how God provides the answer for them.
   - 1 Corinthians 2:1–5
   - James 1:5
   - Philippians 4:6
   - Exodus 4:1–14

Leaders Are to Be Committed to Scripture

Read Acts 20:32 again.

1. What does Scripture accomplish in the lives of people?
2. What do the following verses tell us about the importance of Scripture in ministry?
   - 1 Timothy 4:13–16
   - 2 Timothy 2:15
   - Hebrews 4:12

Read Joshua 1:8 and Deuteronomy 17:18–19.

1. Why was it necessary for the leaders to write down a copy of the Book of the Law?
2. Why is understanding biblical truth critical to leadership?
3. How does this guide us in our understanding of our priority as leaders?

Application

1. How can we make sure that as a board we are growing in our relationship with Christ?
2. What are some ways that we can provide better oversight of the health of the congregation?
3. How can we make Scripture more central in our decision making?

LESSON 4
THE RESPONSIBILITY OF PRAYER

The Critical Task of the Board

As we look at the New Testament, we discover that prayer was central to the responsibility of the leadership. When the church was just beginning in the book of Acts, the leadership did not allow themselves to become bogged down in organizational issues. Instead, they gave these tasks to others so that they might give their "attention to prayer and the ministry of the word" (Acts 6:4). In other words prayer and the study of Scripture are central to guiding the church toward spiritual maturity and discipline.

The Necessity of Prayer

Read 1 Thessalonians 5:17.

1. How do we pray "continually?"
2. What implications does this have for how we spend our time in board meetings discussing issues?

Read 1 Samuel 12:23.

1. What did Samuel see as a sin?
2. Why is it important that we pray for the people we serve?
3. How does the attitude of self-sufficiency hinder our prayer life as individuals and as a board?

Read Joshua 9:14, Isaiah 30:1–2, and Jeremiah 10:21.

1. Why does God condemn the leaders of Israel?

2. What is the result when leaders do not pray?
3. What should we do before we make decisions within the church?

Read Acts 6:1–7 and James 5:13–20.

1. If ministry is ultimately spiritual, requiring spiritual means to accomplish spiritual ends, what is the role of prayer in achieving this goal?
2. What does James reveal concerning how we turn people back from sin and have an influence in their lives?

Read Psalm 73:13–17.

1. How can the apparent success of ungodly people cause us to lose perspective about our relationship with God?
2. What did the psalmist do that helped him regain perspective?

Read John 17:20–23.

1. How are prayer and unity united within the church?
2. Why does division arise in the church when we do not pray?

The Content of Prayer

As we examine the prayers of Paul in the New Testament, we discover a pattern for the focus and content of prayer. Often when we pray, our prayers tend to be general and superficial, rather than specific and transformational in focus.

Look at the following prayers of Paul, and write down the requests that Paul made for the people he was leading.

- Ephesians 1:15–23
- Philippians 1:3–11
- Colossians 1:3–14
- 2 Thessalonians 1:3–12

Read James 5:14 and 3 John 2.

What do we find James and John praying for?

Application

1. How much time do we spend in our board meetings praying for the spiritual needs of people? The emotional needs of people? The physical needs of people?
2. How can we further develop the priority of prayer within the board meeting?
3. How can we further develop the priority of prayer within the church?

LESSON 5
THE ROLE OF A WATCHMAN

In Ezekiel 3:17, God calls Ezekiel to be a watchman for the house of Israel. Like a modern-day police officer, watchmen were stationed on the wall surrounding a city to warn the people of any internal or external danger. So vital was their responsibility that a watchman who failed in his duty faced the death penalty. In Hebrews 13:17, we too are given the responsibility to be the watchmen of the congregation. God holds us responsible to oversee the well-being of the congregation.

Protecting the Church from Dangers Without

We live in a world that suffers the damaging effects of sin, and if we are not careful this corruption will enter the church. This does not mean that we are to isolate ourselves from the world. Rather, we are to protect the church from doctrinal error that can undermine our faith.

Read John 17:15.

1. What is to be our attitude toward and relationship with the world?
2. What is the difference between being "in the world" and being "of the world"?

Protecting the Church from the Rejection of Truth

Read Genesis 3:1–7.

1. In what way was the temptation an attack upon the truthfulness of God?
2. In what ways is that attack still prevalent today?

Read Matthew 24:5–14.

1. What will become more prevalent in the last days?
2. What will happen even within the church?
3. In light of the dangers of false teachers, what are we to do (v. 14)?

Read John 14:6 and 16:13.

1. Many today deny that there is any absolute truth that is to govern our lives and behavior. How does John 14:6 speak to these individuals?
2. How does John 16:13 answer the claim that we cannot know any absolute truth?
3. How can we better prepare people to deal with the question of absolute truth?

Protecting the Church from the Compromise and Distortion of Truth

Read Jude 4.

1. How does the rejection of truth result in a license for sin?
2. In what ways is liberalism a threat to the church?

Read 1 Timothy 1:8–11.

1. How does the right use of the law prevent liberalism?
2. How is liberalism an abuse of freedom?
3. How does theology affect our behavior?

Read Galatians 5:1, 6, and 16–26.

1. How is legalism a distortion and abuse of freedom?
2. In what ways is legalism manifested in the church?

Protecting the Church from Dangers Within

Read Acts 20:29–31.

What are some of the "wolves" that can come into the church?

Protecting the Church from Control Freaks

Read Galatians 2:11–13.

1. How did the power brokers influence Peter's actions?
2. What is the difference between people of influence and people who are controlling in the church?

Protecting the Church from the Infiltration of Sin

Read Hebrews 12:5–11.

1. What is the motivation for discipline?
2. What is the purpose of discipline?

Read Matthew 18:10–35.

1. In what way does the parable of the lost sheep illustrate church discipline?
2. What is the procedure that is outlined by Christ for church discipline?
3. How are we to respond when someone repents of his or her sin?
4. Why is conducting church discipline difficult in the small church?
5. When should we conduct church discipline?

Application

1. What are the specific dangers you are facing in your own life?
2. What are the dangers that the church is facing?
3. What does the leadership need to do to protect the church from these dangers?

LESSON 6
THE ROLE OF A SHEPHERD

Often we view the board from an organizational perspective. However, when we examine Scripture, we discover that the primary role of the board is not organizational but spiritual. Although we are responsible to oversee the structures, programs, finances, and facilities, our ultimate responsibility is to oversee the spiritual health of the congregation. The board is responsible to provide for the care of people, ministering to them in times of difficulty, encouraging them in their spiritual growth, and strengthening those who are spiritually weak.

Spiritual Decision Making

Spiritual care begins with making decisions on a spiritual basis rather than just an organizational basis. While our desire is to be godly leaders who spiritually lead the church, our natural tendency is to become pragmatic (What will get the best results?), or traditional (How have we done it in the past?), or even political (What will the congregation want? What will make the congregation happy?). When we make decisions as spiritual leaders, we are to utilize spiritual principles in order to make sure that we are following God's direction.

Making Spiritual Decisions Involves Prayer

Look up the following verses in Nehemiah, and identify the crisis that Nehemiah was facing and how he prioritized prayer before he acted.

- Nehemiah 1:3–4
- Nehemiah 2:4
- Nehemiah 4:7–9

In what ways can the board make prayer a more central part of the decision-making process?

Making Spiritual Decisions Involves Scripture

Read 2 Timothy 3:16.

1. How is Scripture central to everything we do in ministry?
2. How does Scripture provide everything we need?

Read 2 Timothy 2:15.

What is our responsibility regarding the Scriptures?

Read John 14:26 and 16:13.

1. What role does the Holy Spirit have in helping us understand what Scripture says?
2. How does this give us confidence, even if we have not had formal training?
3. Why do we often neglect going to the Scriptures before we make decisions?
4. How can we integrate Scripture more into our decision-making process?

Making Spiritual Decisions Reflects the Character of God

Read 2 Corinthians 5:20.

1. What does Paul tell us we are?
2. How does this define our role as Christians and as people within the church?

Read 1 Peter 2:12.

1. When we glorify God with the decisions and actions we take as a church, what will be the end result?
2. Why is it critical that before we make decisions we ask, "How will God be glorified and what will bring the most glory to God?"

Making Spiritual Decisions Involves the Counsel of Others

Read Proverbs 11:14, 15:22, and 24:6.

1. Why is it important that we seek the counsel of others?
2. What happens if we fail to get the counsel of others?

3. What are some ways that we can obtain wise counsel before we make decisions?

Making Spiritual Decisions Results in the Transformation of People

Read Colossians 1:28–29.

How does this provide the goal for all decisions we make within the church?

Providing Spiritual Care

What is the priority of the leadership of the church according to 1 Peter 5:2 and Hebrews 13:17?

Look up the following verses, and identify the ways that we are to provide spiritual care for people.

- 1 Corinthians 11:1
- Ephesians 4:14–15
- 1 Timothy 4:13
- 2 Timothy 4:2
- James 5:14–15
- Proverbs 17:17, 22

Application

1. How can the board provide care for people within the church?
2. How can the board improve its care for people?
3. What are some hindrances to the board's providing shepherding care for people within the church?

LESSON 7
SERVANT LEADERSHIP

Within the pages of Scripture, we find the priority of leadership is not the exercise of authority but the work of equipping people for effective ministry. In Ephesians 4:10–13, Paul teaches that the overriding purpose of leadership is to equip others for works of ministry. Because the work of ministry is the task of the whole church, we are to provide them with the foundation so that they understand and are equipped to fulfill the ministry God has given them. A spiritually healthy congregation is one where people are utilizing their gifts for the benefit of others. It is the role of the board to assist them in this process.

Equipping People with Spiritual Foundations

Healthy churches and effective leaders equip people for ministry by providing the spiritual foundation for ministry. This means we must equip people with a proper theological foundation and an in-depth biblical foundation.

Read John 9:2–5.

1. How did the disciples' incorrect understanding of God distort their understanding of the needs of people?
2. In what ways do people today have a distorted view of God?

Read Acts 15:15–21.

1. Why was it important that the early church have a right theological understanding of the relationship of the Gentiles to the Old Testament Law? How would an incorrect understanding have derailed the advance of the gospel?
2. What are some incorrect perspectives people have today that can hinder the outreach of the church?

Read 1 Timothy 4:16.

1. Why did Paul tell Timothy to watch his doctrine closely?
2. What would be the result?
3. Why is it important that we teach people doctrine?

Read 1 Timothy 3:9.

1. Why is it important that the leadership have an understanding of right doctrine?
2. In what ways do we set the example for the church?
3. In what ways is the board responsible to oversee the teaching of the church?

Read Ezra 7:10.

1. Why did Ezra make it his priority to teach the law of God?
2. What were the three things that he sought to do?
3. How does this provide a model for us in training within the church?
4. In what ways are we preparing ourselves to train others, and in what ways are we equipping others for ministry?

Training People for Ministry

Read 1 Corinthians 12 and 1 Timothy 3.

1. In what ways can a small church restrict people in ministry?
2. How do these restrictions relate to what Paul teaches in 1 Corinthians 12 and 1 Timothy 3?
3. What are legitimate restrictions we should place on people with regard to ministry? What are some illegitimate restrictions?

Read 1 Peter 4:10–11.

Why is it necessary for us to develop our gifts? How does our development of our gifts reflect our attitude toward God and toward our spiritual gifts?

Application

1. What are some ways the board can provide spiritual support for people in ministry?
2. What are some ways the church can improve the training of people for ministry?
3. Why is it important that we hold people accountable in ministry (see Matt. 25:14–30)? What are some ways that people should be accountable in ministry?

LESSON 8
UNDERSTANDING THE PURPOSE AND MISSION OF THE CHURCH

Steering the Ship

To oversee the ministry of the church, we are to lead the church in the accomplishment of its God-given mission. In doing so there are two critical questions we must answer. The first is, "Why does the church exist?" This deals with the purpose of the church. The second is, "What is it to accomplish?" This deals with the mission of the church. The answers to these two questions distinguish the church from every other social and community organization.

Fulfilling the Purpose

The church is a spiritual organism that exists for a spiritual purpose. Its purpose is neither sociological (to make the community better) nor psychological (to make people feel better); rather, it is spiritual (to bring people into a vital relationship with Christ).

The Church Is to Glorify God

1. In Isaiah 43:6–7, what do we find is the reason we are created?

2. Look up the following references, and identify the ways that we glorify God.

- Romans 15:7–9
- John 14:15
- Proverbs 3:9
- 1 Peter 2:12
- 1 Peter 4:10–11

Westminster Larger Catechism

Question 1: "What is the chief and highest end of man?"
Answer: "Man's chief and highest end is to glorify God, and fully to enjoy him forever."

The Church Is to Maintain Theological Integrity

The term *theology* comes from the Greek words *theos,* meaning "God," and *logos,* referring to "discourse, language, or study." In other words, theology is the study of God as he has revealed himself and of how we are to respond to him.

Read the following verses, and identify the responsibility of the board regarding the development of theology within the church.

- 1 Timothy 4:16
- Acts 20:29–30
- Titus 1:9
- Ephesians 4:11–14

> "The highest science, the loftiest speculation, the highest philosophy, which can ever engage the attention of the child of God, is the name, the nature, the person, the work, the doings, and the existence of the great God whom he calls his Father."
> —Charles Spurgeon

The Church Is to Develop Godly Character in Others

Genuine theology is lived theology. It moves from the understanding to the realm of daily life.

Read Matthew 22:37–40.

What are the two qualities that are to characterize the disciple of Christ?

Read Deuteronomy 15:5 and John 14:15.

What is the standard by which we can measure our love for God?

Read 1 John 4:8.

What is the relationship between loving God and loving others (see also 1 John 2:9–11; 3:11, 14; 4:20–21)?

What do the following verses tell us about the kind of love we are to have?

- Matthew 18:21–35
- James 2:1–13
- 1 Timothy 3:2
- 1 John 3:17–18

Fulfilling the Mission

While the church is to be grounded in a theology that transforms our life and character, we are also given a task to do. The church exists to accomplish a mission that is mandated by God and is to govern all its activities. This mission is set forth in Matthew 28:19–20 and Acts 1:7–8.

The Mission of the Church Is to Reach People for Christ

Read Matthew 28:19–20 and Acts 1:7–8.

What is our responsibility to the world? What does it mean to be a witness?

Read Matthew 9:36–37.

1. What does this passage tell us about what our perspective is to be regarding the unsaved?
2. List some ways that the church can improve evangelism?

The Mission of the Church Is to Disciple People

Read Philippians 3:10 and John 14:15, 21, 23–24.

1. What does it mean to be a disciple of Christ?
2. What are some ways that the church can improve its discipleship of others?

The Mission of the Church Is to Recruit and Equip People for Service

Read Ephesians 4:11–13.

1. What is the responsibility of the leadership in the church?
2. Why is training important? How can the leadership better equip people for ministry?

Application

1. Is the church being effective in leading people toward transformation? How can we improve in this area?
2. How can the church be more effective in reaching out to people? In what ways can we as a board set a better example of outreach?
3. Are people being discipled? How can we improve our discipleship within the church?
4. In what areas do people need to be trained in order for them to be more effective in ministry?

LESSON 9
TEAMWORK

Ministry is never meant to be a one-person show where the pastor does all the work. God designed the church to be a team ministry, where people are working together, with each exercising their spiritual gifts for the growth of the body of Christ. The ability of the pastor, board, and congregation to work together as a team will greatly influence whether the church is healthy or not.

Defining Team Ministry

A team ministry occurs when the pastor, board, and congregation are working in harmony for the spiritual growth and well-being of others, with each understanding their own gifts, roles, and responsibilities while valuing and utilizing the gifts, roles, and responsibilities of others.

Read Ecclesiastes 4:9–12.
1. Why is it important that the church work together as a team?
2. What will happen when they are not working together?
3. Why is it important that leaders work together and listen to one another (look up Prov. 11:14; 15:22; 24:6)?
4. What important attitude does Paul tell us in Ephesians 5:21 is necessary for an effective church?
5. How is this attitude evident in the development of a team?

6. Why is it important that we trust one another in the church and in the ministry of the church (see 1 Cor. 13:7)?

Read Ephesians 5:22–33.

What attitude of Christ is reflected in the marriage relationship, and how does this reflect the type of attitude we are to have toward the church?

Avoiding the Team Killers

While building upon the right foundation for team leadership is critical, it is also important to identify and avoid those things that will destroy an effective team. How can the following team killers be evident in a team?

- *Pride.* When people take pride in their own achievements and fail to recognize the value of others, especially of those not as trained or talented.
- *Lack of Acceptance.* When we see someone new in the church or someone who is culturally different as an outsider.
- *Suspicion.* When problems in the past make us suspicious of others in leadership.
- *Inflexibility.* When someone always says "no" to any new idea and refuses to accept any opinion or proposal that is not in full agreement with his or her personal ideas.
- *Docility.* When someone always goes with the flow and is always a "yes" person.

Benefits of Team Ministry

For the pastor and board to work as a team, they need to understand the immense value of working together. It is critical that we understand that a team ministry is not only the cornerstone of effectiveness; it is God's desire for the church.

Read Acts 15:5–21.

1. When a potential conflict arose, what did the early church do?
2. How is this a model of effective teamwork?
3. How did this prevent the church from becoming fractured?

Read Acts 11:22–27 and 15:36–41.

1. How were Paul and Barnabas different?
2. How did their differences make them stronger as a team?
3. How did it challenge them as a team?
4. In what ways do our differences make us stronger?

Read Exodus 17:9–14 and Deuteronomy 1:38.

1. How did Joshua's previous work with Moses prepare the people for the time when Moses was no longer the leader?
2. How does an effective team provide greater stability during leadership changes?

Read Proverbs 12:15.

1. According to this verse, what is characteristic of a wise person? A fool?
2. In what way is the wisdom and input of many people beneficial in making decisions?

Application

1. How well are we working together as a team on the board?
2. How well are we working with the pastor as a team?
3. How well is the congregation functioning as a team?
4. In what areas do we need to improve our teamwork?
5. How can we as a board help develop greater teamwork within the church?

LESSON 10
THE BOARD AS CHANGE AGENTS
Keeping the Church Alive

As much as we find change disquieting, the reality is that if we do not change, we will not grow. The church is ultimately an agent of change, for we are not to maintain the status quo but to lead people into spiritual transformation so that they manifest the character of Christ. This implies that we are not just making changes on a superficial level (as in the order of the worship service), but we are to make radical changes that alter the very core and essence of our being. If we do not change individually and corporately, then we have signed our own death certificate, for without change we will die spiritually and organizationally. The task of the church is not to maintain the status quo but to lead the congregation into profound change in all aspects of life and ministry.

1. What do the following verses tell us about the nature and importance of change?
- Matthew 18:3
- Romans 12:1–2
- 2 Corinthians 3:18
- Ephesians 4:22–24
2. Why are people reluctant to change within the church?

The Necessity of Change

There are times when changes are not only helpful but also necessary.

Read Acts 6:1–6.
1. What was the problem confronting the early church?
2. What change was needed?
3. What did the leadership do in light of the problem?
4. What issues do we confront in the church today that reflect the same problem confronted by the early church?

Read Matthew 21:12–17.
1. What was the problem that Jesus was confronting?
2. Why did Jesus initiate the change?
3. What areas in the church today are not in line with biblical truth?
4. What must we do in response?

Read Acts 16:3.
1. What was hindering the ministry of Timothy?
2. What did Paul do in response?

3. In what areas of our ministry might our practices and methods be hindering the work of the church?
4. What changes can we make to remove those hindrances?

Read John 4:39–41 and Acts 18:1–11.

1. How did new ministry opportunities result in a change of plans?
2. When changes occur within the community, how does that necessitate change in the ministry of the church?
3. What are some areas where the church needs to change to be more effective in reaching its community?

Application

1. What changes do we need to make to be more effective as a church?
2. Before we make any changes, what must we do?
3. Who are we to communicate the changes to?
4. Why is it important that the board be agents of change within the church?

LESSON 11
THE RESPONSIBILITY OF ADMINISTRATION

Ministry is not to be conducted haphazardly and inefficiently; rather, we are to recognize the seriousness of the ministry and organize the ministry so that it is effective. This does not mean that we must manage the church like a large corporation. We are to recognize that in the small church we can be effective without making everything completely efficient. However, this is not an excuse for becoming sloppy in administration. Our task as leaders is to assure that the church is working together to accomplish its biblical mission.

Overseeing the Planning

Providing administrative oversight begins with overall planning and strategy of the congregation. This begins with the conviction that every small church has the potential to accomplish great things for God simply because it can be used by God and is called by God to accomplish his will.

What do the following verses teach us about the importance of planning?

- Proverbs 16:3
- Proverbs 19:21
- Proverbs 21:5
- Proverbs 24:27
- Romans 12:1–2

> The goal of planning is not efficiency, but discerning the will of God and channeling our activities, resources, and energies in that direction.

Read 1 Corinthians 16:5–9.

What do these verses tell us about the plans and goals of Paul? Why is it important for us to set goals for the church?

Read Acts 16:6–10.

What does this passage tell us about the relationship between goals and planning and the will of God?

Read Matthew 22:37–40 and 28:19–20.

We find the purpose of the church in Matthew 22:37–40 and the mission of the church in Matthew 28:19-20. How are goals and specific church plans to reflect and fulfill the church's mission and purpose?

Overseeing the Budget

Setting goals and establishing ministries will have little value if we do not have the finances to fund the programs. Because we have limited finances, how we handle the finances is all the more critical.

1. Look up the following verses, and write down the principles they teach regarding our perspective on finances within the church:

- Proverbs 10:16
- Proverbs 13:11
- Proverbs 28:8
- Matthew 6:21
- 2 Corinthians 8:5
- 2 Corinthians 8:7
- 2 Corinthians 9:6–8
- Philippians 4:17–19

2. What does Scripture teach us about providing for the financial needs of the pastor (see Gal. 6:6; 1 Tim. 5:17–20)?

3. How does caring for the pastor relate not only to the financial needs of the pastor but also to the emotional needs as well? How can the church provide for the emotional needs of the pastor and the pastor's family?

Principles for Developing a Sound Budget

- Prayerfully develop goals for each area of ministry.
- Have each ministry formulate a budget for its ministry goals.
- Have the board review the goals and needs of each ministry to assure that they are consistent with the goals and ministry of the church.
- Develop a budget that reflects the goals, vision, and ministry of the church and each ministry.
- Challenge people to commit to the ministry rather than just the budget.
- Pray and trust God for his provision.
- Maintain flexibility within the budget.

Overseeing the Policies

The purpose of policies is to indicate the church's position and values on specific issues. They contain guidelines that inform people what is expected of them in specific situations. Policies are broad guidelines that establish the course of action needed to make a decision.

Procedures inform people how they are to perform their ministry in a way that is in line with the values, beliefs, and doctrines of the church. Procedures provide the specific steps for how policies are to be implemented.

Policy statements should answer the following questions:

1. Why is the policy being implemented?
2. What does the policy cover, and what actions or decisions does the policy apply to?
3. What is the policy?
4. What is the procedure to be followed in implementing the policy?

Application

1. What goals has our church set in order for us to be more effective in accomplishing our purpose and mission? Write down two or three short-term goals the church needs to accomplish in the next six months to a year.
2. Write down one or two long-term goals the church needs to accomplish in the next two years.
3. What actions will need to be taken to accomplish these goals?
4. What are the specific issues that need to be addressed within the church in a policy statement?
5. Who will write and approve the policies?

LESSON 12
MAINTAINING THE STRUCTURE

While many people regard the constitution as either a sacred document that can never be changed and must be meticulously followed or as a man-made document that has little bearing upon the church, it does serve to provide critical structure and oversight for the ministry of the church. A well-written constitution serves to set the guidelines of the church while allowing for flexibility within the ministry so that the church can be effective in an ever-changing world.

The Role of the Constitution

To understand the importance of the constitution, we must understand the role it plays within the life and organization of the church. It is neither an inspired text that cannot be changed nor a man-made institution that should be ignored.

Read Exodus 23:14–19 and Deuteronomy 17:14–20.

1. What do these verses tell us about the importance that God places upon order?
2. When establishing Israel in the Promised Land, why did God set down guidelines and rules that governed not only their spiritual life but their social life as well?
3. What lessons can we draw from this for the church today concerning the importance of order and organization?

Read Acts 6:1–7.

1. What was the problem confronting the early church?
2. How did the church rearrange its organizational structures to deal with the problem?

Read 1 Corinthians 14:40.

1. Why did Paul write that everything should be done in a fitting and orderly way?
2. How does this relate to the present ministry of the church?
3. How can the constitution protect the congregation?
4. In what ways can the constitution provide direction for the congregation?

When to Revise the Constitution

1. What are some of the occasions when it would be advisable or necessary to revise the constitution?
2. In what way, if any, is the present constitution hindering the ministry of the church?
3. What areas within the structures of the church need to be clarified further?

Developing or Rewriting an Effective Constitution

1. How can the church's constitution better reflect biblical theology?
2. How can the structures of the church better reflect the structures revealed within Scripture?
3. Does the constitution reflect current values and structures of the church?
4. How can the constitution be simplified in order to allow for more effective ministry?
5. What is the difference between the constitution and a policy manual?

Application

1. Are there areas in the church's constitution that need to be changed or rewritten?
2. What aspects of the church should have clear, written policies?

Notes

Introduction

1. Aubrey Malphurs, *Leading Leaders* (Grand Rapids: Baker, 2005), 63.
2. Homer A. Kent Jr., *The Epistle to the Hebrews* (Winona Lake, IN: BMH Books, 1972), 288.

Chapter 1: The Biblical Offices of Leadership

1. G. Bornkamm, "Presbys, presbytos, presbytes, sympresbytes, presbyterion, presbeuo," *Theological Dictionary of the New Testament, Abridged,* ed. Geoffrey W. Bromiley (Grand Rapids: Eerdmans, 1992), 931.
2. John MacArthur, *The Master's Plan for the Church* (Chicago: Moody Press, 1991), 182.
3. L. Coenen, "Bishop, presbyter, elder," *New International Dictionary of New Testament Theology,* ed. Colin Brown (Grand Rapids: Zondervan, 1975), 1:189
4. MacArthur, *The Master's Plan for the Church,* 185.
5. Robert L. Saucy, *The Church in God's Program* (Chicago: Moody Press, 1972), 156.
6. Aubrey Malphurs, *Leading Leaders* (Grand Rapids: Baker, 2005), 40–42.
7. For further discussion see Saucy, *The Church in God's Program,* 148–50.
8. For a discussion regarding the "double honor," see Thomas D. Lea and Hayne P. Griffin Jr., *1–2 Timothy,* The New American Commentary (Nashville: Broadman Press, 1992), 155; and Homer A. Kent Jr., *The Pastoral Epistles* (Chicago: Moody Press, 1958), 182–83.
9. Malphurs, *Leading Leaders,* 74.
10. H. B. London Jr. and Neil B. Wiseman, *Pastors at Risk* (Wheaton: Victor Books, 1993), 22.
11. Malphurs, *Leading Leaders,* 70.

Chapter 2: Character

1. H. Muller, "Type, pattern," *The New International Dictionary of New Testament Theology*, ed. Colin Brown (Grand Rapids: Regency, 1976), 3:904

2. See L. Goppelt, "Typos, antitypos, typikos, hypotypsis," *Theological Dictionary of the New Testament, Abridged*, ed. Geoffrey W. Bromiley (Grand Rapids: Eerdmans, 1985), 1193.

3. Homer A. Kent Jr., *The Pastoral Epistles* (Chicago: Moody Press, 1958), 219.

4. John Harris, *Stress, Power and Ministry* (Washington, D.C.: Alban Institute, 1979), 3; quoted in James Means, *Leadership in Christian Ministry* (Grand Rapids: Baker, 1990), 34.

5. Means, *Leadership in Christian Ministry*, 34.

6. Robert L. Saucy, *The Church in God's Program* (Chicago: Moody Press, 1972),149.

7. Bill Kemp, *Holy Places, Small Places* (Nashville: Discipleship Resources, 2005), 41.

8. N. J. D. White, "The First and Second Epistles to Timothy and the Epistle to Titus," in *Expositors Greek Testament*, ed. W. Robertson Nicoll (Grand Rapids: Eerdmans, 1983), 4:114.

9. Josh McDowell and Dick Day, *How to Be a Hero to Your Kids* (Dallas: Word, 1991), 16.

10. For an examination of the view that this prohibits a divorced person from serving as an elder, see J. Carl Laney, *The Divorce Myth* (Minneapolis: Bethany House, 1981), 91–101. For a rejection of this view and support of an elder serving even though divorced, see Stanley A. Ellisen, *Divorce and Remarriage in the Church* (Grand Rapids: Zondervan, 1980), 101–3, 123–24.

11. William Hendricksen, *1 Timothy*, New Testament Commentary (Grand Rapids: Baker, 1979), 127.

12. Thomas D. Lea and Hayne P. Griffin Jr., *1–2 Timothy, Titus*, New American Commentary (Nashville: Broadman, 1992), 110.

13. John MacArthur, *The Master's Plan for the Church* (Chicago: Moody Press, 1991), 222.

Chapter 3: The Priority of Leadership

1. John MacArthur Jr., *Shepherdology* (Sun Valley, CA: Grace Community Church, 1975), 44.

2. Thomas D. Lea and Hayne P. Griffin Jr., *1–2 Timothy, Titus*, New American Commentary (Nashville: Broadman, 1992), 111.

Chapter 4: The Responsibility of Prayer

1. Charles Hodge, *Systematic Theology*, 3 vols. (Grand Rapids: Eerdmans, 1979), 3:692.
2. John MacArthur, *The Master's Plan for the Church* (Chicago: Moody Press, 1991), 63.
3. Quoted in Eugene Habecker, *Rediscovering the Soul of Leadership* (Wheaton: Victor Books, 1996), 227.
4. Gary L. McIntosh and Robert L. Edmondson, *It Only Hurts on Monday* (Saint Charles, IL: ChurchSmart, 1998), 15.
5. Peter H. Davids, *The Epistle of James: A Commentary on the Greek Text*, New International Greek Testament Commentary (Grand Rapids: Eerdmans, 1982), 193.
6. Simon J. Kistemaker, *James and 1–3 John*, New Testament Commentary (Grand Rapids: Baker, 1986), 176.

Chapter 5: The Role of a Watchman

1. John E. Hartley, "צָפָה" in *Theological Wordbook of the Old Testament*, ed. R. L. Harris, G. L. Archer, and B. K. Waltke (Chicago: Moody Press, 1980), 2:773. Hartley goes on to state that the watchman refers to "one who was stationed on the wall and was responsible to inform the nation's leadership of any danger (cf. I Sam 14:16; II Sam 18:24ff.; II Kgs 9:17–20)." So critical was the responsibility of the watchman to the overall security and well being of the city that death was the punishment for failure to fulfill the duties assigned to him. "The prophetic office is sometimes described in this language. To Ezekiel God says, 'I have made you a watchman for the house of Israel; whenever you hear a word from my mouth, you shall give them warning from me' (3:17; cf. 33:7; Jer 6:17; Hab 2:1). If Ezekiel failed to give them God's warning he was liable for their lives; but if he faithfully proclaimed the message, he was free from any further responsibility regardless of the people's response (Ezk 3:18–21). Although God was faithful in sending Israel watchmen, many became blind to their mission (Isa 56:10). The failure of these watchmen and the rejection of the true ones were major reasons for the downfall of Israel. Conversely, the true prophets will be the watchmen who are first to sing of the advance of God's new saving deeds (Isa 52:7–10)."
2. Millard J. Erickson, *The Postmodern World* (Wheaton: Crossway, 2002), 13.
3. D. A. Carson, *Becoming Conversant with the Emerging Church* (Grand Rapids: Zondervan, 2005), 13.

4. Harry Blamires, *The Christian Mind* (Ann Arbor: Servant Publications, 1968), 12.
5. Os Guiness, *Dining with the Devil* (Grand Rapids: Baker, 1993), 56.
6. Charles Swindoll, *Grace Awakening* (Dallas: Word Publishing, 1990), 81.
7. Ibid., 81–82.
8. John MacArthur, *Matthew 16–23*, The MacArthur New Testament Commentary (Chicago: Moody Press, 1988), 133.

Chapter 6: The Role of a Shepherd

1. Rowland Forman, Jeff Jones, and Bruce Miller, *The Leadership Baton* (Grand Rapids: Zondervan, 2004), 78.
2. A helpful resource for verses you can use is *The Billy Graham Christian Worker's Handbook* (Minneapolis: World Wide Publications, 1984).

Chapter 7: Servant Leadership

1. R. C. H. Lenski, *The Interpretation of St. Paul's Epistles to the Galatians, Ephesians and Philippians* (Minneapolis: Augsburg Publishing House, 1961), 530.
2. See Edward Goodrick, *Is My Bible the Inspired Word of God?* (Portland: Multnomah, 1988).
3. There are a number of books that provide an overview of biblical interpretation. For example, see Howard Hendricks and William Hendricks, *Living by the Book* (Chicago: Moody Press, 1991).

Chapter 8: Understanding the Purpose and Mission of the Church

1. Quoted in J. I. Packer, *Knowing God* (Downers Grove, IL.: InterVarsity Press, 1972), 13.
2. For a further discussion on foundational theological issues and minor theological issues, see Rex Koivisto, *One Lord, One Faith: A Theology for Cross-Denominational Renewal* (Wheaton, IL: BridgePoint, 1993).
3. Alan F. Johnson, "Revelation," in *The Expositor's Bible Commentary*, ed. Frank Gaebelein (Grand Rapids: Baker, 1981), 12:434.
4. Cornelia Butler Flora and Jan L. Flora, *Rural Communities: Legacy and Change* (Boulder, CO: Westview Press, 1992), 288–89.
5. Dann Spader and Gary Mayes, *Growing a Healthy Church* (Chicago: Moody, 1991), 157.
6. Win Arn and Charles Arn, *The Master's Plan for Making Disciples* (Pasadena: Church Growth Press, 1982), 43.

7. Kevin Ruffcorn, *Rural Evangelism: Catching the Vision* (Minneapolis: Augsburg, 1994), 90.

Chapter 9: Teamwork

1. For an excellent discussion of the group commitment, see Patrick Lencioni, *The Five Dysfunctions of a Team* (San Francisco: Jossey-Bass, 2002).
2. Ibid, 195.
3. Rowland Forman, Jeff Jones, and Bruce Miller, *The Leadership Baton* (Grand Rapids: Zondervan, 2004), 89.
4. Lencioni, *The Five Dysfunctions of a Team*, 202–3.
5. Aubrey Malphurs, *Leading Leaders* (Grand Rapids: Baker, 2005), 109.
6. Linda Miller and Chad Hall, *Coaching for Christian Leaders* (St. Louis: Chalice Press, 2007), 116.

Chapter 10: The Board as Change Agents

1. Leonard Sweet, *Soul Tsunami* (Grand Rapids: Zondervan, 1999), 73.
2. See Randall K. Crandall and L. Ray Sells, *There's New Life in the Small Congregation* (Nashville: Discipleship Resources, 1983), 12–20.
3. Lyle Schaller, *The Change Agent* (Nashville: Abingdon, 1978), 38.
4. John MacDonald, *Calling a Halt to Mindless Change* (New York: Amacom, 1998), 5.
5. Donald Kirkpatrick, *How to Manage Change Effectively* (San Francisco: Jossey-Bass Publishers, 1985), 120.
6. Ray Comfort, *The Way of the Master* (Orlando: Bridge-Logos, 2006).

Chapter 11: The Responsibility of Administration

1. Robert H. Mounce, *Romans*, The New American Commentary (Nashville: Broadman and Holman Publishers, 1995), 235.
2. David Ray, *Small Churches Are the Right Size* (New York: Pilgrim Press, 1982), 158.
3. Lyle Schaller, *Creative Church Administration* (Nashville: Abingdon, 1975), 122–26.
4. Abe Funk, *Hope For the Small Church* (Ontario: Essence Publishing, 2005), 97.

Chapter 12: Maintaining the Structure

1. Harold Longnecker, *Building Town and Country Churches* (Chicago: Moody Press, 1973), 51.

Study Guide

1. John MacArthur, *The Master's Plan for the Church* (Chicago: Moody Press, 1991), 182.

About the Author

Glenn Daman (M.A. in New Testament Studies and M.A. in Old Testament Studies, Western Seminary; D.Min., Trinity Evangelical Divinity School) serves as director of the Center for Leadership Development and is an adjunct professor for a number of Bible colleges and seminaries in the area of small-church studies. He has served as the pastor of small churches in Washington, Oregon, and Montana, and is the senior pastor of First Baptist Church in Stevenson, Washington.

He is the author of *Shepherding the Small Church* (2002) and *Leading the Small Church* (2006), also published by Kregel.

The Center for Leadership Development (http://www.small churchleaders.org) exists to strengthen and encourage small-church leadership by providing educational and ministry training for those who serve the small church. For more information contact:

Center for Leadership Development
151 SW Iman Cemetary Road
Stevenson, WA 98648
E-mail: smallchurch@gorge.net

ALSO BY GLENN C. DAMAN

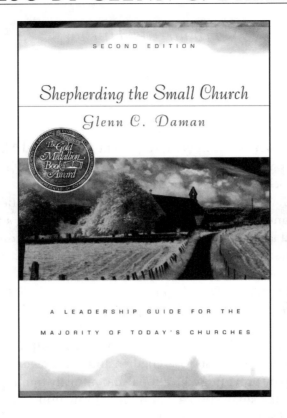

An indispensable source of advice and encouragement

In the U.S., 75 percent of churches have a weekly attendance of 150 or less. Glenn Daman reminds readers that "the vitality of a congregation is not found in its size or its programs or budget. The vitality of a congregation is found in its fulfillment of God's purpose for the church." Offering neither trivial clichés nor quick fixes, *Shepherding the Small Church* gives point-by point suggestions for small church ministry, mission, unity, and more. Several appendixes of helpful assessment tools help pastors and lay leadership work through the book together.

978-0-8254-2500-4 • Paperback • 288 pages

ALSO BY GLENN C. DAMAN

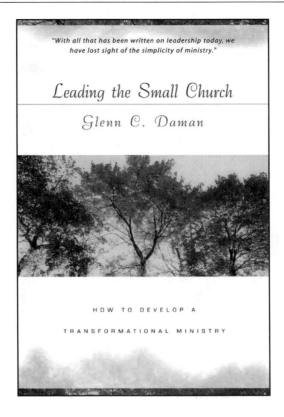

Exhorts pastors to take leadership to a different level

This follow-up book to *Shepherding the Small Church* addresses the essentials for spiritual leadership in the small church. Daman shows that contrary to today's prevailing wisdom, the pastor's role is not to be a visionary or organizational leader. The pastor's primary responsibility is spiritual leadership through preaching and godly role modeling. Readers will come away with insights into the important contribution small churches can make in the spiritual development of people in the church and in the community.

978-0-8254-2447-2 • Paperback • 240 pages

A PASTOR'S ESSENTIAL TOOL FOR LIFE'S FORMATIVE SITUATIONS

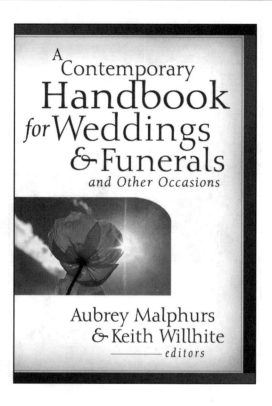

A compilation of ideas and resources to help new and veteran pastors

Weddings and funerals, like few other occasions, offer pastors the opportunity to give direction and encouragement to individuals when their hearts are more open to God . . . and to those individuals attending these events who may otherwise never hear God's message. This handbook, a compilation of tested ideas and resources by pastors, provides just the tool pastors need. Young pastors will appreciate the advice of experienced ministers to help them get started, and veteran pastors will benefit from fresh ideas that add meaning to services they've performed dozens of times. Includes difficult situations like the death of a child and second marriages.

978-0-8254-3186-9 • Paperback • 368 pages